All About Sergio Leone

«CineOmnibus»
Book Series edited by ENRICO GIACOVELLI

Oreste De Fornari

All About
SergioLeone

Edited by
ENRICO GIACOVELLI

With the contribution of
FRANCO FERRINI and DIEGO GABUTTI

GREMESE

To Michela

Acknowledgements
My thanks to Enrico Appetito, Guia Croce, Gloria De Antoni, Gianluca Farinelli e Rosaria Gioia (Cineteca di Bologna), Emma Ferrini, Massimo Ghirlanda e Sabina Meini (Centro Studi Commedia all'Italiana), Marco Giusti, Anna Guedy, Angelo Humouda, Raffaella Leone, Paolo Luciani e Cristina Torelli (Officina Filmclub), Massimo Marchelli, Piero Messori, Carmelo Milone, Giorgio Navarro, Nicola Petralia, Valeria Paniccia, Antonietta Pizzorno, Claver Salizzato, Aldo Tassone, Patrizia Viola, Alejandro Villareal.

A special acknowledgement to Enrico Giacovelli who edited this book showing great knowledge and creativity, enriching it with remarks, materials and photos.

Cover artwork: Francesco Partesano

Photos on the cover: From the left, on the top: Clint Eastwood in *For a Few Dollars More*, Lee Van Cleeff in *The Good, the Bad and the Ugly*; in the middle: Claudia Cardinale in *Once Upon a Time in the West*, Rod Steiger in *Duck! You Sucker*, Elizabeth McGovern in *Once Upon a Time in America*; below: Charles Bronson in *Once Upon a Time in the West*, Eli Wallach in *The Good, the Bad and the Ugly*, Robert De Niro in *Once Upon a Time in America*.

Page 2: Close up of Clint Eastwood in *A Fistful of Dollars*.
Page 319: Lee Van Cleeff in *For a Few Dollars More*.

Most of the photos in this book are from Leone's films. For Leone's childhood photos we thank his daughter Raffaella Leone. As for other photos we have tried unsuccessfully to locate rightful owners. We apologize for any incovenience and will make revisions in future editions, as stated in Article 70 of Italian law n. 633 1941.

Revised by: Alexei Cohen

Traslated from the Italian by: Charles Nopar and Shula Atil Curto

Printed by: MIG s.r.l. – Bologna, Italy

2019 © Gremese International s.r.l.s. – Rome, Italy

ISBN: 978-88-7301-784-4

"What does good, bad and ugly mean?
We are all a little good, a little bad, and a little ugly."

SERGIO LEONE

CONTENTS

Leone's Westerns summed up in the opening credits of *A Fistful of Dollars.*

INTRODUCTIONS

When the Audience Applauded
by Oreste De Fornari

There is the story of that winter afternoon in 1966 when Sergio Leone, in his office, sees three menacing types burst in, demanding in Roman dialect: *"Perfessor – we seen the movie twenny times, we bet our shirts an' ya gotta tell us – was she the daughter or the sister?"*. Their curiosity regarded Leone's most recent movie *For a Few Dollars More,* and in particular the relationship between Lee Van Cleef and the girl who was raped in the flashback scene, whose portrait he keeps in his pocket watch, and whom he avenges by killing her assailant. Despite an explanatory exchange of remarks (Eastwood: "There's a family resemblance in this picture." Van Cleef: "It can happen between brother and sister sometimes."), the three Romans hadn't gotten it. Perhaps the lines were drowned out by cries or applause – that was something that often happened during Westerns, especially when they were directed by Leone. It is well known that the popular cinema in Italy had very brief seasons of success. The Western boom went the way of the horror film, the mythology film, the opera film, etc. Not exactly genres, just barely veins.

The genre is an industrial product which requires a steady flow of investment. The vein belongs to a get rich quick economy: intensively exploited, it is soon exhausted. Furthermore, a vein is aimed at a circumscribed audience, at times only regional, as in the case of the Neapolitan movies of the fifties. Only the Italian-style comedy, an average product par excellence, has escaped this precarious situation: regular teams of directors and writers, recurring characters and actors, the constant popularity among a heterogeneous audience.

Leone's movies also enjoyed the very same success as this type of comedy, in both the big movie houses and the neighborhood dives. Unlike Dino Risi or Luigi Comencini, Leone does not try to tone down the more sophisticated or vulgar elements, but rather intensifies them: there are farce-like lines that stand next to those of an almost hermetic refinement.

Faced with certain prolonged silences (Lee Van Cleef entering the Mexican farm in *The Good, the Bad and the Ugly*), the exasperated audience would be known to cry out, "When is he gonna make up his mind to talk!" – something that otherwise would only happen occasionally in the films of Antonioni. But these were more symptoms of impatience than of discontent. On the other hand, certain critics literally detested Leone. They called him a "mannerist" which in those austere days was an insult. Now thirty years later, mannerism is in vogue and the borderlines between cultivated and popular genres have finally been abolished. Leone is now considered a classic. One speaks of *Once Upon a Time in the West* as a metawestern, a deconstructionist Western, as the cinema reflecting upon itself. Umberto Eco compared Leone's "godless nostalgia" for the West to that of Ariosto's for the Middle Ages.

But such high-flying phrases are not suited to his work. One risks forgetting that the public once practically wrecked movie theaters to see his films, chat moralists accused Leone of being an apologist for violence, and that some film buffs learned his dialogues by heart. It even reached the point where the music of *Once Upon a Time in the West* was played at weddings in place of Mendelssohn's *Wedding March*.

INTRODUCTION 1983 (II)
Who Betrayed Italian Cinema?
by Luc Moullet

In Italy there are two kinds of cinema worthy of interest: on the one hand there is auteur cinema, that of Rossellini, Visconti, Antonioni, Fellini, Pasolini and Bertolucci which, though much applauded by critics, was for a long time ignored by the public; and on the other hand there is a kind of cinema based on the conventions of genres, such as that of Cottafavi, Bava, Matarazzo, and Jacopetti, despised by Italian critics but loved by moviegoers. Within this genre-type of moviemaking Sergio Leone beats all the records for provocation. At the very moment when Italian cinema was fighting the invasion of American films with all the means it commanded, Leone almost exclusively made Westerns, all set in America and shot in American English. Whereas the quality of an Italian movie is often judged by its quota of neorealism, Leone makes fun of reality and is interested only in the past, never in the present. The cinema of social commitment dictates the rules of the game, yet Leone never takes sides (*Duck! You Sucker*). Leone is the traitor of the Italian cinema par excellence.

And yet – as De Fornari's book well shows – these two kinds of moviemaking are closely connected: Mario Monicelli and Dino Risi suddenly switch from the second type to the first, just as De Sica returned at the end of his career to making genre movies. Bertolucci collaborates in writing the script for a film of Leone's; Pasolini acts in a Western and casts the dubious comedians, Franco Franchi and Ciccio Ingrassia, in one of his pictures; Leone works as an assistant and an extra in *The Bicycle Thief* while Cottafavi goes from melodramas and historical costume movies to adaptations of Conrad and the Greek classics.

Nevertheless these genre films often turn out to be even more personal and artistic than the films of auteur cinema which nowadays are reduced to a kind of left-wing reminiscence or fanciful flight of the aesthete (Scola, Brusati, Pontecorvo, Cavani, Bolognini, Petri, Vancini, Maselli, Lizzani, Zeffirelli, etc.).

With his aggressive editing, Leone is the principal heir of Eisenstein. He reaches the levels of the most modern moviemaking structured upon the film's length. Like Rivette, Leone cannot make a successful movie if he does not stretch it out to at least two and a quarter hours. His first pictures were too short, and only with *The Good, the Bad and the Ugly* was Sergio Leone able to really be himself.

There is a new concept of time in him which contains the essence of his genius and is based on extension.

Above and beyond the differences that the size of the audiences or hasty labelling might seem to underline, Marguerite Duras comes to mind. But whereas in Duras the extension of time expresses everyday reality, material or moral, in Leone it infiltrates genres – action films, Westerns – where speed reigns supreme. Another provocation, more provocative than Duras. Speed exists in Leone's work, excessive, preposterous speed: in the wink of an eye several gun-loads of bullets are fired, but only after an unlikely ceremonial, five minute long pause, articulated by countless close-ups contrary to narrative logic, where no action takes place. This rhythm is contradictory, as is the constant accumulation of vulgar with majestic elements. We are not far from Menotti and his opera of the dismal. It is a rare example of avant-garde moviemaking understood and adored by a vast public.

Admirable and precarious work, like that of Syberberg or Jancso, it relies upon the discovery of new formal principles (I almost wrote new formulas) whose interest may wane very quickly, and this helps us understand Leone's "fear of filming."

Introduction 2018
The Man Who Corrupted the Western
by Oreste De Fornari

It took a very long time to win me over to the cult of Sergio Leone. The first time I wrote about him was in a school magazine, more than fifty years ago, thanks to the promptings of a young Jesuit who was later to become an expert on Kurosawa. The intention was to applaud the samurai film *Yojimbo,* which we had just seen at the high school film club, and slate *A Fistful of Dollars*, basically because the former, being a black and white Japanese film, was Art, while the latter, being a technicolor Spaghetti-Western, was a mere money-maker. Anyway, every-one at the time spoke badly of Spaghetti Westerns.
My scepticism grew over the years, especially as I saw myself as a sort of "Frenchified" film buff with a penchant for things American, you might say a worthy child of *Cahiers*. And the measured style of Ford, Hawks, Mann was incompatible with any form of admiration, not even mild indulgence, towards the baroque approach favored by Leone and his followers (as far as the followers are concerned, I still haven't changed my mind). Only *The Good, the Bad and the Ugly*, released on Christmas Eve 1966, possibly because of its historical background, (the American Civil War), caught my attention. I was encouraged in my view by Enzo Natta's review in *Cineforum*, the magazine I read at the time. Later, however, I found *Once Upon a Time in the West* unoriginal and too solemn, a view shared by my friends at *Cinema e Film*. Years later, when I had occasion to write a short book on Leone for the publisher Moizzi, I jumped at the idea. I was particularly drawn to the possibility of making comparisons with American Westerns. Comparisons like this are the critic's daily bread, they give our job the aura of a specific science (but the style, lofty and verbose, left a lot to be desired). Over time, my artistic conservatism mellowed. On the occasion of the publication, by Ubilibri, of *Once Upon a Time in America*, I attempted to transform the book into a sort of all-inclusive album, enriched with photographs and stories provided by the director and his team. I think it was worth the effort because *America*, for many including myself, is Leone's masterpiece. In the meantime, Leone has left us, far too soon, in 1989, taking with him his dream for a film about the Siege of Leningrad.
In 1997, Ubulibri brought out a revised and corrected re-edition, of which Gremese Editore published French and English adaptions.
Twenty years later, Leone's influence can be recognized in an ever-growing number of films and more and more directors admit the debt they owe him. Not least among them the post-modern directors, aces of the *pastiche* such as Tarantino who claims that his favorite film is *The Good, the Bad and the Ugly*. Even one of the fathers of Neorealism, Carlo Lizzani, has denied his earlier misgivings, explaining that Leone's mannerism was in reality a way to affirm an Italian identity.
In truth, as I see it, the only justification I can invoke for the re-edition of this book, which now sports a new layout (the photographic content is different, there are new sections, and even the old ones have been up-dated and enhanced), is a sense of proportion. I do not be-lieve it does a filmmaker any good to receive praise for every aspect of every one of his films. Better to leave the emphasis to Leone, who was a genius, there is no point in imitating him with assessments that are equally emphatic. Moreover, Leone himself was more than capable of self-criticism, for instance regarding *Duck! You Sucker. Once Upon a Time in America*, for example, never fails to captivate me, despite the passing years, with its mesmerising flash-backs and its ambiguous hero, so generous as to forgive the friend who betrayed him, but so contemptible as to rape the girl of his dreams. However, other aspects have always seemed to me weak and loose-ended, such as the depiction of the syndicates or the lacklustre nym-phomaniac played by Tuesday Weld (Leone himself was none too pleased with her). There are other unsettled questions, too, above all the death of Max. I cannot believe he would have

jumped into the garbage disposal van of his own accord (only the tragi-comic humor of a Fantozzi film could conceive of such a suicide). I would suggest that the apocryphal, abbreviated American version, however appalling it may be (I haven't seen it myself, Mary Corliss was the only person to speak well of it, in an article that appears in the third section of this book), can at least boast the gambit of the gun shot off-screen that tells us Max has committed suicide, which settles the matter once and for all. After all, even Hitchcock had settled an ending in the same way, suggesting with his off-screen gunshot Michel Piccoli's suicide at the end of *Topaz* (it was nonetheless a somewhat slipshod conclusion, and was added during post-production). It must be admitted, however, that Leone was not adverse to a bit of mystery, or so he told me on one of the last occasions we met. He also confessed that, if he had to do that film again, he would make it even more intricate, with more hithers and thithers in time. So we must not be too surprised that there are at least three different versions around, which make the intricacies all the more hermetic. Hermeticism, mannerism, postmodernism, alessandrinism, byzantinism. Maybe the best way to describe Leone is what I heard many years ago from Alberto Ongaro: he saw Leone as a corrupter of stories, a splendid corrupter of Western stories. What exactly this is supposed to mean I have tried to explain in these pages.

Part One
LIFE AND FILMS

Once Upon a Time in America.

Biography – Leone's Life Story

Towards Life

Early twentieth century. Sergio Leone's maternal grandfather, Milanese of Austrian origins, was the director of the Hotel de Russie in Rome, in Piazza del Popolo; his paternal grandfather was a person of note from Avellino. His father, Vincenzo Leone, who had studied law and spent time among the Neapolitan artistic milieu, soon became an actor with the company of Eleonora Duse, adopting the screen name of Roberto Roberti. He moved to Turin, one of the capitals of the up-and-coming film industry, and from 1904 he worked as an actor and director for Itala Film, the film production company created by Giovanni Pastrone. In 1913 he directed the first Italian Western, *Indian Vampire*, starring Edvige Valcarenghi, stage name Bice Waleran. The two married the following year. Up until 1928 Vincenzo Leone directed eighteen films starring the diva Francesca Bertini.

His father Vincenzo, stage name Roberto Roberti.

It all started with the film: *Indian Vampire* (1913), the first Italian Western.

1923. Benito Mussolini was Prime Minister. Leone joined the National Fascist Party. Four days later the treasurer ran off with the money and Leone didn't renew his party card. That same year Mussolini invited him to make a film from a story he had written in his youth, *Claudia Particella, the Cardinal's Mistress*, but Leone refused (according to Gian Piero Brunetta he actually agreed, and wrote the screenplay). As president of the Italian directors' association, in response to the critical situation of the film industry, he proposed to the Minister of Corporations, Giuseppe Bottai, the creation of a cooperative system. Bottai rejected the project (it smacked of communism) and threatened him with forced confinement. He was saved by Forges Davanzati ("the only honest Fascist minister").

1928. Pola Negri invited Leone to move to Berlin to work with her, but Leone declined the invitation: his wife after 14 years of marriage was finally pregnant.

His mother Edvige Valcarenghi, stage name Bice Waleran.

Sergio Leone in 1929.

Little Sergio in his car.

1929-1989: Sixty years of life (and forty in films)

1929. On 3 January Sergio was born at the Palazzo Grimaldi Lazzeroni, Rome, near the Trevi Fountain. He was brought up in the old, colorful Trastevere neighborhood.

1935-1939. He attended primary and middle school at the Institute of St. Giovanni Battista de la Salle. As it so happened one of his class mates was Ennio Morricone, whom he was to meet again – initially without recognizing him – twenty five years later. In order to get his son out of Fascist Saturdays, his father enrolled him in a fencing class. He hated dead languages. He enjoyed Italian, philosophy, geography and above all history. He also had a real passion for the Neapolitan puppet shows that were staged at the Gianicolo hill. The epic "boys will be boys" scraps that Sergio and his pals got into on the steps of Viale Glorioso gave him an idea for a story (abandoned after the release of Fellini's *I Vitelloni*). Like all boys of that era, Sergio was mad about American films: his heroes were Errol Flynn and Gary Cooper, but also Warner Oland of the Charlie Chan series. And Chaplin, of course. His favorite comic book was Cino and Franco. Meanwhile, his father was going through a period of forced unemployment. In order to make ends meet he sold his collection of antique furniture. Sergio never forgot those Sundays when he went with his dad to the Caffè Aragno, a meeting place for the left-wing intelligentsia, shadowed by two police officers.

1939. After a dozen or so years of ostracism (suspended once in 1930 for *Assunta Spina*), Leone's father was back behind the movie camera, again thanks to Forges Davanzati, to shoot *The Silent Partner*, a film of Pirandellian overtones starring Carlo Romano and Clara Calamai.

School pals, still unaware of the lofty future ahead: Sergio Leone (back row, 2nd from left) and Ennio Morricone (back row, 2nd from right) in third grade, 1937.

One of the earliest adventures (the title of which inspired Umberto Eco to write a novel of the same name in 2004) of *Cino and Franco*, little Sergio's favourite comic book.

1941. Sergio went to Naples to watch his father shoot *La Bocca sulla Strada*, by the Roman writer – and future leader of the political party known as *The Common Man's Front* – Guglielmo Giannini. The cast included Armando Falconi and, in a small part, Carla del Poggio.

1942. These were days of war and deprivation: Sergio helped in the struggle for survival and exchanged an old pair of his father's shoes for 25 kilos of flour.

1943. He made plans, together with a group of friends, to join the partisans in the mountains, but then changed his mind so as not to upset his mother.

1944. The arrival of the Americans. A positive binge of American films, novels, comic books. Sergio had a penchant for *noir* films. His father tried to persuade him to study law, but Sergio dreamed only of cinema. Still at high school, he worked during the holidays as an assistant director, his first job being on one of his father's films, *Il folle di Marechiaro* (The lunatic of Marechiaro), in which he played the part of an American Sub-Lt. He was then assistant to Carmine Gallone on the opera-films *La Forza del Destino*, *La Leggenda di Faust* and *Il Trovatore*. By the way, he hated opera! («When I see an actor singing sitting on a horse, fall off the horse and then climb back on again singing all the time, I really can't help laughing»).

1946. De Sica signed him up as assistant for the film *Bicycle Thieves*. He played one of German priests of the Propaganda Fide who take shelter from the rain at Porta Portese together with Lamberto Maggiorani and his son. The film is a perfect example of neorealism, at once melodramatic and extemporaneous. Leone never forgot the yellow pullover he wore under his red cassock, which stained a yellowish-red thanks to the rain. De Sica eventually succumbed to his pleas and refunded him for the damage.

1948. These were the days of the Constitution of the Italian Republic. General elections were held on 18 April (the first since the establishment of the Constitution). Sergio's father was a communist, he himself had socialist leanings. But when Socialist Pietro Nenni partnered with the Communist Party (PCI) to form the Popular Democratic Front, Leone turned against him. Later, he was to describe himself as a moderate anarchist. He was convinced you could not be a communist if you owned a villa. He always admitted he had a soft spot for Giulio Andreotti because of his sense of humour.

1949. Sergio dropped out of his college law studies. His parents left Rome and retired to Torella dei Lombardi in the province of Avellino.

1950-1958. He worked on several projects with Mario Bonnard (*Frine, Courtesan of Orient*, *Night of Love*, *La*

La Bocca sulla Strada (1941) by Leone senior, assisted by a twelve-year-old Leone junior.

Leone Junior's first film as assistant director: *The Mad Marechiaro* (1944), which, due to the war was not released until 1952.

Surprise, surprise, Sergio Leone (2nd from right next to the leading man Lamberto Maggiorani) in *Bicycle Thieves*.

Mario Bonnard, in the golden years of silent pictures, in the pose echoed by Alberto Sordi in his film *Gastone* (1959), the film that indirectly led to the beginning of Leone's career as a director.

Ladra, Allow Me, Daddy, Aphrodite, Goddess of Love, Il Voto). Bonnard was like a father to Sergio and invited him to stay at his home for a while. Sergio claims it was he who discovered, and later introduced, Brigitte Bardot first to Bonnard (*Night of Love*) and then to Robert Wise (*Helen of Troy*), but this is highly unlikely[1]. In just a short while, he had gained a reputation as a very reliable assistant, dynamic, unrelenting with the members of the cast who were always stirring it up: they knew they would not work with him again. For certain films, he was actually paid more than the director. He met Walsh (second unit for *Helen of Troy*) and also Welles, who played the part of the husband in Steno's *Man, Beast and Virtue.* They worked together for a few days in an unidentified film that was never finished (possibly *Mr Ackadin*).

1959. He assisted Fred Zinnemann on *The Nun's Story.* During his stay in the Congo he met Lumumba, future independence leader, who was at that time working in a Stanlyville post office, and he experienced first-hand the truth of colonialism («The blacks are treated worse than animals, no small wonder there was a revolution»). For Wyler he directed the chariot race in *Ben Hur,* two and a half months of filming, and every evening obliged to watch the silent version of *Ben Hur* with Ramon Novarro. He worked again with Bonnard for **The Last Days of Pompeii**, then went off to Spain to stand in for the director who was on sick leave (more probably he "ran away" and went back to Italy to direct *Gastone*; Leone chose Sergio Corbucci as the director of the second unit and Duccio Tessari as his assistant. Even though his name did not appear, this was, for the most part, the first film he actually directed. The cinema was his only passion. But he was not above flirting with some of the starlets. He said he was attracted most by physical beauty. Maybe he was afraid to fall in love. He saw intelligent women as friends and nothing

---

[1] Brigitte Bardot was not exactly a "discovery", given that she had already appeared in 13 films, both as the star and co-star, before *Helen of Troy*, with directors such as Willy Rozier, Anatole Litvak, Sacha Guitry, Marc Allégret and Rene Claire…[Ed.]

The famous chariot race in William Wyler's *Ben Hur*.

more. He was head over heels for years, after they met in 1950, for Silvana Mangano, but she was never to know. Like many men of his generation, he was a regular customer of brothels and he also fell in love with one of the girls who worked there. But his longest relationship, eight years, was with Miss Somalia, daughter of an Italian man and a Creole from Zanzibar.

1960. He married Carla Ranalli, a ballet dancer, whom he met in his teenage years (he fell in love with her because of her sense of humor). They were to have three children: Raffaella (1962), Francesca (1964) and Andrea (1969). The producer of *The Last Days of Pompeii*, namely Procusa (financed by Opus Dei), asked him if he was interested in directing a blockbuster, that eventually became **The Colossus of Rhodes**. Leone did not like the sword-and-sandal genre, but he accepted in order to pay for his honeymoon. First choice for the leading role was John Derek, who proved, however, to be undisciplined and arrogant. Leone objected and refused to be swayed even by the pleas of the actor's wife (a certain Ursula Andress). They chose Rory Calhoun, "a poor man's Cary Grant". The film had several "autobiographical" elements, one of which was fire («Flames have fascinated me ever since I was a kid...I must have arsonist side to me»).

1961. There was no lack of offers, but Leone refused more than 20 films with the name Maciste in the title. But had a hand, among other things, in the screenplay for Corbucci's *Romulus and Remus*, starring Steve Reeves. The cast also included Virna Lisi (the good girl) and Ornella Vanoni (the bad girl). He worked for a week on Giorgio Bianchi's *Il Cambio della Guardia*.

1962. He was second unit director for Robert Aldrich's Italian-American film *Sodom and Gomorrah*. "We needed an Italian director in order to get state funding". He was supposed to direct the second crew and he did in fact direct the battle scenes, but he soon became fed up with the American director, whom he had so admired as a filmgoer in the days of *The Big Knife* and *Vera Cruz*, and, annoyed at the waste of resources to the detriment of the producer (Lombardo), he walked out. (Aldrich later gave his own version of the facts, attributing the delays to Leone's unbearably slow working method.)

1964. The popularity of the sword-and-sandal genre was on the wane. Given the success of German-produced Westerns based on the novels by Karl May narrating the adventures of Winnetou, there was talk in Italy about the possibility of filming a Western here, too. Twenty-six were made before someone mentioned to Leone the idea of a Western based on Akira Kurosawa's *Seven Samurai*. This film, **A Fistful of Dollars**, was produced by Jolly Film (owned by Papi and Colombo) back to back with Mario Caiano's *Bullets Don't Argue*, but with a lower budget.

Impossible love, Silvana Mangano (seen here in *Bitter Rice*, 1949).

... and possible love, Carla Ranalli (seen here in a photo from 1968).

The Spanish poster of *Sodom and Gomorrah*, the direction of which was attributed solely to Leone.

Bullets Don't Argue, the forgotten higher-budget "twin" of *A Fistful of Dollars*.

Clint Eastwood, superstar of *A Fistful of Dollars* (set photo by Enrico Appetito).

The co-star Leone would have liked for *For a Few Dollars More*, Lee Marvin (1ˢᵗ left), and the actor he got, Lee Van Cleef (2ⁿᵈ left), side by side in a scene from *The Man Who Shot Liberty Valance*, directed by John Ford (1962).

Both films, in fact, used the same set designs and costumes. Director and cast all adopted American pseudonyms, Leone choosing Bob Robertson, meaning "son of Roberto Roberti". The lead role, after they had ditched James Coburn on the grounds he was too expensive, was offered to a little-known TV actor, Clint Eastwood; the bad guy was an Italian actor, Gian Maria Volonté, who became famous some years later in the politically focused films of Rosi and Petri. For the music Jolly Film suggested Ennio Morricone, Leone's old classmate at primary school. The soundtrack was ground breaking, apart from the "Deguello" bugle call (that of *Rio Bravo* and *The Alamo*), which the director wanted to include at all costs, albeit with some small changes so as not to contravene the copyright. (For this Morricone chose an old lullaby played by a trumpet.) The film was released at the end of the summer in a minor theatre in Florence but, thanks to word-of-mouth, in just a few months, it had unexpectedly achieved widespread success. The Japanese filed suit for plagiarism. And they won. Papi and Colombo refused to pay Leone. *A Fistful of Dollars* turned out to be a very bad deal for Leone.

1965. At this point in time producer Alberto Grimaldi approached Leone with a particularly advantageous offer for another Western: all expenses paid, his director's salary and 50% of the takings. Leone accepted. He also felt it helped to make up in part for the deceitful way he had been treated by the previous producers. It was a sequel entitled: ***For a Few Dollars More***. Screenplay by Luciano Vincenzoni and Sergio Donati, from a story written together with Enzo dell'Aquila and possibily Fernando Di Leo, best known for his *poliziotteschi* films, both uncredited. Alongside the successful duo of the earlier film, Leone would have liked Lee Marvin (who was unfortunately busy on the set of *Cat Ballou*) but in the end settled for Lee Van Cleef, little-known character actor from many American Westerns (*High Noon, Bravados, The Man Who Shot Liberty Valance*). Rosemarie Dexter, who had starred in De Seta's *Almost a Man and Half a Man*, appeared in flash back sequences as Van Cleef's sister, but asked that her name be omitted from the credits, feeling it might undermine her reputation as an "intellectual" actress. The film was a commercial success and became the highest-grossing film of any nationality in the history of Italian cinema. The critics were lukewarm to decidedly derogatory. But Leone began to enjoy the fruits, especially financial, of success. He bought a 15ᵗʰ century house in the shade of the Gianicolo hill, which John Huston had had his eye on too, and he was finally able to unbridle his taste for antique furniture and 17ᵗʰ and 18ᵗʰ century silverware (a predilection he had inherited from his father. He was mortified in the thirties when they had been forced to sell everything in order to survive). «If I hadn't become a director I'd have become an antiquarian.» Given the films he made, that's easy to believe. Among his favorite artists were Degas, Goya, Velàzquez and Grosz. His private collection included paintings by Matisse, Mirò and De Chirico.

1966. For the third film of what became known as the "Dollars Trilogy", **The Good, the Bad and the Ugly**, United Artists joined the project. Screenwriter Vincenzoni recommended the comedy-writing team of Age and Scarpelli to work on the script, too, but Leone was disappointed with the result, judging it to be too comedic. But in fact the humor in the script worked well. Equally brilliant was the new co-star, Eli Wallach as the histrionic gunslinger, dubbed by Carlo Romano («You were better than me» the

American said.) There were shades in the script of Monicelli's *The Great War*, also written by Vincenzoni with Age and Scarpelli, and *Sardinian Brigade*, a Great War memoir by Emilio Lussu. Ennio Morriconi's music was even more pervasive than before, and was sometimes played on the set (someone compared the film to a baroque opera, but Leone preferred to call it a concert). The film was shot in Spain, near Burgos in the north, where Francisco Franco had established his first government in 1938: so Leone was filming the American Civil War where the Spanish Civil War had taken place. Another box office success, critics more objective, even the French. Moralists were still indignant over the excessive violence and by the bad language. For a few days it was rated +14. The *Centro Cattolico Cinematografico* rated it "unfit for all".

Eli Wallach (on the right), the third co-star of Leone's third Western *The Good, The Bad and The Ugly*, seen here in a scene from *How the West Was Won*, the film that first brought him to Leone's attention.

1967. He had a small part in the French-Italian film *Cemetery Without Crosses* directed by Robert Hossein. He played the hotel employee, but he did not have much faith in himself as an actor. The president of the conglomerate Gulf & Western, which controlled Paramount, approached Leone for another western. Leone came up with his own proposal for a film version of *The Hoods,* written by former gangster, Harry Gray, from which Giuseppe Colizzi had just stolen a scene for his film *Ace High*. He would have to wait 15 years to fulfil his dream. Two years later Mario Puzo's book *The Godfather* was published in America. Fulvio Morsella, brother-in-law of Leone's wife Carla, and the director's personal interpreter and assistant, had read the typescript and advised Leone to leave it alone (according to other sources it was his wife who warned him against it).

A Leone-style shot from *Cemetery Without Crosses*, an excellent French-Italian Western directed by Robert Hossein, in which Leone had a small acting part (cut during editing).

Leone teaching self-defence to Claudia Cardinale on the set of *Once Upon a Time in the West.*

Group hanging from *Hang 'Em High*, the film starring Clint Eastwood that Leone refused to direct.

Peter Bogdanovich [bottom left, together with director of photography László Kovács] at the time of his most critically-acclaimed films (*The Last Picture Show, What's Up, Doc?, Directed by John Ford*) and his irreconcilable conflict with Leone.

1968. Leone founded his own production company, Rafran, an acronym created from the initials of the names of his three children. He had decided to have a change of style after the "Dollars Trilogy". The new film was entitled **Once Upon a Time in the West** and he invited two promising young film buffs, Dario Argento and Bernardo Bertolucci, to write the screenplay. He was, however, disappointed in the two young men, and turned for help to Sergio Donati, who had been a ghostwriter for the previous films. The bad guy was Henry Fonda, whom Leone had wanted for *A Fistful of Dollars* («The exciting thing was how he walked in life, exactly as he did in films, like in slow-motion. He had the grace of a ballet dancer. Even if you tried to make him look uncouth with hairpieces and period costume, he still had a princely air about him.») Clint Eastwood refused the role of Harmonica, which went to Charles Bronson, and he also refused a cameo appearance as one of the three men who wait for Harmonica at the station (the other two were supposed to be Van Cleef and Wallach). In turn, Leone refused to direct Eastwood in *Hang 'Em High* and *Two Mules for Sister Sara.* The two were in competition, each one claiming merit for the successes of the other. They never worked together again.

1969. *Once Upon a Time in the West* was a box office success, despite its lack of humor and slow pace. It was hugely popular in France and Germany, where it outshone *Gone With The Wind*. Critics were enthusiastic, from the American critic Andrew Sarris to the French Serge Daney and Michel Ciment, but in Italy not everyone agreed (Kezich and Grazzini: «Leone is a slow pedaller», «there's a shortage of exclamation marks»). Admiring comments came from colleagues such as Ferreri, Kubrick, Boorman and Peckinpah.

1971. The year of **Duck! You Sucker.** The film describes the friendship between a Mexican bandit and an Irish revolutionary at the beginning of the Mexican Revolution in 1913 – not a particularly original subject at the time. Leone never intended to direct the film, he was only supposed to produce it, together with United Artists, Peter Bogdanovich being his original choice for director. But the two did not see eye to eye. For the two leads, Leone would have liked Malcolm McDowell and Jason Robards who, among other things, had just the right age difference, but he was obliged to agree to Rod Steiger and James Coburn. Giancarlo Santi was supposed to direct, but the two stars insisted on Leone himself. Directing Steiger turned out to be difficult, he was too over the top (and not peasant enough!), but by having him repeat scenes over and over again, Leone managed, most of the time, to get him to abandon his Actors Studio idiosyncrasies through sheer exhaustion. The film was initially to be called *Once Upon a Time...the Revolution*, which it retained for the French version. "It's not my favourite film, but it's the one that cost me the most money. I'm fond of it like I'd be fond of a disabled child." It was reasonably successful in Italy, but did poorly in America. Leone's reputation continued to grow and a first book about him was published, a monographic issue of "Bianco e Nero" [*L'antiwestern e il caso Leone* (The anti-western and the Leone case)] written by Franco Ferrini.

1973. The popularity of comedic Spaghetti Westerns was growing, thanks to the success of the duo Terence Hill/Bud Spencer (*They Call Me Trinity* and *Trinity Is Still My Name*). Leone did not like them, but decided to produce a film that was intended to be like a sort of epitaph for the genre, **My Name Is Nobody**, where the young gunslinger Terence Hill competes with the legendary older gunslinger Henry Fonda. Tonino Valerii, former assistant to Leone in *For a Few Dollars More*, was chosen to direct, but Leone was not going just to stand back and watch. "I directed the opening scene at the barber's, the battle with the Wild Bunch, and the final shoot-out." I was obliged to do it because Henry Fonda had to leave the set for another film. The film was a bit of a disappointment. Valerii failed to bring a poetic element to the meeting between the legend, Henry Fonda and his caricature, Terence Hill. (Valerii claimed that Leone shot two different, less important, scenes: the saloon scene with Nobody showing off his gunslinger skills in the glass contest and parts of the sequence of the village festival.)

1974. Leone moved to a villa in the EUR neighborhood of Rome, which had an underground film theater. ("This is where I watch the bad films, the good ones I want to see in a proper theater with an audience.")

1975. The next production was another spoof Western with Terence Hill (*A Genius, Two Partners and a Dupe*). Damiano Damiani was chosen to direct. It was intended as a Western version of *The Sting*, but Damiani had no talent for irony. Leone himself directed the scene that precedes the opening credits with the attack of the bogus Indians, while Giuliano Montaldo directed the siege of the Indians. A total let-down.

1977 and beyond. Leone produced Luigi Comencini's *The Cat*, Giuliano Montaldo's *A Dangerous Toy*, Carlo Verdone's *Fun is Beautiful* and *Bianco Rosso e Verdone*. For the first of these two, he helped Verdone in his directorial debut and with the editing, but with such zeal that he actually slapped Verdone in the face in front of everybody. He refused a number of biographical miniseries for TV (*Marco Polo*, *Garibaldi*) and instead agreed to shoot TV commercials (Gervais ice-cream, Renault 18, J&B Whisky, Europ Assistance, Palmolive, Talbot Solara, Renault 19 etc.): because it was fun, and he could travel and because it gave him an opportunity to put to the test his ability to be concise.

The first book about Leone, written by the future co-scriptwriter of *Once Upon a Time in America*, Franco Ferrini.

Leone on the set of *My Name Is Nobody* looking very much the Director (with Henry Fonda, on the ground, and Terence Hill, standing up).

Leone at his villa in EUR, with Carlo Verdone.

Leone's commercial for Renault.

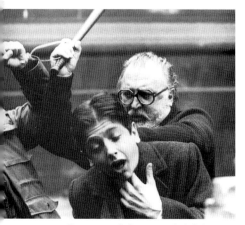

Leone explains a cop's job to the boys of *Once Upon a Time in America*.

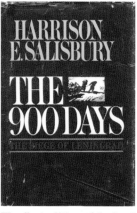

The first edition of the book that gave Leone the inspiration for the film he never managed to make.

1982-1983. Shooting began of ***Once Upon a Time in America***, Leone's pet project that he had been working on for some time (after having met the author of the book Harry Gray, in New York, and having convinced Grimaldi to buy the rights). Originally, he had wanted an international cast, with Jean Gabin and Gérard Depardieu in the role of the old and the young Max, Richard Dreyfuss as grown-up Noodles and Claudia Cardinale as Carol (the nymphomaniac). The screenplay had been written by Enrico Medioli, Franco Arcalli, Franco Ferrini, Benvenuti & De Bernardi. Then, after the split with Grimaldi (in trouble after the commercial and critical failure of Bertolucci's *1900* and *Fellini's Casanova* and sceptical of the script, which he thought too long and with too negative a hero), the Israeli producer Arnold Milchan joined the project, acquiring the rights. De Niro enthusiastically accepted the role of Noodles and the rest of the cast was chosen with the New York setting in mind. Shooting took place in America (only a few weeks, blocked by the unions), Canada and Italy (the background in Noodles and Deborah's last evening scene was the Hotel Excelsior at the Lido di Venezia).

1984. *Once Upon a Time in America* was released first in Canada and France, then in the United States and Italy. The 281-minute version, judged too long and enigmatic after the American previews, was shortened to 139 minutes by the American distributors and the scenes were rearranged in chronological order, without Leone's involvement. It received favorable reviews at the Cannes Film Festival and enjoyed success in Europe, but not in America (where only the shortened version was released). It won no Oscars. But Leone earned recognition as a master film-maker even by those critics who had once been hostile to him. More amazing still was the enthusiastic approval of the *Centro Cattolico Cinematografico*.

1985 and beyond. Leone had long been toying with the idea of a film about the Siege of Leningrad and at last the project seemed about to take off. It told of the love story between an American cameraman and a Russian girl during the three-year siege of the city that brought terrible suffering to the population. With the easing of tensions in the Soviet Union during the Gorbachev era, the project seemed less of a pipe dream. De Niro was considered for the lead male role; while the screenplay was to be a collaborative effort involving a Russian, Arnold Yanovich Vittol, an American, Alvin Sargent and two Italians Benvenuti and De Bernardi. The Soviets themselves were to provide extras, sets and tanks. And, just in case the Leningrad project fell through, there was a standby: a remake of *Gone with the Wind...*

1988. Leone was a member of the jury at the Cannes Film Festival. He endorsed Ermanno Olmi's *The Legend*

The jury of the 1988 Venice Film Festival (Sergio Leone is second from the right in the back row, towering over Lina Wertmüller).

of the Holy Drinker, which went on to win the Golden Lion.

1989. Sergio Leone died of a heart attack, or, in the words of Christopher Frayling "because his heart just stopped beating", on 30 April in Rome. He was in bed with his wife, watching the Robert Wise film, *I Want to Live* on TV.

P.S. [For Sergio]

1989. He was buried on 3 May in the little cemetery at Pratica di Mare, in the province of Rome. The Annecy International Animated Film Festival created a Sergio Leone prize for the best up-and-coming Italian or French film maker (Pupi Avati, Gianni Amelio, Fabio Carpi, Giuseppe Bertolucci, Carlo Mazzacurati, Daniele Luchetti are among past winners).

Susan Hayward, awaiting her execution, in the last film Leone saw, *I Want to Live.*

a b

Two graves for Sergio Leone: one in the cemetery at Pratica di Mare [a] and one – a temporary tribute (2016) from the director's fans – at the cemetery of Santo Domingo de Silos [b] where the final scene of *The Good, The Bad and The Ugly* was filmed.

Life (and the cinema) goes on: Andrea and Raffaella Leone.

1992. Clint Eastwood dedicated to Sergio Leone and Don Siegel (who died in 1991) his award-winning *Unforgiven*.

1993. Torella dei Lombardi became the home of another award dedicated to Sergio Leone.

1999-2002. Several books on Leone were published, among which *Tutto Il Cinema di Leone* by Marcello Garofalo and the monumental biography *Sergio Leone: Something to do with Death* by Christopher Frayling.

2012. The Cineteca di Bologna restored a long version (245 minutes) of *Once Upon a Time in America*, adding the scenes that Leone himself had chosen to omit in 1984. The Leningrad film was never made, and never would be. Giuseppe Tornatore re-evaluated the project, writing a screenplay that was very different from Leone's original idea (the love story between the American and the Russian girl was cut), but in the end he, too, gave up on the idea (the screenplay was published in 2018 with the title *Leningrado*).

Today (2018). Andrea and Raffaella Leone are president and managing director of the Leone Film Group, established by their father in 1989 (and quoted on the stock exchange in 2012). It has produced films by Paolo Genovese (*The Place, Perfect Strangers*) and Paolo Virzì (*Like Crazy*). Projects on the agenda include *Colt*, a western series written and directed by Stefano Sollima from an idea by Serio Leone.

IL MIO MODO DI VEDERE LE COSE
TALVOLTA E INGENUO, UN PO' INFANTILE.
MA SINCERO
COME I BAMBINI DELLA SCALINATA
DI VIALE GLORIOSO

SERGIO LEONE

✝ S P Q R   1999

«**My way of seeing things may be naïve and a little bit childish, but it's sincere. Just like the kids of Viale Glorioso. Sergio Leone**». Commemorative plaque to Sergio Leone in Viale Glorioso (Rome, Trastevere), where the future director used to play as a child.

Sergio Leone's Films

Legend for Cast & Credits

✏ Screenplay

🎥 Photography

♫ Music

🎬 Cast and Characters

📖 Plot summary

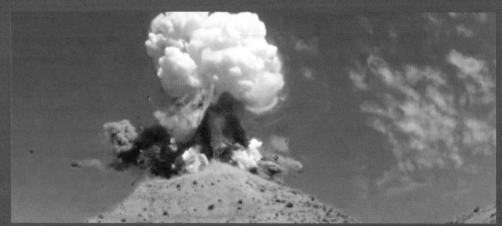

The Last Days of Pompeii.

The Colossus of Rhodes.

1. Before the West
The Last Days of Pompeii
The Colossus of Rhodes

There was a time in wich to become a good director you needed to "pay your dues", namely a wanna-be director had to work as an assistant for a very long time.

Us, as contemporary of Nanni Moretti, we look back on that time with regret, because back then, films were well-made at least. Obviously, if films from the fififties and sixties gave off that sense of reality and wholeness it wasn't just because of the directors' skills and professionalism. Unluckly for the viewers, italian cinema never recovered its greatness: nowadays Italian films are of low quality even if they're produced by skillful directors.

However, Sergio Leone must've been adamant about the value of a long training and maybe that's the reason it took him so long to direct his first film. In fact, Leone worked as an assistant director to more or less fififty films before making his debut.

Sergio's parents both worked for the cinema. His mother, a silent movie actress, Edvige Valcarenghi (stage name: Bice Waleran), marries a veteran film director, Vincenzo Leone (alias Roberto Roberti) and from this union is born a son, Sergio, on January 3, 1929.

Leone makes his official debut as an assistan director to De Sica's *The Bicycle Thief*, the film-symbol of Italian neorealism, and in which he also plays one of the young German seminarists of the Propaganda Fide walking around Trastevere under the heavy rain. For ten years he is an assistant to many Italian directors: Bonnard, Camerini, Soldati, Comencini, Gallone... and some Americans: Wise, Walsh, Wyler, Zinnemann (who come to Hollywood-on-the-Tiber to shoot spectacular productions). Leone had many fathers and will have many sons: Corbucci, Argento, Giraldi, Colizzi, etc. got their start with him.

In 1959 Bonnard interrupted the scarcely initiated shooting of *Last Days of Pompeii* to return to Rome in order to direct Alberto Sordi and Vittorio De Sica in *Gastone* (one of the few decent portrayals of the Italian Belle Epoque) and entrusted the direction of the historical film to Leone. At first glance *Last Days of Pompeii* might seem like a pale copy of the American spectacular epics about persecuted Christians, like *Quo Vadis?* without the spiritual beauty of Deborah Kerr / Lygia and without the amusing perfidies of Peter Ustinov / Nero. But the lack of humor and the wooden acting are compensated for by certain muscular dynamics that are absent in the American models. We see Steve Reeves rip his chains out of the walls of his cell, fight with a shark in the consul's pool, and confront a

THE LAST DAYS OF POMPEII
1959

✎ Ennio De Concini, Luigi Emmanuelli, Sergio Corbucci, Sergio Leone, Duccio Tessari (from the book by Edward Bulwer-Lytton, 1834)

🎥 Antonio Ballestreros
♫ Eraldo da Roma

Steve Reeves .... Glauco
Christine Kaufmann .... Elena / Jone
Fernando Rey .... Arbace
Anne-Marie Baumann .... Julia
Barbara Carroll .... Nidia

Cast and credits page 287
Director's statements page 132

The good girls and the bad girls of Mervyn LeRoy (*Quo Vadis?*, 1951) and Leone & Bonnard (*The Last Days of Pompeii*, 1959): Deborah Kerr [a] vs Christine Kaufmann [b], Patricia Laffan [c] vs Ann-Marie Baumann [d].

lion in the arena. The movie had phenomenal success: 830 million lire, very close to the 900 million record established the year before by Pietro Francisci's *The Labors of Hercules*. From 1958 to 1964 more than 150 of such costume films were produced. They were low-budget productions with great ambitions as spectaculars that compensated for the poverty of means with exhibitions by champions of muscle power and the eroticism of Sapphic queens, sadistic tortures and a pastiche of styles (baroque, comedy, parody, fantasy). Often they were too timid, but sometimes rather foolhardy as in Cottafavi's *Hercules and the Conquest of Atlantis*. Their success was limited to neighborhood movie houses and to certain Parisian film magazines. Another curious fact: the cast of *Last Days of Pompeii* brings together the future fathers of the Spaghetti Western – Sergio Leone, Duccio Tessari, Sergio Corbucci and Enzo Barboni.

Steve Reeves showing off his muscles and his courage: *The Last Days of Pompeii*.

30

a

b

The Last Days of Pompeii [a, c] vs *The Colossus of Rhodes* [b, d]: like a bad and a good copy of the same film. Even though Rhodes and Pompei are 300 years and 800 miles apart, the dead look just the same...

c

d

THE COLOSSUS OF RHODES
1961

✎ Luciano Chitarrini, Ennio De Concini, Carlo Gualtieri, Sergio Leone, Luciano Martino, Aggeo Savioli, Cesare Seccia, Duccio Tessari

🎬 Antonio Ballestreros, Emilio Foriscot
♪ Angelo Francesco Lavagnino

Rory Calhoun .... Darios
Lea Massari .... Diala
Georges Marchal .... Peliocle
Mabel Karr .... Mirte
Angel Aranda .... Koros
Mimmo Palmara .... Ares
Roberto Camardiel .... Xerses

📖 Military hero Darios visits his uncle on the island of Rhodes for a holiday. He flirts with the beautiful Diala and becomes involved with a group of rebels, seeking to overthrow the tyrannical king Xerses, who has just finished constructing the famous Colossus. He seeks Diala's aid but then realises that she, longing for power, has betrayed him and is in cahoots with Xerses's evil second-in-command, who is secretly preparing to overthrow the tyrant with the help of Phoenician agents. Spies, duels, human sacrifices, fire and brimstone raining down on enemy ships, prisoners suspended over the lions' den and, best of all, an earthquake that lays waste to the city. Diala, plagued with remorse, is killed by falling debris.

Cast and credits page 235
Detailed plot page 236
Director's statements page 132
Press review 237
Quotes and dialogues from the film page 185-210

After this success Leone receives an offer to make his official debut in a large production where the true protagonist is not a man but a monument: *The Colossus of Rhodes*.

This time all the Hollywood film conventions are present: duels fought while balancing on the shoulders of the Colossus, prisoners suspended above the lion pit, parties with gossip exchanged among guests at the triclinium, the poisoner who is himself poisoned, cathartic catastrophes, sensational occurrences at just the right moment (Xerxes exclaiming "as long as there is the breath oflife in me..." and in-

Never say "as long as there is breath in me": Serse/Roberto Camardiel in *The Colossus of Rhodes.*

terrupted by an arrow piercing his breast); exquisite tortures (one prisoner has molten metal poured on his back, another is shut up in a bell and deafened). Dialogue full of solemn wishes ("I hope all Olympus is on your side"), heroic precepts ("the freedom of a people is worth six human lives"), inspired gallantries ("Women here exude a special fragrance: they seem made of sunlight"), senile pleasantries ("At your age one's sufferings are only due to women; at mine you suffer because women no longer make you suffer"). Even the hero, a down-to-earth bon vivant, is of American manufacture. However, we are far from the great models of the genre. A comparison with *The Ten Commandments*[1] could be instructive.

Story elements: In the American movie, the Exodus was an indirect consequence of the jealousy of Ramses / Yul Brynner when the beautiful Nefertiti / Anne Baxter prefers Moses /

---

[1] Cecil de Mille, 1956.

The beautiful ladies of Rhodes, made of sun and stone: Lea Massari [a,c] vs Mabel Karr [b,d] (*The Colossus of Rhodes*).

Charlton Heston to him. Leone's movie lacks a central conflict and an interesting villain, the characters have almost no private concerns, the action is artificial and the about-face of the heroine gratuitous (the script was partly re-written during shooting).

Credibility: To make it seem that his boulders were not made of cardboard, De Mille invented a dramatic episode: the old Hebrew woman who falls during the transporting of the stones and would be crushed if Charlton Heston did not intervene. Leone's devices for faking big-budget scenes are more naive, e.g. the interminable final catastrophe which leaves us rather cold since the victims are all anonymous.

Glamour: Anne Baxter on board her boat tries to seduce a mud-covered and semi-nude Charlton Heston. The Italian film lacks this quality; there's an unconvincing-looking Rory Calhoun and a miscast Lea Massari, with her schoolgirl air, playing the part of the deceiving vamp. Only the film's sets are glamorous, with their strange mixture of different periods.

In short, Leone's idea of Hollywood style was so approximate as to make one wonder what use his ten-year apprenticeship had been (which then continued when he was director of the second unit in Aldrich's *Sodom and Gomorrah*, a sorry biblical epic whose only light came from the eyes of Anouk Aimee as the perfidious, incestuous queen). Or else mythology was simply not his genre.

In fact he only found a personal style when he turned to the Western. Among other things, his first Westerns became for the public the equivalent of these gladiatorial spectacles – bloody, exciting, immoral – that his classical epics so dismally evoked.

33

a

b

c

d

Views of the Colossus (*The Colossus of Rhodes*).

In the previous page. *The Ten Commandments* (1956) [b, d] vs *The Colossus of Rhodes* (1961) [a, c]:
Charlton Heston and Rory Calhoun are seduced by Anne Baxter and Lisa Gastoni; Heston and the elderly
slave he saved together like mother and son and the unknown victims of the earthquake in Rhodes.

A Fistful of Dollars.

For a Few Dollars More.

The Good, The Bad and The Ugly.

2. THE DOLLAR TRILOGY
A Fistful of Dollars
For a Few Dollars More
The Good, the Bad and the Ugly

Westerns are as familiar and as remote as the moon. You recognize them at once, but they are not easy to define (epic style? Stoic morality? Historical? Horses and guns?). All the more because it is hard to find one in its pure state (they are often mixed with melodrama or film *noir* elements). And despite their American origins, for a long time they have also been produced in Europe: from the Belle-Epoque France of Joe Hamman-Arizona Bill to the Nazi Germany of Luis Trenker's *Der Kaiser von Kalifornien (The Emperor of California)*, to the Germany of the sixties of the Winnetou cycle inspired by the novels of Karl May, to Spain...

The first Italian writer of Westerns, Emilio Salgari, was a contemporary of the Lumiere brothers. Starting in 1896, this highly popular writer wrote a cycle of three Western novels without ever setting foot outside Italy. Every now and then we note historical events in them. For example, in *La Scotennatrice* [The Scalptress] (1909) there is a description of the Indian massacre at Sand Creek perpetrated by Colonel Chivington's troops on November 29, 1864. "The warriors were scalped, killed or wounded, the women disemboweled and their fingers cut off to get at their rings, the children's heads smashed by stones." And this, sixty years before *Soldier Blue*!

But the Italian Western does not have only literary precedents. At the beginning of the century, during the European tour of Buffalo Bill's circus, the American cowboys were challenged by the Tuscan *butteri* and the rodeo challenge ended in a sensational victory of the latter.

In December 1910 the Metropolitan Opera of New York presented the world premier of Giacomo Puccini's *The Girl of the Golden West* based on David Belasco's drama. It is the love story of a saloon proprietress and an outlaw, the film abounding in manhunts, poker games, attempted lynchings and horses on the stage. There is even the blood dripping from the ceiling which leads to the discovery of the bandit as in *Rio Bravo*[2].

More than half a century later Leone was asked to stage *The Girl of the Golden West*, but strange as it may seem, he never really liked the opera. Between 1910 and 1949 a few Westerns were made in Italy such as Carl Koch's melodramatic *Una Signora dell'Ovest* [A Lady from the West] (1942) with Valentina Cortese, Michel Simon and Rossano Brazzi, and the parody *Il Fanciullo del West* [The Kid from the West] by Giorgio Ferroni (1943) starring Macario. One of the very first was *La Vampira Indiana* [Indian Vampire] (1913) directed by Leone's father[3] and starring his mother.

One cannot omit two pictures by Pietro Germi from the list, undeclared tributaries of the Western: *In Nome della Legge* [In the Name of the Law] (1949) on the conflict between an upright and fearless judge and an old-fashioned Mafioso (on horseback); and, above all, *Il Brigante di Tacca del Lupo* [Brigand from Tacca del Lupo] (1952) which seems distantly inspired by *Fort Apache*[4] in its depiction of the fight between Piedmontese blue jackets and pro-Bourbon brigands.

In 1948 the first issue of *Tex* by Bonelli and Galeppini came out, one of the most popular Western comic books. Exported to various European and South American countries, it is still published today. In it one finds law-abiding Indians, baroque villains à la Cagliostro, lots of people killed, and few female characters.

---

[2] Howard Hawks, 1956.

[3] Who used the alias Roberto Roberti.

[4] John Ford, 1948.

A 1912 edition of the score for *The Girl of the Golden West* by Puccini [a] and a scene from the 2016 production of the opera at La Scala [b]; the first edition of *La Scotennatrice* (The Scalper) by Emilio Salgari (1909) [c]; the posters of near-Westerns *The Emperor of California* (1936) [d], *Girl of the Golden West* (1942) [e] and *The Bandit of Tacca del Lupo* (1952) [f]; the first issue of *Tex* by Bonelli and Galeppini (1948) [g].

Life and Films

Further to be included among the sources of the Italian Westerns are some American productions, mainly from the fifties, that helped form the taste of Leone and his followers. First of all there is *Shane*[5] with its pale-clad hero and black-clad, taciturn villain seen through the fascinated eyes of a little boy. The film has certain realistic details such as bullets that make the men they hit jump backwards. Other adult Westerns Leone may have remembered only for an object, a gesture, an actor's face and which he transferred to his own films denuded of any ethical historical values – the watch of the avenger in *Bravados*[6], the treasure hidden in the cemetery in *The Law and Jack Wade*[7], the long raincoats of the bandits in *My Darling Clementine*[8], Charles Bronson playing the harmonica in *Vera Cruz*[9], James Coburn whittling a whistle in *The Magnificent Seven*[10], Henry Fonda giving a paralytic's crutch a kick in *Warlock*[11]; a businesswoman who thinks of exploiting the railroad passing through her land (*Johnny Guitar*[12]), three killers who wait for their victim at the station (*High Noon*[13]).

And then, for the sake of completeness, we should cite the James Bond series that preceded Leone's Westerns and which share with them a high rate of violence combined with a low rate of emotional involvement and moral implications. Then, too, there are certain comedies of the sixties that recount the cynicism and lust for riches by Italians during the economic boom with a mixture of complicity and disapproval. Exoticism, cynicism, melodrama, the comic-strip, parody – all these are elements that we find in the Italian Western. But the first ones were nothing but apocryphal versions of American originals where the directors used slightly fraudulent pseudonyms such as Terence Hathaway, John Fordson and Frank Garfield.

Leone enlisted in this foreign legion under the name Bob Robertson meaning "the son of Roberto Roberti". He had more imagination than his colleagues and instead of imitating the Americans, he imitated the Japanese. For *The Magnificent Seven*, John Sturges drew inspiration from Kurosawa's *Seven Samurai*[14]. Leone repeated this operation with *Yojimbo*[15], one of that director's distinctly minor films.

---

[5] George Stevens, 1953.

[6] Henry King, 1958.

[7] John Sturges, 1958.

[8] John Ford, 1946.

[9] Robert Aldrich, 1954.

[10] John Sturges, 1960.

[11] Edward Dmytryk, 1959.

[12] Nicholas Ray, 1954.

[13] Fred Zinnerman, 1952.

[14] *Shinchinin no Samurai*, Akira Kurosawa, 1954.

[15] Akira Kurosawa, 1961.

Once Upon a Time there was the (American) Western.

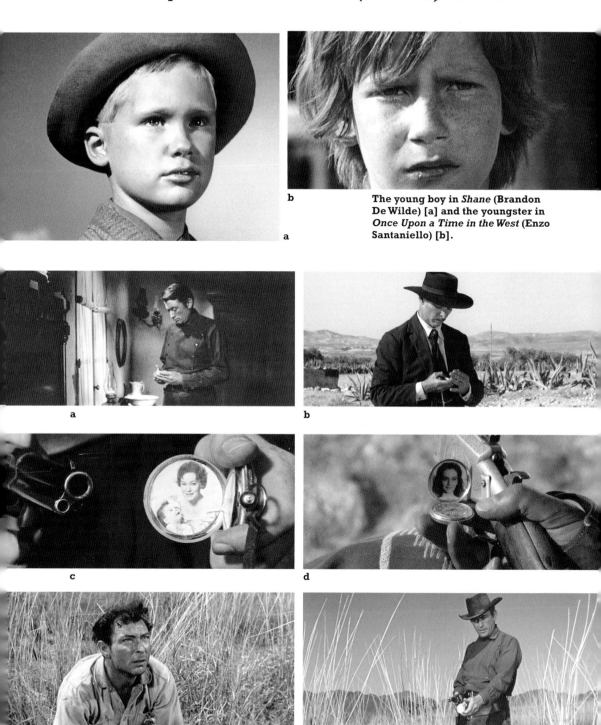

b

The young boy in *Shane* (Brandon De Wilde) [a] and the youngster in *Once Upon a Time in the West* (Enzo Santaniello) [b].

a

a

b

c

d

e

f

Gregory Peck looks at his watch in *The Bravados* [a, c, f] and Lee Van Cleef in *For a Few Dollars More* [b, d]. Strangely, in the 1958 film it is precisely Lee Van Cleef who plays the outlaw involved in an episode with the watch.

a

The loot hidden
in the cemetery
in *The Law and
Jake Wade* [a] and
the cemetery in
*The Good, The
Bad and The Ugly*
[b].

b

a

Charles Bronson
plays the
harmonica in *Vera
Cruz* [a] and in
*Once Upon a Time
in the West* [b].

b

A FISTFUL OF DOLLARS
1964

✎ Sergio Leone, Duccio Tessari, Victor A. Catena, G. Schock, Jaime Comas Gil, Fernando Di Leo, Tonino Valerii
(from *Yojimbo* by Akira Kurosawa, 1961)

🎬 Massimo Dallamano, Federico Larraya
♪ Ennio Morricone

🎭

Clint Eastwood .... The Man With No Name
Gian Maria Volonté .... Ramon Rojo
Marianne Koch .... Marisol
"Pepe" Calvo .... Silvanito
Wolfgang Lukschy .... John Baxter
Sieghardt Rupp .... Esteban Rojo
Antonio Prieto .... Benito Rojo
Margarita Lozano .... Consuelo Baxter

📖 Riding a mule, The Man With No Name enters the Mexican village of San Miguel in the midst of a power struggle between the three Rojo brothers and the Baxter family. He proves his speed and accuracy with a gun and offers his services to the highest bidder, but he then works alternately for both families. His clever plan is to play each family against the other in order to gain maximum profit for himself. He succeeds and the two families end up annihilating each other. He also has a good side to his character, but only on one occasion, when he rescues a concubine-slave from Ramon Rojo and takes her back to her family. The Rojos capture and torture him, but he escapes. In the end, protected by a home-made steel chest-plate hidden beneath his poncho, he challenges Ramon to a shootout and kills him, before riding off again.

Cast and credits page 237
Detailed plot page 238
Director's statements page 133
Press review 240
Quotes and dialogues from the film page 186-210

A Fistful of Dollars is a very faithful remake. It adds to the original massacre of the soldiers and the cemetery caper and deletes a few hold-ups and the intervention of a corrupt government official who takes bribes from both clans. But despite the almost identical subject matter, the two films have little resemblance.

The first break with tradition is the hero's appearance, which is very un-Hollywood. His unshaven cheeks and the *cigarillo* that hangs from his lips give him a certain squalid charm. But the impassive mask of a poker player does not hide the hard-won self control of a Bogart or a Cooper, but only the indifference of a killer. If the hero of the American Western lived on the brink between solitary adventure and the possibility of social integration, and if he took the side of the weak with a certain condescension, Leone's hero alternates incoherently between venality and gallantry. He sells himself to the highest bidder and kills for money, but he protects defenceless mothers and never shoots anyone in the back, keeping to a code of honor even stricter than that of Hollywood heroes who ride in the shadow of the Hays Office. Above all he is astute, but in a rather mechanical, take-it-for-granted way, quite in the style of James Bond. In the following movie, in order to win the confidence of El Indio / Volonté and penetrate his gang, Clint Eastwood decides to free one of the brigand's old buddies from prison. In an American movie we would probably have been treated to an intricate episode wherein the hero gets himself imprisoned to arrange the escape, or else to become friends with the convict and extort some secret from him that will win him admission to the gang. But Clint Eastwood chooses a quicker, easier way: he blows up the prison wall with a load of dynamite, thus allowing the prisoner to escape. Inventive storytelling was definitely out.

The scene in which Eastwood sells information to the Baxters would probably have been

A Fistful of Dollars *(1964)* vs
Yojmbo *(1961)*∗

∗ Many thanks to
Vimeo and Alejandro
Villareal.

treated by Hollywood in *noir* style. The hero is received in the boss' office in the presence of a bodyguard; an exchange of repartee, the boss is suspicious, the hero impertinent, the bodyguard looks grim and is impatient to use his fists. The boss' blonde enters and winks at the stranger. In Leone's picture there is more suspense and less humor. Mrs. Baxter comes home and goes up to her room where Eastwood, hiding in the shadows, surprises her from behind, puts a hand over her mouth and calms her down by telling her of the rival family's intentions. The husband enters and Eastwood disarms him. This rudimentary kind of drama is aggravated by a lack of definition (and charm) in the secondary characters: the villains who, except for

The ragtag charm of Clint Eastwood in *A Fistful of Dollars* and the troubled self-control of Gary Cooper in *High Noon*.

A somewhat unorthodox method to sell information (Clint Eastwood and Margarita Lozano in *A Fistful of Dollars*)**.**

Volonté are practically extras; the old tavern owner who makes us greatly miss the humor of Walter Brennan and George "Gabby" Hayes; the inexpressive mother, Marisol.

Aside from the hero's cynicism, the most startling novelties are, perhaps, the nonchalance of the shoot-outs and certain *Grand Guignol*-style torture scenes. In the American Western

The Mexican family is reunited. A frame from the film with a set photo by Enrico Appetito as a two-shot: *A Fistful of Dollars.*

a too frequent use of pistols was a sign of weakness. In Samuel Fuller's *Forty Guns* (1947) and Sturges' *Gunfight at the O.K. Corral*[16], the sheriff advances unwaveringly on the neurotic young outlaw or the drunken cowboy without drawing his Colt, and this example of cool courage is enough to paralyze his adversary. Leone's heroes, on the other hand, are glad to show off their ballistic abilities, not against bottles, tin cans or coins thrown into the air, but directly against human beings in duels which despite the preliminary suspense (long silences, menacing looks) resemble target practice. The most original shot is taken from the viewpoint of the crackling pistol that lets us see the enemies in long-shot dropping like flies.

This does not reach the sadistic refinements of the finale of *Rio Bravo* where dynamite explosions alternate with witty remarks, but to compensate there is a vague air of sportsmanship at least in the final duel pitting pistol against rifle where the winner is the one who reloads first.

The meticulous style in which the torture scenes are filmed are a milestone in the history of cinema cruelty. The giggles of the torturers, deforming close-ups of their faces, cigars squashed out on people's hands, fists emphasized during the mixing, details of the victims' swollen face (reduced, as Leone would have put it, to an *"ecce homo"*).

The Americans were capable of greater dramatic economy. When in Anthony Mann's *The Man From Laramie* (1955) Alex Nicol has his men immobilize James Stewart and then coldly shoot him in the hand, what is most moving is the close-up of James Stewart's anguish because of the atrocity he has to undergo, rather than a detail of the wounded hand. And one can say the same of the scene where Stewart is dragged by horses.

---

[16] John Sturges, 1957.

Blood-thirsty torturers (Clint Eastwood and Pepe Calvo) in *A Fistful of Dollars* [a-c] and the long close-up of fear and pain on James Stewart's face when he is beaten up in *The Man from Laramie* [d-g].

But it is not obligatory to be allusive. Homer described with surgical precision the most lacerating blows, even if he never forgot to precede the descriptions with some genealogical details about the fallen. And there is nothing more explicit than Toshiro Mifune's body pierced by a hail of arrows in the final scene of *Throne of Blood*[17] but by dint of the physical, of whistling arrows and of strangled cries, one reaches the point of total abstraction and the monarch ends up resembling an impaled animal.

Leone does not have Mann's sense of proportion nor the extravagant imagination of Kurosawa. The differences between *Yojimbo* and *A Fistful of Dollars* are primarily differences of taste. Take the hero's entrance into the village. In the first movie a dog crosses the street

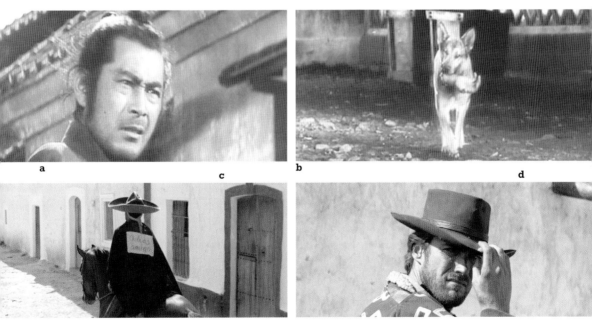

The difference between the grotesque (Toshiro Mifune and the dog with the dead man's hand in its mouth in *Yojimbo* [a, b]) and the humorous (Clint Eastwood and the dead man on his horse, in *A Fistful of Dollars* [c, d]).

---

[17] *Kumonosu-jo*, Akira Kurosawa, 1957.

holding a dead man's hand in its mouth; in the latter the corpse of a Mexican rides erect on horseback with a sign on his back saying "Adios amigo!" Kurosawa is grotesque, Leone merely ironic. Nevertheless his direction, a little neglected, has not destroyed the Elizabethan seductiveness of the material: the Machiavellian intrigue, the macabre humor, the theatrical decor with the homes of the two rival families on the opposite sides of the square as on a stage. Even the archaic nature of the human relationships remains (Marisol is a kind of slave-concubine, which, if it was almost obvious in the Japanese film, is enough to give an exotic flavor to the Italian one).

When the film was released, movie buffs lamented the loss of Hollywood's laconic pistols. But the general public loved it precisely because it did not resemble American Westerns and instead resembled the way one reinvented them in one's childhood games: a series of gunfights where the *pistoleros* never stop conceding encores. Leone has stated that what most fascinated him in the Western was "the possibility of taking justice into one's own hands: bang bang!" Even if it is not the first Western produced in Italy, it is certainly the first Italian-style Western. It is no accident that it was able to conquer both the middle and working-class audiences, something that rarely happened. And even more unusually, it succeeded in doing so without any kind of advertising campaign, but only by word of mouth (on this point see Tonino Valerii's testimony, page 175).

If from time to time even low-budget productions become box office champions, it means that in the movie industry free competition still exists. But even free competition has its rules and regulations, first and foremost those of copyright. Someone recognized in Leone's picture a pirated remake of *Yojimbo* and the case went to court. The Japanese film's producers were awarded the exclusive distribution rights of *A Fistful of Dollars* in Japan, Taiwan and South Korea and 15% of its commercial profits in the rest of the world.

Before the judge, Leone defended himself with a structuralist sally, affirming that in any case the copyright should go to Carlo Goldoni for *Harlequin, Servant of Two Masters.* Later he found a more plausible work to attribute Kurosawa's inspiration: Dashiell Hammett's *Red Harvest,* which is also the story of a very cunning, double-crossing avenger (a private eye in a detective agency) who cleans up a town in the clutches of gangsters by pitting one gang against the other. On a philological level it is a weak thesis (the only scene vaguely in common with the movie is the raid on the bootleggers' hide-out) however interesting it may be on a cultural one, demonstrating, as it does, how plots and cliches can travel from one continent to another with the authors being unaware of it. Leone seems to have unwittingly put a hard-boiled novel onto the screen.

Contrarily, it was excessive awareness that was responsible for making Walter Hill's terribly serious remake such a disappointment: *Last Man Standing* (1996) with Bruce Willis in the role that had been Toshiro Mifune's and Clint Eastwood's. One feels nostalgia for the Western background that justified the provocations, reprisals and, above all, Leone's approximative style. This too played its part in making *A Fistful of Dollars* so special: a cross between American brutality, Japanese ritualism, and Roman swagger.

FOR A FEW DOLLAR MORE
1965

✏ Sergio Leone, Luciano Vincenzoni
🎬 Massimo Dallamano
♪ Ennio Morricone

Clint Eastwood .... Monko
Lee Van Cleef .... Col. Douglas Mortimer
Rosemarie Dexter .... His sister
Gian Maria Volonté .... El Indio
Klaus Kinski .... The Hunchback
Josef Egger .... The old "prophet"
Luigi Pistilli .... Groggy
Mario Brega .... Nino
Mara Krupp .... Mary, the hotel manager's wife

📖 A sharp-witted young bounty hunter and an older man, a former army colonel, join forces and decide to go after a ruthless Mexican psychopath who has been broken out of prison by his gang. The Mexican carries with him a musical pocket watch that he took from a young girl he raped in his youth, and he smokes an addictive drug to cloud his memory of the incident. After a succession of chases, bank robberies, ploys and capers, poker games and shootouts, the bandits eventually eliminate each other and the colonel, who turns out to be the brother of the girl the Mexican bandit raped (who shot herself during the aggression), kills the bandit in a final shootout, while the other bounty hunter arbitrates. Having appeased his thirst for revenge, the colonel departs leaving his share of the bounty to his young companion.

Cast and credits page 257
Detailed plot page 258
Director's statements page 134
Press review 261
Quotes and dialogues from the film page 185-210

By now it seemed that the future of the Italian cinema lay west of the Missouri. Leone had discovered a successful new genre: the Spaghetti Western. (The slightly pejorative term was coined by the American press.) In 1965 alone, thirty such movies were made. Their ingredients are well-known: much gunfighting, lots of violence, no sentimental distractions and a pinch of irony.

Other directors added some variants. In *Django*, Sergio Corbucci tried to break all records for sadism. The hero, dressed in black, travels with a coffin from which he now and then takes out a machine-gun and mows down dozens of adversaries. The bad guys are crueler than usual: when they take the hero prisoner they do not stop with beating him up, they crush his hands to a pulp under the hoofs of horses. It also has culture: a quote from Eisenstein's *Alexander Nevsky,* with the Ku Klux Klanners swallowed alive by the mud. Everything is gratuitous, monotonous, shapeless – but at the time, the abuse of violence seemed scandalous. *Django* was the first Western to be banned to young people under eighteen and in England the censor refused to let it be shown at all. With *Il Grande Silenzio* [The Great Silence] Corbucci established another first: the first Western where in the end the bad guy (Klaus Kinski) kills the good guy (Jean-Louis Trintignant).

In *A Pistol for Ringo*, Duccio Tessari takes the Goldonian inspiration of Leone's movie for his own. Ringo, alias Angel Face, is a double-crossing hero, infallible with a pistol, and gallant with the ladies. His adversary is a grotesque Mexican bandit who has fun decimating his hostages by making them play Russian roulette. In the background there is the flirtating between the bandit's woman and a prisoner, the aristocratic hacienda owner. The attempts at rakish comedy are compromised by a constant play of juvenile jokes. For example, in the end Ringo kills the bandit with the astuteness of a billiard player: he shoots at a bell hanging from the ceiling, calculating the trajectory of the bounce and hits his target. In compensation, Tessari does not

a   b   c

In *A Fistful of Dollars* [a, b] coffins were a lucrative business and a secure hiding place, while in *Django* [c] the hero Franco Nero towed one behind him like a caravan or a dog.

lack ambitious cultural alibis. In a letter to the magazine *Cinema Nuovo* he writes: "My Ringo is a character full of doubts, of fears, who is constantly polemicizing (perhaps he is futilely anarchic, a nihilist steeped in Sturm und Drang) with a society which he does not accept but which, unconsciously, he wants to improve."

At the time it was fashionable, even among the literati, to discuss James Bond and the Spaghetti Western. Moravia thought that the success of the genre was the unconscious fear of over-population. The massacres carried out by Clint Eastwood and his likes were a lightning solution to the problem. Mario Soldati made sarcastic remarks at the expense of his ex-assistant Leone, but, curiously, he loved Giorgio Ferroni's *One Silver Dollar* because of the moving melancholy with which it represented the South after its defeat.

The Good (Clint Eastwood), the Ugly (Lee Van Cleef) and the Bad (Gian Maria Volonté) in *For a Few Dollars More*.

Leone sought more solid attractions than sadism or parody. For one thing, the quality of the faces. In the cast of his new movie *For a Few Dollars More*, along with Eastwood and Volante, there is a little-known American character actor, Lee Van Cleef, (*High Noon, The Man Who Shot Liberty Valance*) whom Leone promoted to co-star, creating a part made to measure for his sculptural profile. Another novelty with respect to the preceding film is the antiquarian's taste for period firearms, reflecting a hobby widely pursued in Italy. In addition there is a fine and studied approach to choosing locations and costumes. But most of all, the characterizations are an improvement over the earlier picture. This time there are two heroes. Clint Eastwood has a profession: bounty hunter. In Anthony Mann's movies [*The Naked Spur* (1953) and *The Tin Star* (1957)] this was a rather infamous profession. Leone rehabilitates its image in order to bring the figure of the hero into line with the public's new taste, making him decidedly cynical and venal. The happy ending which sees him load the outlaws' corpses onto a cart, not to take them for burial but to cash in the reward, even scandalized a critic of the *Cahiers du Cinema*. The other hero, Colonel Mortimer, is an all Bible-and-pistol type whose self-control hides bellicose intentions of vengeance. The villain is a psycopath Mexican with self-destructive tendencies.

The moral of the American Western was often based on a compromise between free will and predestination. For example, Borden Chase's friendly enemies (in *Bend of the River*[18] and *Vera Cruz*) are free to choose between good and evil, to yield to or resist the temptations

---

[18] Antony Mann, 1952.

The cynically tongue-in-cheek wagon-load of corpses in *For a Few Dollars More* [a], brings to mind the carts that carried the dead to be buried during times of pestilence: Domenico Fiasella, *La Peste di Genova*, 17th century [b]; an illustration from a 19th century edition of *The Betrothed* [c].

strewn along their paths, even if it is easy to guess from the start what their choices are going to be. Leone adopts a more elementary Manicheism. His heroes have faces like primitive masks. It is enough to see what they smoke to guess their characters. The pipe smoked by the colonel, sign of a stubborn and reflective temperament; the short cigar of Monko which gives him his couldn't-give-a-damn air; the marijuana cigarette that explains El Indio's hal-

lucinatory look. One of the movie's themes is the celebration of vengeance according to a Latin and melodramatic tradition. This will be a constant of the Spaghetti Western.

In American Westerns, vengeance is often expressed euphemistically. The hero has to eliminate the villain because he is a danger to society besides being guilty of having killed the hero's friend (the case of *My Darling Clementine,* among others). Sometimes, as in *Bravados*, a Catholic Western by Henry King starring Gregory Peck, vengeance is openly condemned both during the story and in the finale, when he learns that he was mistaken: the men he killed were not those who murdered his wife.

More interesting are some auteur Westerns, such as *The Searchers*[19] or *Ran-*

Tell me what you smoke and I'll tell you who you are: the Colonel's pipe [a], Monko's half-smoked cigar [b], El Indio's joint [c] (*For a Few Dollars More*).

---

[19] John Ford, 1956.

Gothic Leone

The "Court of Miracles", the pink rape scene and the red suicide scene: *For a Few Dollars More.*

cho *Notorious*[20], where vengeance rather than being condoned or condemned, is transcended by an epic or tragic catharsis. In Ford's film, John Wayne's tenacious hatred of Indians sometimes appears unjust or even absurd, but it is also fatally inscribed in the collective destiny of the conquerors. In Lang's picture, Arthur Kennedy joins forces with the outlaws to find his fiancee's killer, but hatred turns him into a cynic ready to use the love of a woman for the purposes of vengeance. So he too becomes the victim of a universal destiny of guilt.

Leone limits himself to wrapping the story of vengeance in a Gothic novel atmosphere. Brigands straight out of a court of miracles (hunchbacks, giants, scarfaces...), rape photographed through a rose-colored lens, a close-up of the dead woman that brings Poe to mind... Furthermore the tragic event is divided into two flashbacks in the style of the psychoanalytical melodrama (*The Snake Pit*[21], *Marnie*[22]) and we cannot exclude the possibility that it may have left traumas on the two antagonists. In fact the bandit has a strange compulsion to recall it by listening to the music box set in his watch which is identical to the colonel's (even with its own music box and the same music). Thus is the operatic style of the subsequent movies.

It is in the duels that Leone reveals his taste for the ceremonial. If, Hawks, Ford and Mann are concerned about the right dosage of gunfights and about motivating their presence in the story, what seems to interest Leone is mainly to vary the protocol each time. There is the upshot in the deconsecrated church when El Indio takes revenge on a traitor; the semi-serious duel where the two heroes shoot holes in each other's hats under the ecstatic gaze of a group of urchins; the target practice scene where the two bring down a shower of apples to the joy of a little Mexican child; the final clash, with the arena and referee. What is new about these duels is that, since they are rituals, they can be enjoyed both as drama and as parody.

There is an ambiguity which does not regard the film as a whole (weighed down, among other things, by the excessively long robbery episode) but which suffice to make Leone recognized as an unconscious heir of the great mannerist painters, capable of re-designing a traditional subject in an up-to-date and slightly disenchanted way. As in the paintings of that period there is a kind of portrait of the patron which here becomes a pretext for a little private vendetta. In the grotesque guise of the innkeeper, a woman of easy virtue, and her small, nasty-looking husband, it seems we are asked to recognize the wife of a producer who, once upon a time, had not behaved entirely correctly towards Leone.

The hotel owner, a woman of easy virtue (Mara Krupp, *For a Few Dollars More*).

---

[20] Fritz Lang, 1952.
[21] Anatole Litvak, 1948.
[22] Alfred Hitchcok, 1964.

For a Few Dollars More: *protocols*.

a

b

c

d

The revenge shoot-out in the converted church [a];
the semi-serious blowing holes in hats shootout [b-d].

Target practice against a tree [e-g];
the final duel with the referee [h, i].

THE GOOD, THE BAD, AND THE UGLY 1966

✏ Age & Scarpelli, Luciano Vincenzoni, Sergio Donati
(from a screenplay by Sergo Leone and
Luciano Vincenzoni)
🎥 Tonino Delli Colli
♪ Ennio Morricone

Clint Eastwood .... the Good, Blondie
Eli Wallach .... the Ugly, Tuco
Lee Van Cleef .... the Bad, Angel Eyes
Aldo Giuffré .... Clinton, Union capitain
Mario Brega .... Cpl. Wallace
Luigi Pistilli .... father Ramirez
Al Mulloch .... one-armed bounty killer
Rada Rassimov .... Mary, the prostitute

📖 During the American Civil War, a trio of bounty hunters, the straight-faced Blondie, the histrionic Tuco and the ruthless Angel Eyes, team up in search of buried gold. The first two make a pact, though that does not stop them from trying to outwit each other from time to time, while the third works alone. At a certain point we find Angel Eyes dressed in the uniform of a Union sergeant in charge of a prison camp in which the other two are being held, having been captured while posing as Confederate soldiers. The gold is stashed in a military cemetery, the scene of the final shootout in a three-way duel. Blondie shoots Angel Eyes and leaves Tuco half the bountry.

Cast and credits page 262
Detailed plot page 263
Director's statements page 135
Press review 266
Quotes and dialogues from the film page 185-210

In 1966 *A Man and a Woman*[23] wins the Palme d'Or, the Oscar, and is a box office success. It is the first time this has happened with a film shot according to some of the aesthetic principles of the *nouvelle vague*, full of dreams, flashbacks and documentary-style scenes. The audiences continue to be moved when the lovers meet again at the station. But if their embrace is shot with a hand-held camera and moreover in black and white, it is doubly moving for spectators to discover that they themselves have a taste for poetry.

Rather than experimental films, it must have been television and its commercials that created this mass aestheticism. After the commercial success of *Juliet of the Spirits* in Italy even average films were made with rather Byzantine wrappings. Among the box office hits of the season there is *L'Armata Brancaleone* [The Brancaleone Armada] a burlesque saga recited in archaic Italian, which would have expected to appeal only to well-educated audiences, and *Africa Addio!*, Jacopetti's reportage-fiction in *Mondo cane*-style, where lyricism and truculence are cleverly mixed to serve the author's nostalgia for colonialism.

Meanwhile they continue to shoot Westerns, fifty movies – twenty more than in 1965. Even intellectuals promenade on the Main Streets of Cinecittà, armed with good intentions. Pier Paolo Pasolini plays the part of a revolutionary priest in Carlo Lizzani's *Requiescant* (the hero, also a semi-priest, is Lou Castel, of *Fist in His Pocket*). Tinto Brass shoots *Yankee* in the manner of underground comic books with close-ups of necks, cigar-smoking belly buttons, nude ladies tied to poles; and the producer throws it out of the editing studio. Giulio Questi's *Django Kill!* is inspired by the director's experiences as a partisan fighter during WW II (the bandits in black uniforms represent Fascism). It is sequestered because of certain excessively violent scenes, including one depicting the rape of a young boy.

---

[23] *Un homme et une femme*, Claude Lelouch, 1966.

Not only Leone! The Radical-Pop Italian Spaghetti Western.

a

b

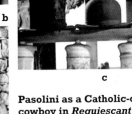

c

Pasolini as a Catholic-communist cowboy in *Requiescant* [a]; Tinto Brass gives a hint of the erotic films he was to make ten years later in *Yankee* (with Mirella Martin) [b]; Tomas Milian peers out from behind the shoes, hats and bottles in the Italian Spaghetti Western horror film *Django Kill... If You Live, Shoot!* [c].

Leone prepares an international spectacular production (United Artists comes up with half a million dollars as an advance on half the box office takings abroad). It is *The Good, the Bad and the Ugly*. What is spectacular about it is the setting of the American Civil War, with its many extras and cannons. The casting adds Eli Wallach to the usual Eastwood and Van Cleef. Vincenzoni, Age and Scarpelli are selected to write the script, specialists of the Italian comedy. The idea was to remake Monicelli's *The Great War* as a Western.

The irony in Leone's movie begins with the tide. If *the Bad* is a hired killer, *the Good* is merely a bounty hunter and *the Ugly* a kind of likeable picaresque brigand. But while the Bad kills for money in cold blood, the Good only shoots to defend himself after having challenged his adversary, and the Ugly tries to kill for vengeance, but never succeeds. (He is about to shoot the Good when the phantom carriage arrives, and he is about to hang him when a providential cannonade makes the ceiling fall.) Despite everything, the stereotypes remain – without stereotypes, no irony. But it is brought up to date and gets complicated. The Good and the Ugly are distinguished from the Bad inasmuch as they are economic animals: they are capable of stipulating contracts and respecting them. On the other hand the Bad, once having killed on commission, eliminates his patron as well.

The Good and the Ugly form a partnership to trick sheriffs and then become allies in hunting for the treasure, ready to betray each other as soon as the occasion presents itself, but also ready to punish the treacherous partner; and to punish him they try to hang him.

In the American Western, from Wellman's *The Ox-Bow Incident* (1943) to Ted Post's

The beginning...

...*and the end of the Good, the Bad and the Ugly.*

A fate similar to that of the Law: Eli Wallach and Clint Eastwood, the Ugly and the Good, the noose and the desert.

Hang'em High (1968), there is much democratic disdain for lynching (in general it is the innocent who pay the price) and a bit of nostalgia for quick procedures. In Howard Hawks's *Barbary Coast* (1935), the San Francisco vigilantes try the killer, Brian Donlevy, while they are conducting him to the gallows in an atmosphere of ferocious judicial mirth. Leone takes up this myth with a certain taste for the absurd. His *pistoleros* send their enemies to meet their creator without much ado ("If you gotta shoot, shoot and shut up" opines the Ugly), but when it comes to punishing the partner who has violated the contract, they imitate the justice of the State and its liturgies: they compel him to make long forced marches in the desert, or, rope in hand, order him to hang himself. One would think the whole penal code had been invented by two brigands who were supposed to divide some loot. At times it seems like a Gothic tale where all the characters have fun betting their necks against the devil (In the prologue we see the Good deliver up the Ugly to the sheriff, cash in the reward and then, at the last moment, save him from the gallows.) As in dreams, one falls but does not die. And like the heroes in silent comedies, who avoid falling into puddles, and Hitchcock's innocents who escape plunging to their deaths, so in Leone's movie the executions are failures. At one and the same time there is a parody of the castrating law and the castration of parody: the shadow of the gallows continues to menace even if the heroes are practically immortal. In the background is the war, the American Civil War in which Ambrose Bierce set his cruel stories.

In American pictures there was an inclination to depict Confederates as prisoners of the past and Yankees as practical builders of the future. In Leone the desert dust confounds the uniforms and perhaps the centuries as well. One sees trenches, concentration camps. One hears pacifist slogans. At fixed times, hundreds of men hurl themselves upon each other to take a bridge whose strategic importance they do not understand. Leone says he was inspired by Lussu the Italian author of a novel on World War I), but Ford portrayed with more depth military grandeur and stupidity – (the suicidal charge of the Confederates in *The Horse Soldiers*, 1959). This way of fictionalizing history is also very European. In American Westerns history is given a moral with the help of star-appeal. In Raoul Walsh's *They Died With Their Boots On* (1941), it would seem that the Indian Wars were provoked by the trader Arthur Kennedy's envy of the handsome general Errol Flynn. From the way in which the liberal Gary Cooper and the slaver Howard da Silva dispute the favors of Paulette Goddard in De Mille's *Unconquered* (1947), one can deduce the causes of the American Revolution; and in Robert Aldrich's *Vera Cruz*, the Mexican revolution against Maximilian is legitimized by the fact that Gary Cooper takes the side of Juarez and Burt Lancaster that of the French – a Manicheism that does not exclude a certain malicious fun (in general villains and bad causes do have their fascination). In Leone there is no connection between history and how it is fictionalized. The three adventurers change uniforms with the same nonchalance as Buster Keaton in *The General*[24] And if they blow up a bridge, thus determining the outcome of a battle, it is only so they can continue to hunt for treasure. They go through the war with the indifference and greed of the lovers in *Senso*. But if in *Senso* when a door is opened by mistake one surprises plotting

---

[24] Clyde Bruckman and Buster Keaton, 1926.

Blowing up bridges: *The Good, the Bad, and the Ugly* [a, b] vs *The Horse Soldiers* [c, d].

patriots (that is, history in the making) rather than a lovers' tryst; here one opens the wrong trunk and discovers the skeleton of a soldier. *Memento mori* is Leone's only message. Only once does one gather that war is a kind of organized banditry. When the Ugly is tortured by the Bad in the barracks of a Union camp, the prisoners' band has to play louder to cover his screams – a use of the chorus that would not have displeased Brecht.

Apropos of Brecht, one knows that Leone's heroes are moved by no other ideal than to get rich (someone baptized his first Westerns as "the dollar trilogy"). In this movie more than all the others, Leone recounts their rapacity with a black humor reminiscent of von Stroheim (Tuco handcuffed to the corpse of the corporal) and goes as far as to associate money and corpses with a rather sacrilegious twist. In *For a Few Dollars More* the hero adds up the amount of the reward he will cash in as he loads the corpses onto a cart. In *The Good, the Bad and the Ugly* the treasure map is found in a diligence full of corpses and the box of dollars buried in a military cemeter.

If you think money brings happiness, remember it also brings danger! *The Good, the Bad and the Ugly.*

Here too Gothic allusions, and possible Freudian readings can be made (the corpse as a source of profit reminds one of the symbolic equivalence of money and feces). But, in Hollywood, corpses were taboo, or almost. At the end of Anthony Mann's *The Naked Spur*, James Stewart, bounty hunter on occasion, pulls the body of Robert Ryan out of the river in order to cash in the reward for him; but a horrified Janet Leigh convinces him to desist from this impious commerce. Even a totally unscrupulous outlaw like Hugh Marlowe in *Rawhide*[25] flames with contempt when one of his companions Jack Elam transports the cadaver of one of his victims by dragging it behind a horse rather than loading it onto the animal's back. And not even the feelings of vengeance

---

[25] Henry Hathaway, 1951.

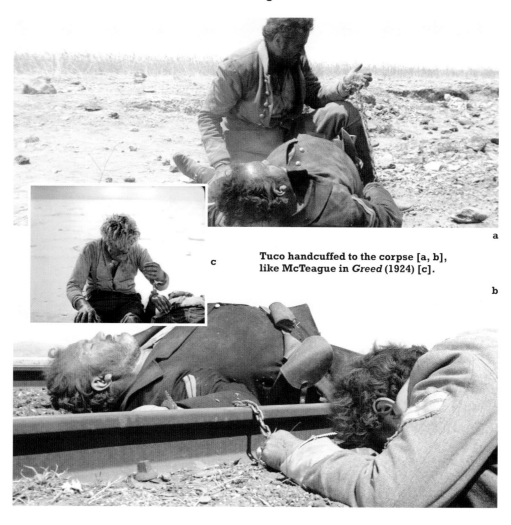

Tuco handcuffed to the corpse [a, b],
like McTeague in *Greed* (1924) [c].

for the Indians nourished by the hero of *The Searchers* can justify the profanation of a grave or a dead man's eyes.

Apparently there is no taboo on dollars. And yet, normally, there figure in Westerns a capital that is morally justified for its civilizing function (land and herds) and by the risks one must run to make it multiply (Indians, landholders, thieves). *Red River*[26] dedicates ten minutes to the building up of a cattle empire and two hours to its defence. Dollars only appear at the poker table: an intelligent hobby (Henry Fonda in *My Darling Clementine*) but a rather shady profession (gamblers often cheat). Sometimes money has sexual symbolism. In *Man Without a Star* (1955) the attractive cattle queen Jeanne Crain hires Kirk Douglas as an overseer and asks him to name his price: he imperiously writes *YOU* in the accounts book – they will end up in bed together. In George Cukor's *Heller in Pink Tights* (1960), Sophia Loren, a gambler momentarily broke, offers herself as the stake when the betting gets heavy. This sudden turning of the female body into money seems to free it from the cage of mere representation (on the screen the nude body of a woman is still only an image of a nude woman). For a moment one has the impression that naming the price is the same as possessing the woman. In Leone's erotic world, a dollar does not buy land, herds or girls, but perhaps it dispenses

---

[26] Howard Hawks, 1948.

tactile pleasures and in any case it inspires a perverse kind of mysticism. The Ugly rushes to the cemetery accompanied by celestial music; he slits open the dollar sacks with blows of his spade shot from below; he rummages for spoils in the pockets of rotting corpses. Here the dollar appears in all its macabre splendor, *stercus diaboli*, which alludes to the vanity of all the galloping rides and treasure hunts of this world. It is a fine cocktail, mixing Carnival and Lent, even if diluted by too much repetition.

And it is a very free re-make of *The Great War*. Monicelli had portrayed the instinct for self-preservation by mixing comedy, realism and drama. In Leone the art of getting by becomes greed and the law of the jungle; the tragic sense approaches the taste for the macabre; realism becomes naturalism and the comic borders on the trivial. Tuco, the Ugly, wanting to leap from the train, asks the corporal if he can go and pee. The peeing man will become a recurring figure in Leone's movies.

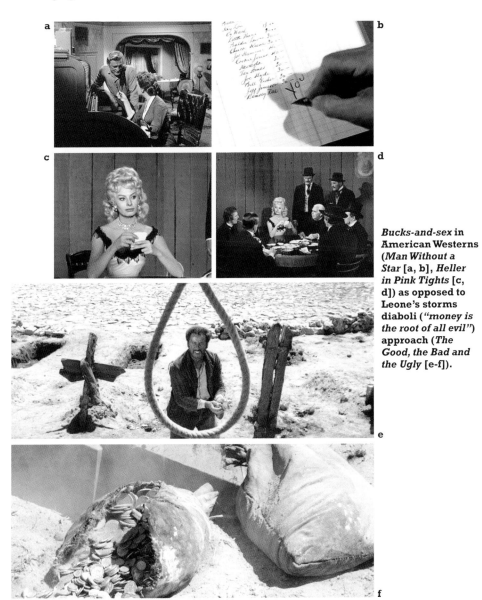

Bucks-and-sex in American Westerns (*Man Without a Star* [a, b], *Heller in Pink Tights* [c, d]) as opposed to Leone's storms diaboli (*"money is the root of all evil"*) approach (*The Good, the Bad and the Ugly* [e-f]).

The Good, the Bad and the Ugly: *three-way duel.*

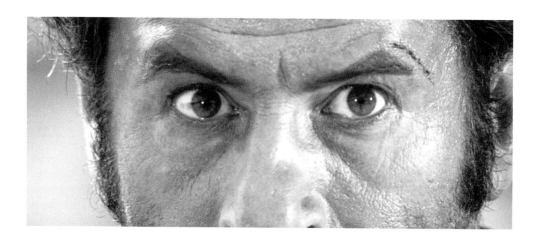

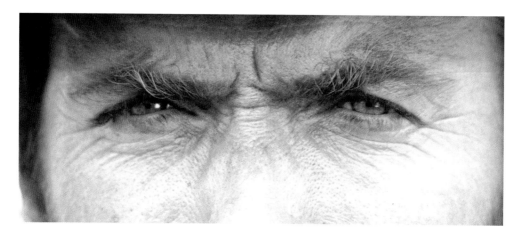

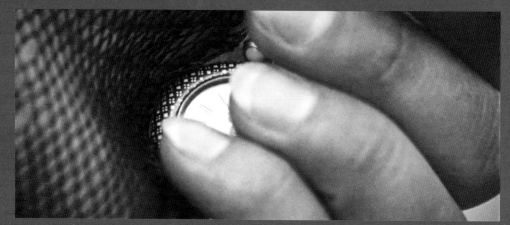

Once Upon a Time in the West.

Duck! You Sucker.

Once Upon a Time in America.

3. THE TIME TRILOGY
Once Upon a Time in the West
Duck! You Sucker
Once Upon a Time in America

ONCE UPON A TIME IN THE WEST
1968

✐ Sergio Donati, Sergio Leone, Luciano Vincenzoni (from a screenplay by Sergio Leone, Dario Argento and Bernardo Bertolucci)

🎥 Tonino Delli Colli
♫ Ennio Morricone

🐎

Claudia Cardinale .... Jill McBain
Henry Fonda .... Frank
Charles Bronson .... Harmonica
Jason Robards .... Cheyenne
Gabriele Ferzetti .... Morton
Frank Wolff .... Brett McBain
Keenan Wynn .... The sherif
Paolo Stoppa .... Sam

📖 A former prostitute named Jill arrives in town saying she is the new wife of Brett McBain and she has inherited his land through which a railroad is to pass. Crippled railroad tycoon, Morton, wants to take the land from her whatever the cost and he sends his hired gun Frank. Frank kidnaps Jill. A mysterious harmonica-playing gunman, who has his own personal reasons for seeking revenge, goes after Frank and in the meantime takes care of Jill, helped by Cheyenne, an amiable bandit full of wise words. The final showdown takes place at the track's construction site. Harmonica shoots Frank and silently leaves. Cheyenne, mortally wounded, (by Morton), dies with dignity.

Cast and credits page 267
Detailed plot page 268
Director's statements page 136
Press review 271
Quotes and dialogues from the film page 185-210

"I don't want the government's money to go to *Once Upon a Time in the West*."

"And I don't want it to go to *Partner*." These are the words of two Italian journalists (Mino Argentieri and Vinicio Marinucci) at a critics' conference in October, 1968. Old arguments. Art vs. industry, ivory tower vs. popularity, state-subsidized movies vs. American capital, molotov cocktails vs. Union Pacific. The reality is more complex. Bernardo Bertolucci, the director of *Partner,* had written the subject for *Once Upon a Time in the West.* The cultural inspiration of the two movies was neither Hanoi nor Washington, but Paris the (then) capital of movie-buffdom.

In 1968 politics and cinema went hand in hand. The youthful public went wild for *Bonnie and Clyde*[27], which was anarchic and retro at the same time, and committed directors were shooting movies that fell between left and pop: *Partner* (Dostoevsky meets Jerry Lewis); *Beneath the Sign of the Scorpion* by the Tavianis (Brecht meets the peplum); *Dillinger e Morto* [Dillinger is Dead] by Marco Ferreri (Marcuse meets Rauschenberg). The Italian Western was running out of steam. From seventy-seven movies made in 1968, production had declined to thirty-one in 1969. Leone's last Western was not so very Italian: Paramount was among the producers; in the cast figured three American stars of different schools (Henry

---

[27] Arthur Penn, 1967.

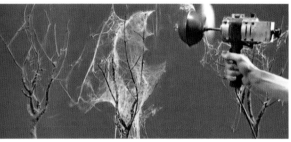

a

b

Echoes of the Western in non-Western films of the late 1960s: Pierre Clémenti gripping a weapon in *Partner* [a, b]; Gian Maria Volonté wearing a white shirt in *Under the Sign of Scorpio* [c]; not much different from his appearance in *For a Few Dollars More* [d].

c   d

Fonda, Jason Robards and Charles Bronson); locations were no longer only in Spain but also in Monument Valley, the very location where *Stagecoach*[28] was shot. Marshall McLuhan said that the subject of all Westerns was "Let's build a city." The game is even more fun when you are linking up the cities with stage-coaches, the telegraph and the railroads. Legendary companies lend their names to these movies: *Pony Express, Wells Fargo, Western Union,* and *Union Pacific*.

"Let's build a town", the focus of all Westerns: *Once Upon a Time in the West.*

Leone too sings the epic of the first transcontinental railroads solemnly and with secret irony. He combines Hollywood sterotypes with classical archetypes.

There is only one woman, a defenceless widow with prostitute past and a future as a businesswoman. In the West all social precedents are abolished and anybody can become somebody. Even a prostitute. The best female parts in Westerns are those of self-made women with an equivocal past who are ennobled more by economic independence than by nostalgia for their lost innocence (*Johnny Guitar* and *Raneho Notorious*). Even the legendary Scarlett O'Hara combines very dubious

---

[28] John Ford, 1939.

70

Self-made women: Claudia Cardinale in *Once Upon a Time in the West* [a, d]; Vivian Leigh in *Gone with the Wind* [b]; Joan Crawford in *Johnny Guitar* [c].

morals as regards men with a Calvinistic sense of business and an absolute worship of land-ed property. Leone's heroine is of the same breed, even if she has a more limited range of expressions (actually only two: amazement and diffidence). To make up for that she is full of dignity. She performs the simplest daily tasks, like warming up the coffee, drawing water from the well and distributing it to the workers, with all the solemnity of a vestal virgin. The good hero, Harmonica, is even more primordial. He floats through the film like a ghost, talks in riddles, smiles sadly, is sparing in gesture and almost totally wordless. He prefers playing the mouth organ, always the same dirge-like tune, thus giving proof on more than one occasion of an impassiveness that is too perfect not to be hiding a deep, deep wound. In the end we learn that Harmonica only lives for vengeance: he is a tragic hero.

His opposite, Cheyenne, the sage brigand, is always ready for a chat and never misses an opportunity to pontificate. Even when courting Jill, he does so with two-bit philosophy lessons and impertinent praise ("You remind me of my mother, the biggest slut in Alameda and the most on-the-ball woman who ever lived. Whoever was my father, for an hour or a month, was a lucky man."). The two villains, in traditional style, do not trust each other and try to wipe each other out. There is a Western-type villain and a film *noir* type. Leone endows the former with a sinister grandeur by "wrong" casting. Henry Fonda's calm presence and clear-eyed glances which have so often portrayed the Olympic serenity of the just man, here give a priestly gravity to the gestures of the evil character. Dressed perpetually in black, he is an elegant sadist who likes to humiliate his victims and see them groveling at his feet.

Morton, the other bad guy, is something halfway between a gangster and a tycoon. Visual-ly, three things characterize him in almost comic-strip style: the chin strap and brass hand-rail he needs for support because he has tuberculosis, and the picture of the Pacific Ocean which is the goal of all his efforts. Even capitalists can be dreamers.

The five founding fathers Leone imagined are no less monumental and monolithic than the ones sculpted on Mount Rushmore. Their individual differences are less important than the gigantic quality they have in common, and in any case the moral differences of the good and the bad count for less than the historical gap between the two generations of pioneers:

The "good guys"... Harmonica/ Charles Bronson [a], Cheyenne/ Jason Robards [b]...

the nomadic adventure seekers and the new settlers determined to build something for themselves and hence more suited to the industrial civilization that is coming.

This would all seem to take us back to Frederick J. Turner's theory of the frontier as a symbol of the perpetual rebirth of American society and to the autumnal Westerns that recount

The opening scenario of *Once Upon a Time in the West* bears similarities to *High Noon* [b]. But in Leone each of the three gunfighters has his own vexation while he waits: one plays with his hands (Al Mulock [a]), another is bothered by a drop of water (Woody Strode [c]), while the third catches flies (Jack Elam [d]).

a

b

c

d

...and the "bad guys" (Frank/ Henry Fonda [c], Morton/Gabriele Ferzetti [d]: *Once Upon a Time in the West* (and still today...).

c

d

the extinction of the courageous breed of men (*Ride the High Country*[29] and *The Man Who Shot Liberty Valance*[30]). We are at the very heart of the American tradition. However, while the heroes of Ford and Peckinpah become legendary even for their weaknesses (a drunken John Wayne who sets fire to the ranch, or a Randolph Scott who tries to escape with the loot from the bank), those of Leone face their destinies with an inhuman dignity. This lack of psychlogical shades isn't so serious if, like in the grand operas, it's the music that suggests the emotions or enhances them. And just that happens in certain scenes of *Once Upon a Time in the West* – for example, when Jill goes down to the station.

To emphasize the vastness of his stage, Leone omits any supporting characters and never allows his five heroes to appear all at once (in three hours of projection time, Cheyenne never meets Frank, and Jill never meets Morton). Nothing could be further from the narrative functionalism of the American Western. Here the length of the scenes is not proportional to their story interest but rather to their

Jill's first night in her new home: *Once Upon a Time in the West.*

liturgical content. Leone's favorite rites seem to be the waiting and the agony. In the prologue three shady characters await the arrival of the train. To kill time, the first patiently maneuvers a pesky fly into the barrel of his gun, the second submits, motionless, to the slow dripping of water from the ceiling into his hat and then drinks it, while the third cracks his knuckles. It is a quote from *High Noon*. Deprived of all suspense (we have no idea who is arriving) it becomes a classic stereotype in an almost pure state, an ironical homage to the proverbial patience of the Westerner.

---

[29] Sam Peckinpah, 1962.
[30] John Ford, 1962.

A carnal duel between *Claudia Cardinale* and *Henry Fonda* in:
Once Upon a Time in the West.

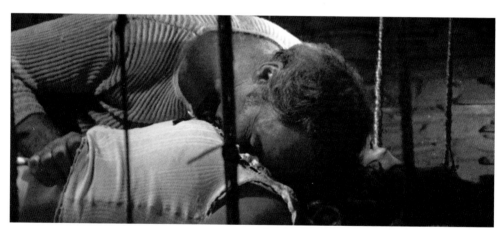

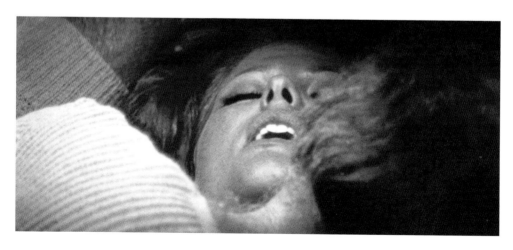

The pain and despair of Morton [a] and Cheyenne [b] while their partners look on: *Once Upon a Time in the West.*

Long waiting again occurs during Jill's first night at the ranch where she is baptized into the immense solitude of the West; typical is the scene on the bed, culminating in a frame a la von Sternberg, in which she is seen through the bed's lace canopy, looking like a frightened queen. To obtain such mythological emphasis, Leone is capable of sacrificing some spectacular effects. For example, he does not shoot the gunfight on the train where Morton and Cheyenne are killed. Instead he dwells at length on their final agony. Morton dies beside his train, creeping with pathetic tenacity towards a pool which the sound of waves in the sound-track transforms into a surrogate for that ocean the tycoon never reaches. Cheyenne dies as composed as a samurai: he drops to the ground and asks his companion to move on. Just as ritualistic are the exchange of threats. Each time it seems the characters are about to attack each other, but nothing happens. Cheyenne does not draw his Colt, Jill does not grab the kitchen knife and Morton closes the drawer where he keeps his pistol. They all give great proof of self control. But too many false alarms are an invitation to smirk. These exchanges

There is no one to watch this gun fight, on the outskirts of the track building site: Charles Bronson vs Henry Fonda in *Once Upon a Time in the West.*

of threats remind us of the swaggering nature of the heroes of the dollar trilogy here wrapped in a vague veil of mystery.

Leone, no less swaggering and mysterious than his characters, is a master in the art of keeping one waiting and reveals the avenger's motives in flashback, and only at the exact moment of his vengeance, which takes on an almost sacred, ritual tone. Here is the operatic Western, hieratic and ironic, which becomes a requiem mass for the Western genre itself Admittedly there is no lack of crowd-pleasing scenes: two prolific gunfights (on the train and in the streets of Flagstone) made vivid by some optical illusions and a sex scene dominated by Henry Fonda's half-cynical, half-bitter words. Here, as in other scenes of the movie, everything is more acted, evoked, than directly lived.

The effect is enhanced by the rather unreal quality of space, where the desert suggests that everything is temporary. Even the images of labor and progress partake in the spectical. In *My Darling Clementine* the whole town dances on the foundations of the church under construction, announcing a radiant future. Here, it is Cheyenne's brigands who measure the ground and sink the piles on which the station will be erected. And they do it only out of gallantry towards Jill. The city being built looks like a phantom city, or perhaps merely a toy city immersed in a deceiving light which slightly alters its proportions to the scale of that model of the station that Jill finds when rummaging in the drawers in a scene shot with an intimate, almost crepuscular flavor. Even the crudest, episode of the whole picture, the lynching at the

Claudia Cardinale and the model of the station looming over her: *Once Upon a Time in the West.*

stone arch, seems to come from some ancient oriental story. Leone has kept the ambitious promise made in the title: to make us continually feel the "once upon a time." Curiously, two movies linked to the legendary past and the science-fiction future, full of nostalgia for the epic and of skepticism regarding the future of humanity, were to become the main cult movies of 1968: *Once Upon a Time in the West* and *2001: A Space Odyssey*.

DUCK! YOU SUCKER
1971

✏ Sergio Donati, Sergio Leone, Luciano Vincenzoni (from a screenplay by Sergio Leone and Sergio Donati)
🎭 Giuseppe Ruzzolini
♫ Ennio Morricone

Rod Steiger .... Juan Miranda
James Coburn .... Sean "John" Mallory
Romolo Valli .... Doctor Villega
Franco Graziosi .... Governor don Jaime
Domingo Antoine .... Colonel Gunther Reza
Rick Battaglia .... Santerna
Maria Monti .... Adelita

📖 Mexican Revolution. Greedy bandit Juan and idealist John, an Irish Republican Army explosives expert, accidentally meet and fall in with a band of Pancho Villa's revolutionaries fighting against Colonel Reza, at the service of dictator Huerta. A patriotic doctor betrays them under torture but later redeems himself with a heroic sacrifice. In the final battle, Juan guns down the colonel with a machine gun and John, mortally wounded, blows himself up with dynamite. The Mexican is left upset on his own.

Cast and credits page 273
Detailed plot page 273
Director's statements page 138
Press review 276
Quotes and dialogues from the film page 185-210

In 1971 the latest box office miracle is Dario Argento's *The Bird With the Crystal Plumage* which inaugurates a new genre, the Italian thriller[31]. The recipe is not much different from that of the Western: multiply the number of homicides, insist on truculence, expand the suspense with music, create an unusual look (American actors in a glass and cement Italy). It is the film *noir* of the age of distraction which involves no one emotionally and which can be followed intermittently like television and which flatters the viewer who feels erudite when he manages to recognize mechanisms and quotations. Argento, though less gifted than Leone, will have a similar destiny: once the detective story scheme of the first films is abolished, he will devote himself to a kind of delirious mysticism of terror *(Suspiria, Inferno* and *Tenebre* [Darkness]). There are already some who propose a return to the private, to sentiment. It is the year of *Love Story* and a lucky Italian melodrama *The Anonymus Venetian* by Enrico Maria Salerno with Tony Musante, condemned by an incurable malady, who tries to win back his wife, Florinda Bolkan, in the setting of a putrefying Venice.

The cultural trend continued to demand serious commitment. There was the commitment of directors such as Montaldo and Damiano Damiani to the justice thriller and with positive heroes (*Sacco and Vanzetti, Confessions of a Police Captain*). And then there was the more sophisticated commitment of Elio Petri (*Investigation of a Citizen Above Suspicion*) with the police commissioner's delusions of grandeur and *La Classe Operaia va in Paradiso* [The Working Class Goes to Paradise], with its workers' nightmares of grandeur, both of them entrusted to Gian Maria Volonté's grotesque actor's mask. But the secondary characters are a shade too wise (and stereotyped) while the dialogues sound like pamphlets. Behind the delirium one smells the committee room.

Even certain master directors seem to be infected with the radical and apocalyptic spirit of these times. Visconti shoots *The Damned* about the relationship between Nazism and

---

[31] Actually, the Italian thriller arose between 1963 and 1964 with Mario Bava's films *La Ragazza che Sapeva Troppo* [The Girl Who Knew Too Much] and *Sei Donne Per L'Assassino* [Six Women for the Killer]. However, Dario Argento will give to the Italian thriller personal and totally new features.

a   b

Mexican revolution Westerns (or maybe Italian revolution?) of the late 1960s: Lou Castel and Gian Maria Volonté in Damiano Damiani's *Quién sabe?* (1968 [a]), Tomas Milian and Franco Nero in Sergio Corbucci's *Vamon a Matar, Compañeros* (1970) [b]).

heavy industry with echoes of Thomas Mann, Shakespeare, Dostoevsky and Wagner, all of them subsumed under a levelling moralizing that diminishes the *chiaroscuro* definition of his anti-heroes. In *Zabriskie Point* Antonioni applied his surface-of-the-world style to the campus students whom he portrayed as rebellious angels trying to share their most audacious dreams. The happy ending shows refrigerators, television sets and other symbols of the consumer society exploding in slow motion.

Even the directors of Westerns discover the revolution, the Mexican one, that was suited to combine spectacle and ideology because of the way it mixed brigandage and class struggle. And yet, despite some interesting subjects by Donati or Solinas (*Face to Face* and *A Bullet for the General*) the films mix the over-ambitious and the sophomoric. Thomas Milian plays the eccentric rebel peon by wearing a Che Guevara-Style beret; Volonté as a Mexican bandit speaks half Italian, half Spanish and sneers all the time; Franco Nero illustrates the idea be-

a   b   c

d   e   f

LA RIVOLUZIONE   NON E'   LA RIVOLUZIONE
                                UN PRANZO DI GALA,   E' UN ATTO DI VIOLENZA.
                                                          MAO TZE TUNG

g   h   i

Duck! You Sucker [d-i] and American classical cinema: *For Whom the Bell Tolls* (1943) [a-c].

Sergio Leone vs Dario Argento

a

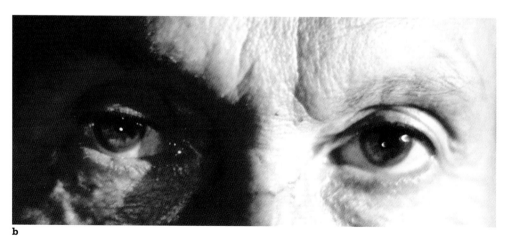

b

c

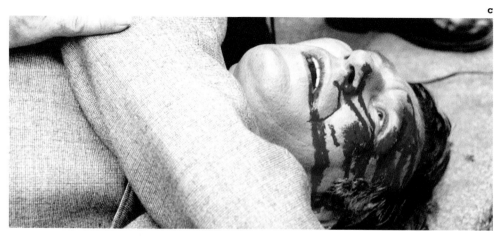

d

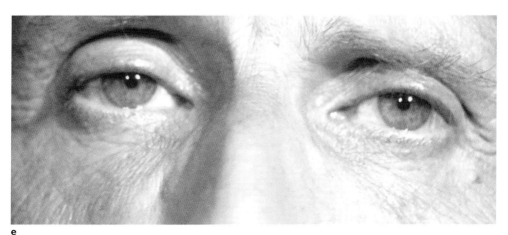

e

f

The Bird with the Crystal Plumage (1970) [a-c] vs *The Good the Bad and the Ugly* (1966) [d], *Duck! You Sucker* (1971) [e] and *Once Upon a Time in America* (1984) [f].

hind revolution to Tony Musante with a parable, using a naked woman ("Keep in mind that the rich are the head, the ones who command and make all the others work; while the poor are the backside, the lower half."); Mark Damon asks himself between tortures and shoot-outs if it is the southern slaves or the northern workers who are most exploited; and a Yankee capitalist threatens: "I don't like people touching my capital." These Westerns seem to be bad copies of political revolutionary films that never saw the light.

The subject of Sergio Corbucci's (*A Professional Gun*), transferred from Mexico to the Antilles, served as a point of departure for Gillo Pontecorvo's *Queimada* (also known as *Burn!*), a chilling lesson on neo colonialism offered by a sluggish Marlon Brando. But perhaps the true, noble father of third-world Westerns is a director himself of the third world: Glauber Rocha, the creator of *Antonio das Mortes,* a barbarous ballad about a kind of Brazilian bounty hunter.

However sensitive Leone may have been to social commitment (he participated in a film of counter–information on the Piazza Fontana bombing entitled *12 Dicembre*), he seems not to have been interested in shooting a populist Western. He limited himself to writing a script for his assistant Giancarlo Santi and arranging for the production. But Rod Steiger and James Coburn insisted on being directed by the master himself and this climate of improvisation may have been salubrious. Leone felt no obligation to direct an auteur film, but only to make a solid movie using a subject that had already been handled before, in the way American directors do.

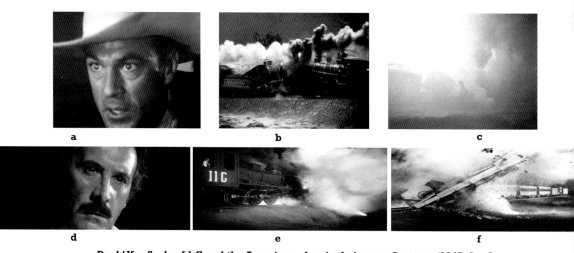

a   b   c

d   e   f

Duck! You Sucker [d-f] **and the American classical cinema:** *Saratoga* **(1945) [a-c].**

It has always been a prerogative of a spectacular epic to mix the sacred and the profane, and in 1971 there was nothing more sacred than revolution. *Duck! You Sucker* juxtaposes in the most nonchalant way quotations from Mao Tse Tung with bridges that are blown up (as in *For Whom the Bell Tolls*[32]); homage to the IRA, and *Saratoga Trunk-type*[33] locomotive collisions.

But Leone has the good taste not to take himself too seriously. His heroes are comic-book style supermen. The Irishman, a professional revolutionary, travels on a motorcycle and wears overalls lined with explosives. At the end, wounded in the back, he kills himself by blowing up the arsenal he carries on him, like a magician or Pierrot "le Fou"[34] (there is also a precedent in Ford's *Three Bad Men*[35]). The Mexican is a histrionic and rough bandit (the movie

[32] Sam Wood, 1943.

[33] Another film by Sam Wood starring Gary Cooper and Ingrid Bergman, 1945.

[34] The main character in Jean-Luc Godard's film *Pierrot Le Fou*, 1965.

[35] John Ford, 1926.

Duck! You Sucker [c-d] **and the American classical cinema:** *Three Bad Men* **(1926) [a-b].**

opens with a detailed shot of him urinating). The villain is a Prussian, a warlord, who travels in an armored car, drinks raw eggs for breakfast and, even on the train, does not forget to brush his teeth. Perhaps he is a shade immortal, to judge by the way he survives the bridge massacre unharmed wearing an irate expression that is a promise of reprisals in the next episode. There is also a traitor, a doctor who cannot stand up to torture. But he redeems himself with a heroic sacrifice. In short, everything must turn out larger than life, but this does not happen all the time. For example, the friendship between the two heroes, carbon copies of those by now standard figures in the political Western, the gringo and the peon, is portrayed in the most predictable paternalistic way. (From this point of view *A Bullet for the General*

Duck! You Sucker [c-d] and European art cinema: *Pierrot le Fou* (1965) [a, b].

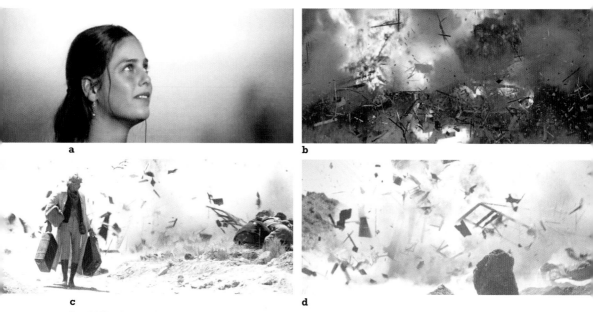

Duck! You Sucker [c-d] **European art cinema:** *Zabriskie Point* (1970) [a-b].

was more interesting, where the peon, disgusted by the gringo's cynicism, ends up killing him.) The Irishman is the teacher, with regard to firearms as well as morality; the Mexican a recalcitrant disciple in whom dwell ferocious instincts, peasant simplicity, and religious faith. Juan speaks with God, like Don Camillo, and loves his family: he converts to the revolution above

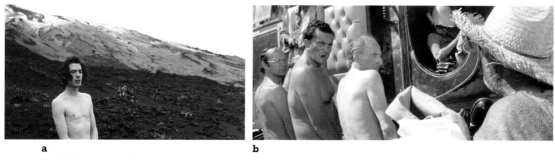

Duck! You Sucker [b] **and European art cinema:** *Pigsty* (1970) [a].

all to avenge his children. (Here there is an allusion to the Italian Resistance: Alcide Cervi and his seven children killed by the Nazis.) He is not even particularly violent. In the end, when he takes the governor's prisoner, he seriously hesitates before killing him; and he makes the decision to do so only after considering all his crimes and after he tries to escape. Before he dies, the Irishman gives back the crucifix that Juan had thrown away in a moment of despair over the death of his sons. An edifying ending which counterbalances the relative irreverence of the beginning, in Buñuel style, where the Mexican robs and strips the passengers in a luxury stagecoach; representatives of the backbone of society, a priest included. In the foreign edition and the restored one, the ending is followed by a relatively libertarian, Lelouch-style epilogue in which the two Irish conspirators kiss the same girl in slow motion under the branches of a tree.

But where Leone's populist, picaresque taste finds original accents is in the Chaplin-inspired bank hold-up where Juan and his men open the safe and instead of money find dozens of half-starved political prisoners. And his mannerist and melodramatic spirit return to splen-

84

a   b

Duck! You Sucker [b] and American classical cinema: *Modern Times* (1936) [a].

dor in the betrayal episode in which some have seen the spirit of Borges. Leone does things in a big way, he shows us almost simultaneously two betrayals (obtained under torture) in two different revolutions, the Mexican and the Irish. A flashback lasting barely a minute is enough for him to suspend narrative time and suggest a metaphysics of betrayal. Leone's originality is also revealed by the fact that whereas the Westerns of Damiani, Sollima and Corbucci entrusted the revolutionary message to dialogue much more than to action scenes in Leone, it is

One-man execution, mass execution: *Duck! You Sucker.*

more or less quite the opposite that happens. The relations between the leads are treated in a comically heroic style (duels, ritual threats, demonstrations of pyrotechnical skill), while the spectacular scenes have an almost funereal gravity that was appreciated even by a critic hostile to Westerns like Alberto Moravia. Mostly they are execution scenes where the hero, not being able to come to the aid of the condemned, watches the firing squad from a hiding place, and so they seem more authentic and inevitable.

This tragic voyeurism is enhanced in the night-time execution, where the traitor identifies the prisoners who are being executed and the Irishman, hidden among the crowd, recognizes the traitor in turn. The night, the rain, the courtyard lit by the headlights of the trucks, the stripes of white paint on the walls, all accentuate the atmosphere of mourning. When the Huerta regime vacillates, a movement of the helicopter crane reveals an apocalyptic scene: dozens of political prisoners massed in parallel trenches hurriedly being shot by soldiers stationed upon the parapets. For once Leone does not take his time, shoots no close-ups, but makes one long take and the effect is even stronger – as if one were passing there by chance. A pity that Leone does not also tell us of the revolutionary terror; but, after all, his film is merely a spectacular where one has to be able to distinguish the good from the bad. Furthermore even an auteur epic such as *1900* is no less schematic with its De Amicis-style stereotypes (vigorous proletarians, intrepid little school mistresses, heartless bosses) brought up to date with sex and scenes straight out of the Grand Guignol. And, in general, it is no longer so easy to distinguish between high-brow

a

The grave in honor of Sam Peckinpah (who was still alive) in *My Name is Nobody* [a]; dedication to the late Sergio Leone and Don Siegal in *Unforgiven* [b].

b

DEDICATED TO
SERGIO AND DON

or low-brow films. How, for example, does one classify Dario Argento's *Le Cinque Giornate* [The Five Days] that narrates the Risorgimento in cynical anti-rhetorical cabaret terms? Not to mention certain rickety black comedies by Lina Wertmüller such as *The Seduction of Mimi* that drip with folklore, ethnic cliches, and bad taste, but which at least do not hide social conflicts.

At times even the usual protagonists of typical Italian comedy visit the real life of the present. In Dino Risi's *Mordi e Fuggi* [Bite and Run], the industrialist Mastroianni is kidnapped by terrorists and makes every compromise to save his neck. In Monicelli's *A Very Little Man*, Alberto Sordi as an office worker takes revenge for the death of his son during a hold-up by kidnapping and meticulously torturing the murderer. Even when he is acting in a vile or sadistic way, the eternal champion of the art-of-getting-by is still the most likeable and vital character since in such films the powers that be are only caricatures and the young are a hostile and incomprehensible race.

Even "Z" movies are on the side of the silent majority, but without humor. The model is Michael Winner's *Death Wish* (1974). Usually there is a hero fed up with the slowness of the legal process who decides to take the law into his own hands and resorts to massacres worthy of the early Italian Westerns.

On the other hand, the few Westerns produced these days are pretentious like Lucio Fulci's *I Quattro dell'Apocalisse* [The Apocalypse Four] which combines Bret Harte's outcasts with the peyote of Castaneda and Corbucci's sadism; or else they are frankly burlesques like the Trinity series with Bud Spencer and Terence Hill, where the Western has by now been reduced to a local-color level to the point that the pair can transform themselves into pirates or cops in other movies. Their most original characteristic is a kind of violence that is both exaggerated and innocuous as in cartoons even while being a little monotonous.

Leone, too, in the thirteen years that separate *Duck! You Sucker* from *Once Upon a Time in America*, directs some TV commercials and produces two Westerns starring Terence Hill for the Rafran Cinematografica (the name taken from the initials of his three children: Raffaella, born in 1961; Francesca, born in 1964; and Andrea, born in 1968).

My Name Is Nobody by Tonino Valerii (1973)[36] is at once a homage to and a parody of Leone's

---

[36] See page 175 to read about the claims between Sergio Leone and Tonino Valerii about the authorship of the movie. In the end they broke up their friendship along with their partnership. Complete Cast & Credits page 287 Critics page 288

One, Nobody and a Hundred Thousand
(My Name Is Nobody).

The Marvellous Pavilion brings down the curtain
on the era of the West: My Name is Nobody.

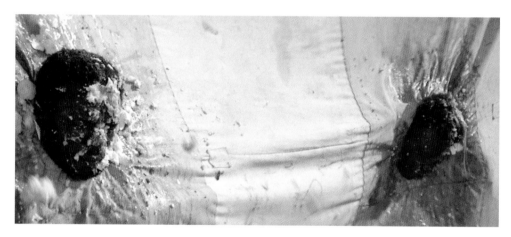

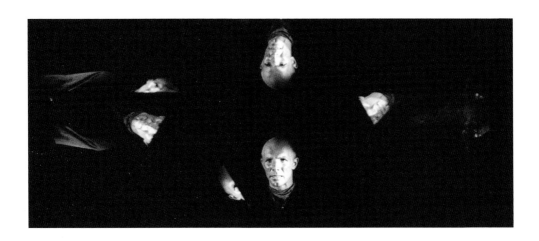

baroque style, with shoot-outs taking place in mirrored labyrinths, its wild bunch charging to the music of *The Ride of the Valkyries*, and Henry Fonda confronting 150 adversaries single-handedly, hoping to go down in history books. His wish is immediately granted. With the magic of editing, every now and then a gunfight freezes into a still shot and ends up printed in the pages of a book. Irony towards mythology, always an undercurrent in Leone, is here made explicit.

Less successful, Damiano Damiani's *A Genius* is a farce where clergymen preach in broth-els, the military is completely corrupt and pistols come out of their holsters and shoot by themselves. The one refreshing note is Miou Miou's emancipated smile.

For a couple of years, while the series that opened with *A Fistful of Dollars* was beginning to run out of steam, one had begun to catch glimpses of its influence in American Westerns, at least in the cruelty of certain scenes and perhaps in a certain desecrating spirit. Already in 1968, for example, there had been the interesting *Hang'em High* by Ted Post (the direction had first been offered to Leone), where the legal hangings of the guilty are no less frightful than the lynchings of innocents and where there is nothing exalting in the vengeance, even if the avenger is Clint Eastwood. And the following year in *The Wild Bunch* (1969), Peckin-pah had recounted with stubborn pessimism (and occasionally sincere feeling) the end of adventurous ideals, celebrating the only remaining form of heroism in the nihilistic violence of the finale. And again, twenty years after *Duck! You Sucker,* two directors of the uncertain Western revival express their debt to Leone. If Sam Raimi in *The Quick and the Dead* (1995), the bloody chronicle of a direct-elimination tournament between gunmen, revives the taste for the macabre pastiche that was typical of the Spaghetti Western, so Clint Eastwood in *The*

From a real life (life?) picture to a print: The West is by now History (or Legend?): *My Name is Nobody.*

Unforgiven (1992, dedicated "to Sergio and Don"), the story of vengeance on commission narrated in a terribly unadorned style, succeeds in overcoming both Puritan moralizing and Italian cynicism. Just as the heroes no longer have such perfect aim, so justice proceeds by inevitable and bloody approximations, and not even the dividing line between good and bad is very clear anymore (even though everyone still fools themselves into thinking they see it). Not even Leone with his funereal skepticism had reached such a degree of lucidity. He had always still believed in the game of heroism a little.

ONCE UPON A TIME IN AMERICA
1984

ONCE UPON A TIME
IN AMERICA

✏ Leonardo Benvenuti, Piero de Bernardi, Enrico Medioli, Franco Arcalli, Franco Ferrini, Sergio Leone (from the novel by Harry Grey *The Hoods*, 1952)
🎬 Tonino Delli Colli
♪ Ennio Morricone

Robert De Niro / Scott Tiler .... Noodles
James Woods / Rusy Jacobs .... Max
Elizabeth McGovern / Jennifer Connelly .... Deborah
Amy Ryder / Julie Cohen .... Peggy
Larry Rapp / Mike Monetti .... Fat Moe
William Forsythe / Adrian Curran .... Cockeye
James Hayden / Brian Bloom .... Patsy
Burt Young .... Joe
Joe Pesci .... Frankie
Treat Williams .... syndicalist Jimmy O'Donnell
Tuesday Weld .... Carol
Danny Aiello .... police chief

📖 1922. Jewish quarter in New York. Two young boys, Max and Noodles, grow up together in a no-holds-barred society: minor theft, small-time jobs for smugglers at the port, playing tricks on the local cops, flirting with girls.
1933. Prohibition. Noodles is released from prison. Max is by now a well-established gang leader. The last night of Prohibition, the friends are caught in a police ambush, all except Noodles. Somebody snitched on them.
1968. Noodles returns to New York after a long absence, a bitter surprise awaits him. His old friend Max did not perish in the ambush and has become a powerful politician. Now he must die (condemned by the organization) and he asks Noodles to kill him, but Noodles refuses...Maybe it was all a dream, dreamt by the young Noodles, in an opium den.

Cast and credits page 278
Detailed plot page 279
Director's statements page 140
Press review 283
Quotes and dialogues from the film page 185-210

A Fistful of Dollars was presented at the Sorrento Film Festival in 1964, but no critic noted its presence. *Once Upon a Time in America* is the big event of the Cannes Festival '84. It is very rare that crime is honored by the cultural world. Maybe there were some who thought this was laughable. But if Olmi sought time past in a rural Arcadia, and Fellini looked for it in a provincial and operatic one, there is no obvious reason why Leone should not seek it in the black Olympus of gangsterdom – that is to say, in our past as spectators. It was these films which gave us our rudimentary instruction in the willfullness of power (*Scarface*[37]), in Machiavellian dealings (*The Rise and Fall of Legs Diamond*[38]), in disenchantment (*High Sierra*[39]).

Leone, the last virtuoso of the film tale, tenaciously conceived a summarizing of these myths. The preparation for *Once Upon a Time in America* took thirteen years of his life. Among the accidents along the road, were: the bankruptcy of a producer, the stealing of ideas by the competition, the monkey wrenches tossed in by American unions during the shooting in the States, the cutting of whole sequences to meet the length agreed upon with the producer, the butchering of the American version which was cut by seventy-five minutes and re-edited in chronological order against Leone's will. Yet one cannot speak of an accursed movie, considering that the director approved the edition distributed in Italy and that the scenes originally sacrificed will be restored in the long edition.

Another colorful aspect is the saga of the screenwriters who adapted Harry Grey's novel *The Hoods-Americans* and Italians,

---

[37] Howard Hawks, 1932.
[38] Budd Boetticher, 1960.
[39] Raoul Walsh, 1941.

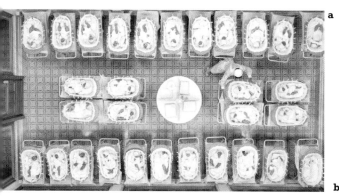
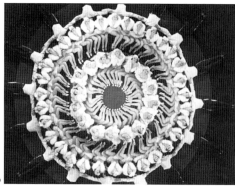

Baby switching in *Once Upon a Time in America* (1984) [a], Busby Berkeley-style shot from above (42ⁿᵈ Street, 1933 [b]).

veterans and beginners, serious writers, detective story writers and movie buffs. In their past is a long row of milestones (as well as scandals) from *The Naked and the Dead*[40] to *Rocco and His Brothers* and *Last Tango in Paris*.

The credits also give Leone's name under the tide "screenplay." For example, the idea of mixing up the new-born babies is not his, but it was he who, dissatisfied with the improbable idea in the novel for resolving the strike (the gangsters took dozens of their adversary-bullyboys out of circulation by giving them drugged whisky), put the problem in terms of a film memory: a solution was needed that was just as strong as the beheaded horse in *The Godfather,* but less ferocious, if possible. So the director functions as head playwright (like Ford, Visconti, Shakespeare...). The length too was established by the director: 3 hours 38 minutes, a provocation in the era of the remote control button.

The Hoods is an autobiographical novel, the story of a small-time gangster told in the first person as in a diary, with its notes of hold-ups, homicides, blackmail, pastimes and ideas... and without forgetting to go back to the origins every now and then with slices of Jewish life and debates between the gangster and his journalist brother. The film is more novelish than the novel itself. The life of Noodles, which in the book only included

The first American edition and the first Italian edition of *The Hoods* by Harry Grey.

adolescence and youth, is prolonged into old age and told in flashback, multiplying memories and comparisons among the three stages of life.

In the book the three boys surprise the local cop having sex underneath the stairs with Peggy, the Lolita of the building complex. They ridicule him and threaten him and let the incident go at that. In the movie the tryst takes place on a roof terrace where Peggy goes to hang out the washing. The boys photograph the couple in a compromising position, then blackmail him into giving them back the watch and obtain his complicity in their future crimes and access to Peggy's

---

[40] Raoul Walsh, 1958.

On the terrace, where only the laundry is clean: *Once Upon a Time in America.*

charms for free. Thus the episode is a reference point to a before and an after, and introduces the themes of blackmail and desire... in short, is placed in a context. Certainly a roof terrace is not as miserable a place as below the stairs, but the roof terrace with washing hanging out to dry is a traditional place of promiscuity in public housing: nothing is better suited to telling a story of survival and celebrating the ferocious vitality of small time delinquents.

The movie is full of such by now archetypal images: the Chaplinesque gag about the char-

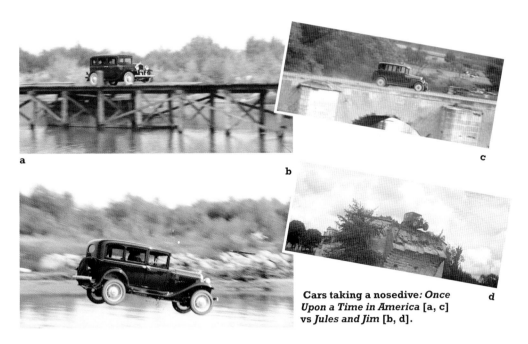

Cars taking a nosedive: *Once Upon a Time in America* [a, c] vs *Jules and Jim* [b, d].

lotte russe; the romantic, Fitzgerald-like dinner of the nouveau riche; the actress taking off her make-up in front of the mirror[41] (*Bonjour Tristesse*); the car that goes flying into the river as in *Jules et Jim*[42]; the Bergman-like "wild strawberry" patch (that here is a toilet); and even the pilgrimage to the crypt a la Joseph Roth. (But the various hold-ups, shoot-outs, beatings and prisoner exchanges are all cliches, worn out and a little too Western-ish.)

---

[41] *Bonjour Tristesse*, Otto Preminger, 1958.

[42] François Truffaut, 1962.

The three ages of Noodles
(Scott Tiler / Robert De Niro)

The three ages of Deborah
(Jennifer Connelly / Elizabeth McGovern)

Noodles "wild strawberry patch": *Once Upon a Time in America*.

Almost no historical factors disturb this compilation of myths (the part regarding the connection between labor unions and gangsters is the least inspired in the movie), nor do ambitions to present such iron-clad heroes as Cagney, Bogart or Mitchum. Noodles is a run-of-the-mill type who is not aware of it, a dreamer who goes through fundamental life experiences such as sex, love, friendship and adventure with an honorable vocation to defeat.

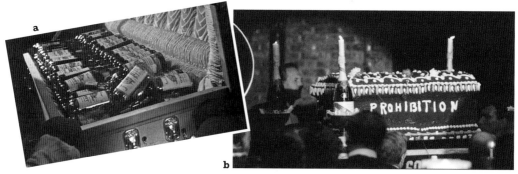

Roaring Twenties and Prohibition: the "funeral" in *Some Like It Hot* [a] and the one in *Once Upon a Time in America* [b].

Life and Films

a

Love and death: The
Colossus of Rhodes
[a] vs *Once Upon a
Time in America* [b].

In *Some Like it Hot*
(1959), Billy Wilder evo-
ked the Roaring Twenties
through transvestism and
the confusion of the sex-
es. Leone goes further and
confounds the impulses.
Erotic desire is identified
with anal instinct (Peggy
and Noodles petting in the
toilet); with gluttony (Patsy
who gives up Peggy for a
charlotte russe); with death
(love-making in the hearse
which recalls the flirtation
among the *sarcophagi* in
The Colossus of Rhodes).
In the orgy, identity is both
lost and found again: Carol

b

only recognizes the four bandits once they have covered their faces and unbuttoned their pants.
Here perhaps the absolute is being pursued along the road of dissipation.

But Noodles, who is secretly reading *Martin Eden*, is also attracted by the American dream
of happiness-beauty-energy which he finds in the form of the aspiring ballerina Deborah and her

a

c

b

d

Noodles and
Deborah like
Montgomery
Clift and
Olivia de
Havilland:
*Once Upon
a Time in
America* [a,b]
vs *The Heiress*
(1949) [c, d].

Dinner...

«Amapola, lindísima Amapola...

...and after dinner.

...será siempre mi alma, tuya sola...»

Noodles (Robert De Niro) and Max (James Woods), Noodles pretends not to recognize Max: *Once Upon a Time in America*.

charms. She graciously grants him the first kiss between o Biblical verses. But when, bleeding, he knocks at her door, she remains stock-still and haughty as if she were acting out the end of *The Heiress*[43] (1949). Ten years later Noodles invites her to dinner in a seaside restaurant that has been opened only for them (in the novel it was crowded), but when she rejects him he shows less class than Gatsby and rapes her: rather than despise him, we feel ashamed for him.

As an old man, Noodles finds himself in a theater admiring Deborah in a play by Shakespeare, just as when, as a child, he spied on her dancing from his hiding place in the bathroom. He has realized that the only place in the American dream for him is as a spectator. The criminal adventure is expressed as an experience of limitations, where violence borders on voluptuousness, terror on the burlesque, omnipotent power on impotence. The big thug runs after the little thugs as in a slapstick comedy, but this time the upshot is a dead man; the hold-up ends with Noodles raping a masochistic secretary; the gangsters blackmail the police chief by mixing up the baby boys with the baby girls (a confusion of orifices, an anatomical carnival); destiny is symbolized by a garbage truck.

Another myth, the one of male friendship, is celebrated here with a play of shoddy complicities, cruel jokes and false betrayals which outline the characters of the loser and the winner – sometimes a bit forced, as in Max's madness. But it is only at the end, probably inspired by Chandler's *The Long Goodbye,* that the theme of friendship becomes wrapped in a veil of myth. After thirty-five years Noodles discovers that the Machiavellian Max has taken him for a ride; and as punishment refuses to recognize him and to kill him as requested. Only then does Noodles cease to be run-of-the-mill and behave like one of the stoic heroes of *noir* films.

How is it that this eccentric saga manages to involve us, to become our past? Everything depends on how time is measured. Scarface made the pages of the calendar fly with machine gun bullets in a pathological version of American activism (in those days gangster stories were also success stories). Noodles prefers madeleines.

And Leone gathers together all the delights of the cinema of memory: symmetries, circularity, retrospective clarifications and violent juxtapositions. The structure of the movie allows us to be two Noodles at once: the one who acts and the one who remembers, the joyful gangster and the melancholy Jew; and to go through his life cycle at a solemn and dizzying pace, but without the uneasiness and absurdiry of those old movies where the characters grow old from one scene to the next. Thanks to the flashback, two minutes in the present are enough to cover a leap of ten years into the past.

Noodles' life seems to be made up of significant moments rhythmically connected to each other. From one epoch to another encounters are renewed (the two returns to Fat Moe's), the goodbyes (in front of the prison and at the station); repeated lines (Deborah's "Mother is calling"), objects (the watch), activities (Max polishing his shoes) and songs (*Amapola*). Each repetition, always in a different key, traces the course of the years and also includes us in the circuit of the characters' memories and feelings.

But the lurches with which Leone shortens the thread of time are more surrealistic than

---

[43] William Wyler, 1949.

Ghosts from the past: David, Max's son/clone and the Roaring Twenties' automobile, a last fling in 1968 (*Once Upon a Time in America*).

pathetic. We visit the station, and a circus motif mural on the wall in 1932 magically becomes a 1968 pop mural. And another no less fanciful detail: the ticket-taker with a white beard is replaced by a young rent-a-car employee. Another gauge of time, accelerated and inoffensive, are the wrinkles on the faces of the characters. One cannot fail to notice that they are young people made up to look old, contrary to what was done in *The Man Who Shot Liberty Valance.* In growing old, Leone's heroes fulfill their destinies as archetypes, becoming their own masks. At twenty-three, Peggy is even creamier and more luscious than she was at thirteen; Max at sixty seems like an even greater scoundrel than he did at twenty-three. Fat Moe never loses his tame and subservient look. Deborah finds eternal youth in the theatrical guise of Cleopatra. These irreducible adolescents never seem to grow up. Maybe they reproduce by cloning. David, Max's son, is the exact copy of his father (the actor is, in fact, the same one) as if he had been generated without the union with a woman. This is an expedient to strengthen the surprise in the scene where Max reappears, thus sparing a few lines of dialogue, but insinuating the suspicion that the present is a time of ghosts and simulacrums. Other clues: the garbage truck, inspired by a true circumstance in the Jimmy Hoffa case and turned into horror fantasy by the fact that the driver is invisible; a Frisbee thrown by an unknown hand.

In a word, the present no more improbable than the past. To be more exact, the present does not really exist at all. If the 1923 and 1932 episodes are flashbacks from 1968, it is equally true that 1968 is a flash forward from 1932 and the old Noodles is a projection that the young Noodles had had in the opium den. There is only the past as seen from the future and the future as seen from the past, memory mixing with fantasy with no points of reference. It is always the pulsation of feeling that expands time. Leone goes into slow motion during a flight of street urchins and prolongs the end of a sequence dwelling on the pensive hero (an adolescent on the terrace, an adult at the seaside); he uses music to make memories blossom and to temper feel-

Noodles' and his cups of coffee: *Once Upon a Time in America*.

Time is captured forever in these murals of the circus [a], the theater (Deborah finds eternal youth in the role of Cleopatra) [b], in the Chinese shadow dancers and opium [c]: *Once Upon a Time in America*.

Little men, big spaces: the house in front of the prison, marooned tugboats, the dawn of Noodle's disenchantment (*Once Upon a Time in America*).

ing (the bellicose march softened by panpipes).

The acting too obeys an inner rhythm. Like the hieratic kiss of the two adolescents, the ineffective attempt of Noodles to hide his embarrassment as he stirs a spoon in his coffee, the pilgrimages to Fat Moe's and the cemetery where the hesitations of De Niro suggest senility, disorientation and emotional upheaval. Nothing could be better for an epic of memory than this falsely lethargic actor hiding a distant hilarity in the depths of his eyes, as if behind the gangster there was a dormant actor.

The construction of the space contributes to this magical atmosphere. Leone could not ignore the fact that even the most deprived of his spectators had entered a Chicago speakeasy and driven the streets of the city in a Ford Model T at least once in his life. The extra emotions he offers are connected to traveling through time, to immensity, and they tend to make us accept even the less vital parts of the story. The opening of every sequence is a curtain rising on

In the end, maybe, (or at the beginning) it's all an opium smoker's dream.

perpetually different, dated and expanded stages: in height (the opium den with its bunk beds); in width (the house facing the prison); in depth (the restaurant on the seaside). Or else they are vaguely spectral like the deserted slaughter house and the outskirts with its beached tugboats. Space is stretched in all directions, but for acceptable reasons. For example, to film Noodles taking Carol bent over the table, there was no more sober and appropriate angle than a frontal one, but with an upward view of the elegant coffered ceiling suggesting the "majesty of the vulgar."

The dolly shot that elicits applause (and, if you will, tears) is the one that begins the sequence of old Noodles' return to Fat Moe's. Through the window we see the old bar owner answering the telephone and sending away the last customers. Meanwhile the camera is elevated, broadens its angle to take in the semi-deserted street and drops onto a telephone booth to shoot a close-up of Noodles talking on the phone. Thus the movement of the camera suggests mystery and ritual by transforming this street corner into the theater of a furtive ceremony in nostalgia which only we are able to understand.

After the various deaths, rebirths, regressions and disillusions, like a time traveler, Noodles chooses the epoch in which to live and goes back, rejuvenated, to take refuge in the opium den of 1933. The end generates the beginning. That is enough to suggest the infinite. In the final shot, De Niro directs an ecstatic and crafty smile right at the public which is destined to endure as one of the memorable acts of anti-stardom along with Jean-Paul Belmondo's dying wink in *Breathless*[44] and Marlon Brando sticking his chewing gum onto the railing in *Last Tango in Paris*. A disconsolate homage to artificial paradises: opium probably stands for cinema (there is a Chinese shadow theater below the opium den) with its low-cost dreams and interchangeable lives in which we are allowed at times to lose ourselves, gaining an illusion of immortality even when the lives are as unfulfilled as Noodles's[45].

---

[44] *À bout de souffle*, Jean-Luc Godard, 1960.

[45] Sergio Leone's cinema ends here. The director died of a hear tattack the night of April 30, 1989.

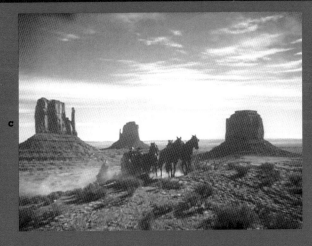

Sergio Leone, *Once Upon a Time in the West* (1968) [a]; John Ford, Henry Hathaway and George Marshall, *How the West Was Won* (1962) [b]; John Ford, *Stagecoach* (1939) [c].

4. Six Ways to Avoid Resembling John Ford

1. Actors

The Western owes a lot to the star system. It transformed the heterogeneous mythology of the Frontier into a concentrated pantheon of figures familiar to the public and capable of expressing themselves with ease and sobriety. (The intense mobility of Gary Cooper's face may even go unobserved.)

During the fifties even intellectual Actors Studio types played in Westerns – unusual roles like Paul Newman's neurotic Billy the Kid in Arthur Penn's *The Left-Handed Gun* (1958). Leone makes a blend of these styles, juxtaposing wooden exponents of understatement (Eastwood, Bronson, Van Cleef, Coburn) with disciples of Lee Strasberg (Steiger, Wallach) in the roles of Mexican bandits. Sometimes Visconti actors (Paolo Stoppa, Romolo Valli) appear in secondary roles, and occasionally Buñuel favorites (Fernando Rey, Margarita Lozano).

a

b

c

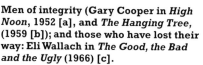

Men of integrity (Gary Cooper in *High Noon*, 1952 [a], and *The Hanging Tree*, (1959 [b]); and those who have lost their way: Eli Wallach in *The Good, the Bad and the Ugly* (1966) [c].

The best of them is Eli Wallach who enriches the ribald nature of his character with subtle shadings. When his brother the monk reproves him for not having helped their parents ("You didn't show up for nine years"), he replies by mimicking him three times ("nine years, nine years, nine years") varying the intonation from contrite, to distracted, to infantile in order to make light of his guilt. Here the histrionics of the actor mix with those of his character. Wallach evidently knows how to act with his whole body, even when shot from above, as he shows when he races around the cemetery looking for the grave. In one scene Leone makes him act in the nude, or rather nude with a pistol. Immersed in the bath tub, Tuco kills a rival by shooting him with a pistol hidden in the suds. Then he gets out and cautiously looks around the room, a beast of prey and of the theater. There is as much of the spirit of Boccaccio here as in the auteur nudes of Pasolini's *Decameron*.

Rod Steiger is more academically histrionic in *Duck! You Sucker*. His bravura moment

Rod Steiger's seemingly unexplained despair in the cave of the dead in *Duck! You Sucker*.

is his long description of the Mesa Verde bank when he is twisted up in a fit of ecstasy ("not a bank, *the* bank, the biggest, most beautiful, fantastic, formidable, magnificent goddam bank in the whole world") and groping with his hands for the right word ("It's like... like... a sign of whatsit... of destiny"). And there is also the scene of pain in the San Isidro grottoes brought to dramatic peak by Leone.

Normally in Westerns when we come across the smoking ruins of a farm attacked by Indians, we discover the corpses of the victims through the eyes of the hero. But here we first see the peon who collapses onto a bench weeping, murmurs a few words ("Six... I never counted them"),

B movie spoof comedy: bullying the little man in *Once Upon a Time in the West*.

rips the chain with the crucifix from his neck and ends by picking up a machine gun and walking heavily towards the mouth of the grotto. The reason for his despair is not totally clear, and consequently his actions take on an air of sacred mystery. Only when he has come out of the grotto do we, together with the Irishman, discover the corpses of his family members while off screen the chatter of the machine gun is heard.

Alongside such refinements Leone is capable of breaching taste, primarily in the choice and direction of the secondary characters. In *Once Upon a Time in the West*, the threatening actions of Frank's henchmen, when they intimidate a little guy who wants to bid at the auction, are too theatrical to seem furtive and make the whole scene seem unreal. There are

The scene with the match (Lee Van Cleef vs Klaus Kinsky) in *For a Few Dollars More* (1965) [a-d] and Thomas Mitchell's blaze in *Stagecoach* (1939) [e].

some memorable provocations: for example, Lee Van Cleef striking a match on Klaus Kinski's hump.

John Ford also liked emphatic gestures, but he filmed them with greater discretion. In *Stagecoach,* for example, one gets a glimpse of Thomas Mitchell in long shot who, having refused to toast with the banker, pours his whisky into the fireplace, causing the fire to flare.

2. Costumes

According to Roland Barthes, a theater costume has two duties: "to be a humanity," which means to give veracity to the character; and to be an "argument," which means to express the symbolic function of the character.

In Westerns perhaps the best humanity-costumes are those of Howard Hawks's drunkard sheriffs (Dean Martin in *Rio Bravo* and Robert Mitchum in *El Dorado,* 1967). A worn-out, much

a

b

The humanity-costumes of Howard Hawkes' drunken sheriffs, Dean Martin's worn-out jacket in *Rio Bravo* (1959) [a] and Robert Mitchum's undershirt in *El Dorado* (1967) [b]; Clint Eastwood's poncho in *A Fistful of Dollars* (1964) [c].

c

"lived-in" jacket and an undershirt which bear witness to the characters' decline and makes more dramatic the effort needed to rise again. In synthesizing the characters' past and present, costumes fit them like a second skin.

Among the most memorable costumes are the ones worn by the captain-reverend Clayton played by Ward Bond in *The Searchers*. He goes nonchalantly from the horseman's overalls to the long, black formal coat and is almost never seen without a top hat that gives him the menacing and slightly ridiculous aspect of a totem. In the same film John Wayne wears a civilian shirt and military trousers: he is a veteran and still considers himself a warrior. In brief, the epic dimension of the American Western can also be read in the accessories.

In the Italian Western, the costume is a often a piece of folklore. In the dollar trilogy one remembers Clint Eastwood's poncho. In *The Good, the Bad and the Ugly*, the hero only wears it in the final duel like a bullfighter's costume. But in *Once Upon a Time in the West* the clothes are all dusty, threadbare, archeological, something never seen in American movie costumes.

The star system, as we know, always preferred the seemingly true to the real. Even with regard to hair-dos. With all-too Victorian ringlets, braids and chignons, the faces of the stars would seem less familiar to us. That is why, for example, Calamity Jane's hair-do in the two versions of *The Plainsman* (Jean Arthur[46] and Abby Dalton[47]) are inspired by the feminine fads of 1936 and 1966 rather than the fashions of the 1800s. But Leone is historically accurate even when it comes to doing Claudia Cardinale's hair. At times, however, authentic detail creates an atmosphere of legend: for example, the famous overalls borrowed from *My Darling Clementine* which give the bandits a rapacious air.

---

[46] In *The Plainsman* by Cecil B. DeMille, 1936.
[47] In *The Plainsman* by David Lowell Rich, 1966.

Ladies' hairdos: Jean Arthur [a] in *The Plainsman* 1936, Abby Dalton [b, set photo] in *The Plainsman* 1966; and Claudia Cardinale [c] in *Once Upon a Time in the West* (1968).

Charles Bronson undresses Claudia Cardinale in *Once Upon a Time in the West*, but not for sex.

Sometimes the costumes can have a narrative function (Harmonica ripping Jill's clothes to make her sexy and confuse the bandits lying in ambush) or an allegorical one Jill, who, when in the desert, renounces the frills of city fashions. Or they can become the objects of semiological comments on the part of the villain. Having to punish one of his lazy and incompetent henchmen who begs to be trusted, Frank makes the disparaging crack: "How can I trust someone who wears a belt and suspenders – someone who doesn't even trust his own pants?" Then he executes him with a kind of poetic justice: three shots, one in the belt and two in each suspender.

This is far from the provincial and prudent good sense of the Americans. In *The Big Carnival*[48], Kirk Douglas placated a newspaper editor with these words: "I have lied to men who wear belts, and I have lied to men who wear suspenders, but I would never be so dumb as to lie to a man who wore both a belt and suspenders."

---

[48] A.k.a. *Ace in the Hole*, Billy Wilder, 1951.

3. DIALOGUES[49]

"Biondo, lo sai di chi sei figlio tu? Di una grandissima puttaaaaa–" ("Blondie, do you know who you're the son of? Of a great big biii–"). At this point the chorus of the Cantori Moderni di Alessandroni pick up and prolong the final vowel in a short musical phrase that imitates the howl of a coyote. In this way, both triumphantly and chastely, the phrase "son of a bitch" officially enters the list of uncensored epithets.

Eli Wallach hams it up with his final scream in *The Good, the Bad and the Ugly.*

Way back in the time of *The Great War* (1959), Leone's three scriptwriters (Age, Scarpelli and Vincenzoni) already managed to get an insult like "faccia di merda" (shit face) past the censor by making it a patriotic act. (Gassman said it to an Austrian officer, thus showing that he preferred to die rather than be a traitor.)

This Rabelaisian taste is a constant factor in Leone. His Westerns have tragic images and comic dialogue. Certain lines seem written in order to be learned by heart. Everyone remembers Volonté's maxim in *A Fistful of Dollars*: "When a man with a pistol meets a man with a rifle, the one with the pistol is a dead man." Macabre humor abounds in *For a Few Dollars More.* After a short poker game where no bets are placed and Clint Eastwood beats an outlaw, the outlaw asks: "What were we betting?" And the imperturbable hero replies: "Our necks." Even the villain is humorous ("Rather than have that pair behind you, it's better to have them in front of you, horizontal and preferably cold").

There are those with a loaded gun...

...and those who dig...:*The Good, the Bad and the Ugly.*

The Good, the Bad and the Ugly has particularly funny and witty dialogue. In the prologue, the entrance of the hero is accompanied by a good line. One of the bounty hunters that has just captured Tuco observes the reward announcement and comments: "Your face looks like that of somebody worth $2,000." "Yeah," the blond guy says as he enters the scene with the camera at his back, "but you don't look like the one who's going to cash it in – a few steps back, please." The whole movie abounds with naughty remarks

---

[49] Collection of dialogues and quotes from Sergio Leone's films, pages 185-210

The groping hand...

a

b

*Once Upon a Time in the West [a-b], Duck! You
Sucker [d], Once Upon a Time in America [c].*

c

d

("Put down your pistol and put on your underpants"); or boastful ("I'm off, I'm going to kill him and I'll be back"); with threatening aphorisms ("The world is divided into two kinds of people: those with a rope around their necks and those who cut it... those with a loaded pistol and those who dig-you dig."); sadistic pleasantries ("I like guys like you because they make so much noise when they fall"). In *Once Upon a Time in the West* the humor is more subtle, putting courtly language into the mouths of naive persons (just as conventionally happens in operas).

Harmonica recounts a shoot-out, describing the bodies of the dead enemies as if they were a set of Russian dolls that fit one inside each the other: "I once saw three overalls like that some time ago. There were three men in them. In the men there were three bullets." And sometimes he took pleasure in aristocratic reflections:

HARMONICA: And so you have discovered you're not a businessman after all.
FRANK: Only a man.
HARMONICA: An old breed. More Mortons will come and make them disappear.
FRANK: The future is something that no longer concerns you and me...

One could imagine one was listening to the Prince of Salina[50]: "We were the leopards, the lions. Those who take our place will be jackals and sheep and all of them, leopards, lions, jackals and sheep will continue to consider themselves the salt of the earth."

Before dying, Cheyenne will leave a spiritual testament: "You know what, Jill? If I were you I would bring those boys something to drink. You have no idea the joy a woman like you gives a man, even just to look at her. And if one of them touches your rump, don't take any notice and let him do it." Whereas in Ford's films men and women reach out in a chummy and mischievous way to spank each other's behinds, Leone's heroes philosophize about it as well.

4. EDITING

There was a time when Hollywood directors took an attitude towards technical aids that some men take towards prostitutes: they enjoyed their favors in private while in public they pretended not to know them. For them editing had to be invisible, fluid, functional to the story. Therefore movement from close-ups to long shots always had to be gradual and the actors never looked us or the camera straight in the eyes but always gazed to one side. In that way they eluded the boundaries of the screen and the presence of the camera, creating depth and continuity, and thus realistic effects. (Yet how many small, exciting discontinuities in the films of Hitchcock, Tourneur, and even Ford!)

But in Leone's movies, techniques are not entirely invisible. Forbidden link-shots from close-up to long shot, etc. are common. One of the most famous examples of this style is the three-man showdown used in *The Good, the Bad and the Ugly* narrated with the interminable repetition of three increasing enlargements (three faces, three cartridge belts, three pairs of eyes, three hands on pistols, then eyes and hands again, faster and faster). There is no real suspense since each new piece of information contains nothing to make us change our expectations about the outcome of the duel. It is pure 'filmic' tautology. Even if the trick is so utterly exposed that Leone – with the compliance of Morricone's music and its bursts of drums, trumpets, guitars, reminiscences of the "Deguello," anticipated explosions – finally involves us in the game of prolonging the wait beyond all reasonable limits.

But in *Once Upon a Time in the West* this dilatory technique works on behalf of the mythological element. The close-ups seem like true icons: Bronson's lined face in sculptured profile as suits the last remnant of an extinct race ready to be engraved on a coin; Henry Fonda's aristocratic face on which a latent uneasiness throbs. One would never tire of looking at it, all the more since the duellists are intent on preliminary maneuvering (the villain circling around

---

[50] In *The Leopard* by Luchino Visconti, 1963.

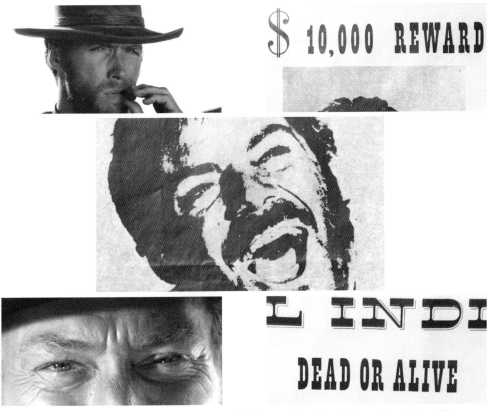

Kuleshov effect: Blondie and the Colonel have different objectives in *For a Few Dollars More*.

the good guy so that the sun will be in the other's eyes) like a macabre dance. Here the slowness does not weigh on the spectator.

This predilection for editing in particulars also includes an involuntary homage to one of his first teachers of theory, Lev Kulesov. In *For a Few Dollars More*, the two bounty hunters study the announcement of the reward on El Indio. Blondie looks at the amount while Mortimer observes the picture of the bandit and the words "Dead or Alive," a sign that the former is motivated by money and the latter by hatred. The significance does not depend upon the acting but only upon the order in which the four shots appear. This is precisely a Kulesov effect.

A nod to Soviet silent films is perhaps intended at the beginning of *Duck! You Sucker* where the arrogance of the rich who despise the peon is made grotesque by editing – in repulsive details of their mouths and fragmentary echoes of their insults that hammer away like futuristic captions ("ugly... like animals... idiots... brutes..."). One does not know whether the source is Eisenstein or Grosz, but one cannot but recall that in Ford's stagecoaches the descriptions of the relation among the social classes were more concisely described – John Carradine offering his silver cup to Louise Platt while refusing it to Claire Trevor who has to make do with drinking directly from the water bag. But Leone's unusual style does not only regard editing. The zoom, if sometimes used in a banal television way to underscore feelings where a simple linking shot from the same angle would be better (Marisol embracing her child during the exchange of prisoners in *For a Few Dollars More*, and the bandit on the train who notices the presence of Cheyenne in *Once Upon a Time in the West*), makes us think in at least one case of the comics (even if the zoom does not exist in the comics). When Ed McBain sees his daughter fall, hit by gunfire, and before running to help her cries "Maureen," Leone zooms onto his shouting mouth rather than his eyes, suggesting a degree of dismay not to be

Long shot to close-up to long shot: the final duel in *Once Upon a Time in the West.*

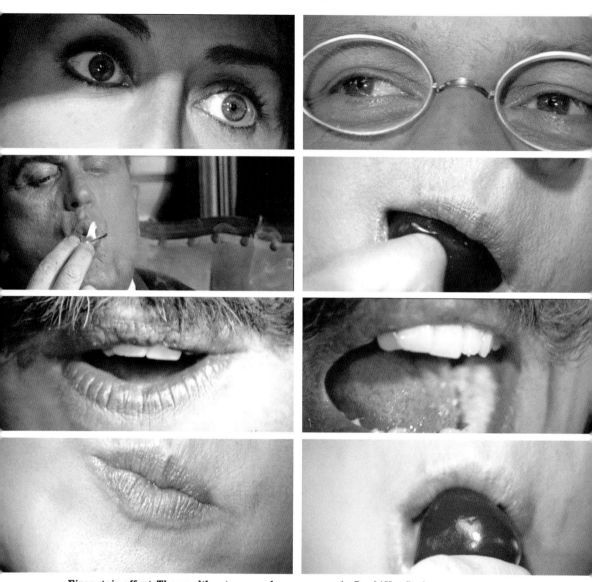

Eisenstein effect: The wealthy stagecoach passengers in *Duck! You Sucker*.

expressed through traditional mimicry. There are also plenty of subjective camera shots, with their unfailing effect of disorientation. In identifying ourselves with what a persons sees, we lose control of the scenic space and are swallowed up.

In *A Fistful of Dollars* there is a subjective camera shot of the dying villain where the site of the duel becomes more and more blurred. In *Duck! You Sucker* there is a subjective camera shot that allows us to look death in the face – that is to say, the firing squad lined up in front of Juan. And in both movies there are also some voyeuristic subjective camera shots where someone unseen spies on a scene of violence. But the most dislocating subjective camera shot occurs in *Once Upon a Time in the West* and announces the entrance on scene of some new character (the McBain child who comes running out of the farm during the massacre, Cheyenne who appears at the auction). Leone assigns us their field of vision even before letting us know who the person is.

The movements of the crane also reveal small differences in comparison to the transparency of Hollywood style. For example, the dolly shot of the title scene in *Singing in the Rain*[51] follows the movements of Gene Kelly and at the same time, creating a certain dizzy feeling, involves us in his euphoria. In *Once Upon a Time in the West* the technique, rather than enhancing the feeling, actually creates it. We know nothing about Jill when she gets off the train; but after the majestic dolly that follows her walking through the unknown town, we have felt the loneliness she will have to face and the courage which she probably has to face it with.

All of this does not exclude a very classic sense of continuity when called for. In *For a Few Dollars More*, after the semi-serious duel in which Mortimer and Monko have shot their hats full of bullet holes, we see the two hats and two cartridge belts placed on a table as a sign of peace. In fact, the camera pans the two leads seated at the table in friendly conversation. At the beginning of *The Good, the Bad and the Ugly*, Blondie has freed Tuco from the three bounty hunters and the latter is already exulting over his close call. But now the hero, without saying a word, pushes a cigar into his mouth rather than untie him. In the following shot we see Blondie delivering the Mexican up to a sheriff to cash in the reward. The gesture of mockery was like a punctuation mark that permitted the transition between the two scenes.

Tilted point-of-view shots for those looking death in the face: the bandit in *A Fistful of Dollars*, who sees the sky falling on him [a, b]; the little boy in *Once Upon a Time in the West*.

A gesture of that kind can sum up the meaning of an entire episode – Tuco ends the hold-up of the old arms dealer by sticking a sign saying "open" in his mouth – or even of an entire picture (the harmonica that Bronson pushes into the mouth of the dying Fonda in *Once Upon a Time in the West*. Sometimes the link between two sequences can be an object (the book by Bakunin

Bullet-riddled hats after the duel in *For a Few Dollars More*.

[51] Stanley Donen and Gene Kelly, 1952.

Gagged
mouths: *My
Name is
Nobody* [a],
*Once Upon a
Time in the
West* [b, c],
*The Good, the
Bad and the
Ugly* [d].

that Sean throws away during a bivouac and which the pursuers find). It can also be a rhythmic analogy: the slapping rhythm made by the Union officer as he cleans off his uniform is echoed by the marching rhythm of the prisoners in the concentration camp; or a referent of sounds: Sean in Dublin shooting at the English patrol links up with the gunfire of the Mexican platoon, Frank is about to shoot his pistol at the McBain child when there is a cut to the whistle of the train Jill is traveling on.

Even less classical and more manneristic than these shock ellipses is the use of alternating editing in the first two Westerns. In *A Fistful of Dollars* the pistol shots exchanged by the Rojos and the Baxters has in counterpoint Joe in the cellar knocking with the butt of his pistols (he was the one to trigger the gunfight) on the barrels, as he hunts for the treasure. At the end of *For a Few Dollars More* El Indio, in order not to share the loot, sends his men out to risk death on the streets of Aguacaliente and the editing alternates shots of the bandit wearing a bored expression waiting to find out the result of the battle and shots of the gunfight in which the two bounty hunters kill off the Indian's men. In both cases the irony subtly corrodes the suspense giving rise to something that could be called "alternating editing with a Machiavellian content." A veiled form of detachment. Leone, more simply, would say it was "the puppeteer's game as an extra excitement."

5. MUSIC

Even before Leone, Westerns had something operatic about them. For example, the highly codified nature of the story elements, the amount of musical interludes provided by singing cowboys, and the musical commentary in the orchestral background. John Ford integrated musical folklore very well into the dramatic structure giving dancing scenes the function of aggregating provisionally different ethnic and social groups (*Wagon Master, Fort Apache*) and used classically inspired compositions to go from the adventurous to the epic – as in the case of Max Steiner's emphatic, largely brass score for *The Searchers* which gives a martial tone to the odyssey of the two heroes.

In Leone the music (written by Ennio Morricone) carries even more decisive weight. In *A Fistful of Dollars*, for example, the irony is suggested mostly by the title theme which comments on Clint Eastwood's astute tricks.

Strange things from the past: the cover of an LP album which includes the sound track of *Duck! You Sucker!* that of a mediocre erotic drama by Piero Vivarelli and Mozart's *Symphony no. 40 in G minor...*

Probably Morricone sees the Western from an even more barbaric and amused point of view than Leone does. One knows that he loves eccentric instrumentation: anvils, bells, whistles, whips, shots, animal noises, human voices used as instruments and passages from Bach and Mozart. It could easily become pleonastic, but everything is so well amalgamated into the sound texture of the film that it is hard to distinguish the natural noises from those electronically imitated, the realistic from the symbolic. For example: those percussion sounds that accent the Mexican's panic as he waits with a noose on his neck in the epilogue to *The Good, the Bad, and the Ugly* are, in reality, nothing but amplified heart beats.

It may happen that the orchestra hides among the actors (the music box in *For a Few Dollars More* and the harmonica in *Once Upon a Time in the West*) or that music replaces dialogue (Harmonica cracks on a note to provoke Cheyenne). Similarities to pure melodrama

Soundtrack

a

b

c

Life and Films

The musical watch in *For a Few Dollars More* [a, b], the gramophone and the little seaside orchestra in *Once Upon a Time in America* [d, e], the harmonica in *Once Upon a Time in the West* [c, f].

d

e

f

are contained in the use of emphasis and in the ritual quality of certain scenes, but they are also present in the leitmotifs that follow the characters with unusual precision (the Cheyenne theme stops abruptly at the very instant of his death), that transform their character according to the situation (in the horror-style flashback of the rape scene in *For a Few Dollars More* the music seems like a tormented version of the music-box motif), that suggest feelings that images alone cannot evoke (when Jill enters the station, the theme for a solo voice expresses the loneliness of the woman from the East coming into contact with the West but also alludes to the director's nostalgia for that lost world). And sometimes the music takes audacious liberties, as when the sentimental tune ("Sean... Sean... Sean") is used as commentary for a massacre and during the collapse of the bridge in *Duck! You Sucker*. There is a realistic pretext for this (Sean put cotton into his ears to protect them from the explosion), a psychological meaning (the dynamiter's memories of Ireland) and an unexpected sense of sweet catastrophe (Kubrick was just as audacious at the end of *Dr. Strangelove* in eroticizing the atomic mushroom with a languid song of Vera Lynn's). No less Dionysian is the music just before the end of *The Good, the Bad and the Ugly* when the "ecstasy of gold" theme transforms Tuco's rush to the cemetery in search of the treasure into an ironic icon of cupidity which encompasses the spirit of the picture – and perhaps of all Leone's pictures – funereal Bacchanals to exorcise the melancholy of the story.

6. Sets

No one seems to have noticed that in *Johnny Guitar* Joan Crawford keeps a bust of Beethoven in her office. The fact is that Americans did not emphasize. Even sets obeyed the rule of understatement. Starting with those wooden villages that had a saloon, a bank, a prison, a barbershop and a drug-store all lined up along Main Street, there was always something interchangeable about them, not to say pre-fabricated, despite the fact that they were inspired by period illustrations.

a   b

The vaguely Sicilian-Andalusian-style ghost towns of the Dollars Trilogy: *A Fistful of Dollars* [a], *For a Few Dollars More* [b].

In Leone's villages, on the other hand, there is no growing civilization to honor, no drugstore, no courthouse and no (or almost no) inhabitants. They look like ghost towns and, sometimes, like Southern Italian small towns. The prevailing connotation is the archaic. The same is true of the interiors. The relay post in *Once Upon a Time in the West* is a kind of *caravanserai* that combines saloon, dormitory, blacksmith's shop and stables. At times one breathes the air of a museum or antique shop there. Leone, whose hobby was collecting antiques (mostly silver and Roman furniture of the 1600-1700s), finds ingenious narrative pretexts for showing off his rare pieces. He is even capable of turning a tobacco box or a clothes press into bizarre instruments of torture. The *piece de resistance* of the antiquarian style is, of course, the private railroad car in *Once Upon a Time in the West* with its lace trimmings, brocades and brass handrails.

a   b

The museum-like interiors of the Time Trilogy: *Once Upon a Time in the West* **[a]**, *Duck! You Sucker* **[b]**.

Leone's movies never lack a groaning board. In American pictures, if food was sometimes inscribed in a moral system as the counterpoise to alcohol [in Anthony Mann's *The Far Country* (1954), the good guys go to the restaurant while the baddies visit the saloon], in the dollar trilogy the scenes of conviviality partake of the baroque, steeped in violence and death.

In *A Fistful of Dollars* the Mexicans play at target practice against a suit of armor while they dine; in *For a Few Dollars More*, the bandits' bivouac in a deconsecrated church near a statue of an angel. In *The Good, the Bad and the Ugly*, Angel Eyes offers Tuco dinner before torturing him.

In *Once Upon a Time in the West* there would seem to be some need of precise period research. As Cheyenne listens to Jill, in order to make his role more active, rather than doing something like smoking, he eats stewed potatoes and peas from a little terracotta pot using a match for a fork.

Even the finest idea for a set in the films of Leone has to do with eating. The farm tables of the McBain's, set for a wedding banquet outdoors (with red and white-checkered table cloths, a symbol of frugal honesty, according to Erwin Panowsky) are turned into funeral altars for the bodies of his family members, underscoring the profound unity of the farmer's life cycle: feasts, flour and funerals. This erudite taste is shared by two predecessors, who are obviously very different from each other: De Mille and Visconti. De Mille loved to fill his scenes with period gadgets (for example, the sort of rudimentary cocktail shaker used by Jean Arthur in *The Plainsman*, 1936). In this way he created a kind of period color, a rather naive kind of exoticism, which kept his historical frescos from becoming pompous. In Visconti's *Senso*, sets

a

Tuco's metaphysical-surrealist sunshade: *The Good, the Bad and the Ugly* (1966) [a, b, d] vs Alejandro Jodorowsky's *El Topo* (1970) [c].

b   c   d

Mealtime with Leone

a

b

c

Meal with target practice in *A Fistful of Dollars* [a], tucking in at the church *For a Few Dollars More* [b], Cheyenne's potato stew in *Once Upon a Time in the West* [c], lunch on the High Sierra in *Duck! You Sucker* [d], cupcakes in *Once Upon a Time in America* [e], table strewn with corpses in *Once Upon a Time in the West* [f].

d

e

f

a

b

c

d

The stone arch in *Once Upon a Time in the West* (1968) [a, b], the Arch of Gallienus in Rome in a drawing by Giambattista Piranese (1756) [c] and a hanging from Tinto Brass' film *Yankee* (1966) [d], which may well have inspired Leone.

full of authentic pieces are filmed in a way to reveal their theatrical nature, since the heroine, without knowing it, is living through a melodramatic passion.

Leone is exotic like De Mille and theatrical like Visconti. He even manages to make the desert theatrical. In *Duck! You Sucker* Juan and Sean have lunch seated on Louis Vuitton chairs set up in the middle of a Mexican sierra; *in The Good, the Bad and the Ugly* Tuco shades himself with a violet-colored umbrella as he escorts his prisoner across the desert. (An allusion to metaphysical painting: Leone loved De Chirico and had some of his works in his house.) But the set that best represents Leone's taste is the stone arch with a man hanging from it in *Once Upon a Time in the West*. Here the nostalgia for the West becomes a romantic, obsessive love of ruins whose most illustrious precursor was Giovanni Battista Piranesi, the creator of the famous engravings that depict Rome's eroded centuries-old monuments from imaginary perspectives. Leone did something of the sort for the heroes of American legends, portraying them magnified by memory, corroded by irony and pursued by the shadow of death.

P.S. (THE NAME ABOVE THE TITLE)

At times the language of credits has its own esoteric effectiveness. *Per un pugno di dollari: regia di Bob Robertson; Once Upon a Time in America*: a film by Sergio Leone. An inverse symmetry that encompasses twenty years of Italian cinema from mimicry to nomadism.

The difference between "directed by" *(regia di)* and "a film by" has lost the heraldic value that it had in Hollywood. (Frank Capra called his autobiography *The Name Above the Title*.) But Leone, who controlled every phase of the production of his movies, would have been entitled to the name above the title even in those days. All the more so in that the results bear the imprint of a highly personal taste. Let us list some of the constant factors:

1) A space that deliberately eschews unity, always too cluttered or too empty, with *very close* close-ups, wrinkled and immobile (evoking masks), and long shots where the depth cracks open suddenly.

2) A subtly entranced rhythm (enervating dilations, traumatic ellipses) sustained by a fusion of drama and music that makes one think of opera.

3) A story evoked in flashbacks, in which a ceremonial tone (highlighted in duels, long waits, and farewell scenes) takes priority over plot construction.

4) A mannerist tendency to exalt popular genres and themes with tragic, precious, and solemn treatment.

5) The insistence on reviving past epochs (the West, Prohibition, but also in unrealized projects like those on Leningrad and the seventeenth century) with a scrupulously realistic and arbitrarily chimerical style.

6) A continuous flowering of Mediterranean mythologies: Trastevere swaggering, rustic vendettas, lacerating martyrdoms, obscene pranks. (Giulio Bollati has written that Christ and Pulcinella are the key figures of the symbolic Italian stage).

All mixed in a *pastiche* that includes American myths (like men friendship). A more rigorous critical period would have cited Auerbach to compare Leone to the late Roman, Ammiano Marcellino and Apuleius, of whom he speaks in a chapter in *Mimesis* ("personages who constantly live inebriated on blood and in fear of death; mixtures of the most subtle rhetorical arts and a strident and contorted realism; a prevailing of the magical-sensual over the rational-ethical."). Today one tends to agree with Baudrillard who called Leone the first post-modernist director. No one, perhaps, expresses skepticism about the representation of reality better than this Roman who, in his early films, thought he was celebrating the American legend of the 1800s and instead ended up describing primarily the Italy of the sixties already resigned to its cynicism. He did it with less subtle shading than greater directors, but also with fewer inhibitions.

In the snapshot album of the boom era, together with Mastroianni pretending to enjoy himself at a party, and Alain Delon who only feels he is alive when he is playing the stock market, and Vittorio Gassman who feels young when he is at the wheel of a sports car, there should definitely be included the scene in which in a desert clearing a man with a gun meets another man with a gun. They are joined by a third man and the three, in order to avoid sharing the loot, prepare for mortal combat, studying each other at length, spasmodically at length – in order to make us understand that they are astute and ferocious, to give us time to listen to the music, and because they think that in the West that was how things were done.

From the Italian opening titles with a fake English name to the English opening titles with the true Italian name: a life and a career in two billboards.

Part Two
WORDS

Indio's sermon in *For a Few Dollars More.*

1. LEONE ON LEONE

Editing of Guy Braucourt's *(g.b.)* interviews with Sergio Leone by Oreste De Fornari *(o.d.f.)*, Franco Ferrini *(f.f.)*, Gilles Lambert *(g.l.)*, Massimo Moscati *(m.m.)*, Noël Simsolo *(n.s.)*, Luca Verdone *(l.v.)*.

THE BEGINNINGS

My father, Roberto Roberti, began his acting career in 1904 with Eleonora Duse. In 1908 he started directing and shot about ninety films in all, quite a few of them with the actress Francesca Bertini. *Contessa Sara* ran for nine months in a Rome movie house. I remember seeing a photo showing the mounted police controlling the crowds at the entrance. He discovered the actor to play Maciste, Bartolomeo Pagano. Pagano was working as a stevedore at the port of Genoa, and my father presented him to Pastrone. He is also the director of a very fine version of *Fra Diavolo* [Friar Devil] with Gustavo Sereni and Lido Manetti, who was killed in Hollywood under mysterious circumstances – apparently by the Mafia because he was threatening to take the place of Rudolph Valentino. When Ernst Lubitsch went to Hollywood, my father was called to replace him as the director of Pola Negri. But my mother was against it and so it is by pure chance that I wasn't born in Germany. [*o.d.f.* 1983]

My father was one of the first to enroll in the Fascist Party. He paid his first dues and after ten days they came to tell him he had to pay them again because the secretary had run off with the cash box. From that moment he became an anti-Fascist. He was saved from internment thanks to an old school chum, Roberto Forges Davanzati, who had become a minister, but for a long time was not able to shoot a film. When we went out on Sundays to the Cafe Aragno we were followed at a distance by two policemen. During that long period of inactivity my father was reduced to misery. This ostracism ended in 1941 thanks to an influential member of the Regime and my father was able to shoot *La Bocca sulla Strada* [Mouth on the Street] in Naples with Armando Falconi. The following year I was his assistant director for *I Fuochi di San Martino* [Fires of San Martino] with Aldo Silvani. That was his last film.[52] Then he gave up moviemaking and retired to Torella dei Lombardi between Avellino and Naples where he had been born and where he died soon after. [*o.d.f.* 1983]

I never had the chance to learn from him. I began as an assistant to Vittorio De Sica, Mario Camerini, Mario Soldati, Carmine Galloni, and Mario Bonnard. I was technical director for an episode of *Questa e la Vita* [This is Life] (from Piraridello's story *La Marsina Stretta)* [The Tight Tailcoat] interpreted by Aldo Fabrizi. [*o.d.f.* 1983]

I also worked with the Americans: Mervyn Le Roy's *Quo Vadis?* in 1951, *Helen of Troy* with Wise in 1958 (I was in Walsh's second unit which had filmed all the battle scenes and the landing, then I was transferred to the first unit with Wise, who hadn't wanted to do the film), and Zinnemann's *The Nun's Story* in 1959. But, above all, *Ben Hur* with Wyler again in 1959. Wyler had signed a contract that stipulated he would in no way concern himself with the chariot race which would be entirely in the hands of the second unit. He would see a projection of the result and if it did not please him it would be shot again until he was satisfied.

I was assistant director in the second unit directed by Andrew Marton. We had two months to prepare the horses and over three to shoot.

---

[52] Leone is referring to a film in progress and left unfinished in 1944, titled *I Fuochi di San Martino*. It was completed in 1950 by adding some sequences and it was released only for few days and just in Naples, in the summer 1951 with the name *Il Folle di Marechiaro*.

I had to see Fred Niblo's version of *Ben Hur* an awful lot of times because they showed it every night and the troupe was obliged to attend the projection." [*g.b.* 1969]

This is the best way to learn. I always tell those who ask to be a voluntary assistant: "You should come and watch me shoot a film and then escape, especially if you love my movies, because you risk becoming an imitator as happened with Zeffirelli under Visconti. It's better to be an assistant to three or four directors whom you esteem and then some less excellent directors in order to make comparisons and decide what you would do in their place." As an assistant director I made some films where I earned more than the director did because he needed me for the technical side. I was the one to tell him where to place the camera.

When I was twenty-five I received a proposal to direct some minor Italian films, but I refused because I wanted to delay my directing debut. I was afraid of ruining my career and involving the producer in an economic disaster. I believe that Loy, Petri, and Bolognini acted similarly. In those days we were more responsible. [*o.d.f.* 1983]

LAST DAYS OF POMPEII

Last Days of Pompeii was begun by Bonnard who then abandoned it to make *Gastone,* and I, who was with the second unit, went over to the first and chose Corbucci (whom at the time no one wanted) to direct the second unit and Duccio Tessari as assistant director.

At first the hero was supposed to be a kind of Scarlet Pimpernel or James Bond, intelligent and witty. Then when we got to Spain, the producers (Procusa, an Opus Dei company) told us they had managed to sign up Steve Reeves. So in ten days we had to rewrite the script to suit this muscular actor.

But *The Colossus of Rhodes,* where the hero is a playboy, is more to my taste. [*o.d.f.* 1983]

THE COLOSSUS OF RHODES

I have no nostalgia for mythological subjects. I made *The Colossus of Rhodes* in 1960 for bread and butter, to pay for my honeymoon trip to Spain. Forced into a choice I said, 'I want to try making a film with the same ingredients but in an ironic vein.' I had been remotely inspired, actually, by a film of Hitchcock's, *North by Northwest:* a person takes a trip to an accursed island for a rest, and in spite of himself he becomes involved in all kinds of things that push him to take action. Certainly it was not the kind of thing I really liked. I do not even like *Spartacus,* however well made it was. The only interesting thing of the kind I have seen was an English television series on domestic life in ancient Rome.

The Colossus of Rhodes was a success, so successful I was forced to refuse six Maciste films a day. When they offered me two of these movies I had 200,000 *lire* [about 200 dollars] in my bank account. I put off signing until the next day. Carla, my wife, said: "If you really don't feel like it, refuse. Something else will turn up." What turned up was a film script and then Robert Aldrich who asked me to be his assistant in *Sodom and Gomorrah.* It was a big disappointment because I had deeply admired the latest things Aldrich had made, *Attack!* and *The Big Knife,* but when I found myself faced with reality it was all different. Then I left, deserted the set, explaining that I didn't want to help bury an Italian producer. I sent a good letter to Lombardo, saying: "Instead of fishing around in the South Seas, come back at once with a machine gun and when you land at Marrakesh, don't worry too much but just shoot, whomever you hit it will be okay, since this is a criminal organization: they're murdering you." And in fact, the movie had those misadventures which, together with the failure of *The Leopard,* led to the bankruptcy of Titanus. [*o.d.f.* 1988]

Words

A FISTFUL OF DOLLARS

Italy was in the midst of a movie-industry crisis. Remember the bankruptcy of Titanus. And so the films taken from Karl May's books, a kind of German equivalent of our Emilio Salgari were successful. On the European level it was thought that to reduce financial risks it would be a good idea to make Westerns. In that case, in fact, Spanish and German producers would be willing to join in. But one thing I must make clear: many people think I am the father of the Italian Western. It's not true. Before me twenty-five Westerns had been made.

When I finished *A Fistfitl of Dollars,* a Roman movie-house owner, with no less than fifty theaters, did not even want to come and see the film because it had been deemed by then that the Western in Italy was totally finished. The other Italian Westerns had already been released and the critics had not even noticed. For three years they had already been doing re-runs of them on the neighborhood circuits and no one had noticed because they were all presented with false names and it was thought that they were minor films, American television releases, and no one guessed for a minute that they were made by Italian and Spanish directors; and so let's say that *A Fistful of Dollars* was the twenty-sixth Italian Western. [*f.f.* 1971]

Ten years ago, when I began to shoot films, coming from a neo-realist school I could not imagine that four years later I would make my debut with such a thing as a Western. One day I noticed that the genre was languishing, I had seen some of the recent American productions that were pretty stale, and I thought: "Why should such a noble kind of cinema have to die?" For, in a Western you can treat such wide-ranging and important themes in such a way as to make the genre truly noble. After seeing *Yojimbo* I thought of bringing back home the American novel on which Kurosawa had based his movie and I dedicated myself with great passion but little means to working on the film. The producers did not realize that a film was in the making that would give a new special direction to movie-making and so I was kind of the little brother. In fact, the same producers were making another movie at the same time, Mario Caiano's *Le Pistole non Discutono* [Guns Don't Talk], which was full of commonplaces, the final charge, etc., and they had given all of the money to him. For example, one American actor alone, Rod Cameron, cost as much as my whole cast put together because they thought it was an A-movie whereas *A Fistful of Dollars* was thought to be kind of a salvage job.

When I spoke with these gentlemen, to be precise with a certain so-called producer Giorgio Papi, I told him that I wanted Gian Maria Volonté as the hero, and he said: "You're nuts, Leone, go away and play, have your fun, I don't even want to see the film – anyway we're ahead of the game to start with." For them it was just a business deal and that was very much to my advantage because I had complete autonomy and there was no interference from the producers. So I went off to Spain and did my seven weeks of shooting and what came out of it was *A Fistful of Dollars*. [*f.f.* 1971]

I was the first to make Westerns without women. I anguished for six long months after having finished *A Fistful of Dollars* (which had cost the Italian producer only 30 million *lire*) because somebody had read the treatment and mistaken it for a comedy, while someone else asked how you could dream of making a film without women. A big Florence movie-house owner who today doesn't have the courage to face me said: "My dear Leone, you have made a film which can never be successful because it is absurd that the only woman in it is an extra." And I replied that I was intentionally shooting a movie without women, that it was all calculated in advance. I had seen John Sturges' excellent *Gunfight at the O.K. Corral* (which was later badly remade[53]) and had asked myself what Rhonda Fleming was doing in it. She stopped the rhythm of the movie. If during the editing they had cut her part it would have been a more serious movie. Maybe her part was inserted for atavistic reasons. The Western was the first

---

[53] Leone is referring to *Hour of the Gun* (1967), that's more a sequel than a remake.

kind of film ever to be made, and so women were considered indispensable for the female public, but it was demonstrated that women liked *A Fistful of Dollars* precisely because there were no women in it. And maybe they even thought: "The hero is the way he is because he never met me!" [*m.m.* 1978]

I wanted Lavagnino, who had composed the music for *The Colossus of Rhodes,* to write the score. At the Jolly they had spoken to me of Ennio Morricone and showed me *Duello nel Texas* [Showdown in Texas] which seemed horrible to me; the music sounded like a poor man's Tiomkin. The producer insisted on my meeting Morricone. I went to his house and he recognized me at once. We had been classmates in fifth grade at Saint Juan Baptiste de la Salle, with the Piarist Brothers where I also did my high school studies. He had me listen to a piece that the producers had rejected and which I was later to use in the finale of the film. Afterwards we listened to a record of something he had written for an American baritone which immediately impressed me. I asked him to keep the basic musical elements. We had the principal motif, only the singer was lacking. I proposed having someone whistle it and thus the firm Alessandroni & Company was born which later worked on many Westerns. [*o.d.f.* 1983]

FOR A FEW DOLLARS MORE

The bounty hunter was an ambiguous figure. In the West he was called "the undertaker." He fascinated me because he represented the way of life in this country: the need to kill in order to survive.

This reminds me of an anecdote about Wyatt Earp. Just after being named sheriff of a small town he goes out looking for a card shark. To demonstrate his power, he provokes him, challenges him to a showdown, and kills him. At that very moment he hears footsteps behind him, turns and shoots his assistant between the eyes, killing him. That is what the period was like and the bounty hunter was a typical figure. [*g.b.* 1969]

I wanted Lee Marvin for the part of Mortimer. I left Rome on a Friday and was supposed to start shooting with him on Monday at Cinecittà. Just before leaving I got a phone call from Marvin's agent: the contract had fallen through because Marvin had signed for *Cat Ballou*. I was desperate. I left for Los Angeles with the production director Ottavio Oppo. I remembered Lee Van Cleef in *Bravados* and in *High Noon* where he was called "machine gun" for the way he used pistols. I remembered him as being a bit like a Roman barber, all dark and curly-haired, and that worried me.

But Lee Van Cleef seemed to have disappeared. They told me he had stopped working. He had gone to dry out in a clinic for alcoholics and had ended up with his car in a Los Angeles canyon. He was covered with silver plates and nails. To earn a living he had taken up painting pictures. He painted like a young lady, all landscapes and seascapes.

When I found him in a hotel foyer he was wearing a dirty trench coat that reached his feet and cowboy boots. His salt-and-pepper hair had a brush cut. He looked like an eagle, he looked like Van Gogh. I said to Ottavio Oppo: "He is so right for the part that I don't even want to talk to him, because if I talk to him maybe I won't find him intelligent and I will make a big mistake. Go and sign him up at once." Instead he is anything but stupid, he is a Dutch Jew and calls himself Van Cleef like the jewelers.

He said he had to deliver a picture. They had given him fifty dollars and he had to go collect another hundred and fifty. He thought we wanted to have him shoot two or three scenes. When he realized he would be the co-lead in the movie he almost fainted. He began sharing the $5,000 advance with his agent as if he had hit a gold mine.

He was very grateful to me, and two years later when we were doing the dubbing in New York, he invited me to a marvelous Chinese restaurant with his wife and ex-nurse he had met in the hospital (he needed someone to keep him under control). I said to her: "What a lovely fur." She smiled at me: "We owe it to you. Two years ago we were having trouble paying the light bill." [*o.d.f.* 1983]

THE GOOD, THE BAD AND THE UGLY

I began this film just like the two preceding ones, with three characters and a treasure hunt. But what interested me was, on the one hand the demystification of words, and, on the other, the absurdity of war. What do good, bad and ugly mean? We are all a little good, a little bad, and a little ugly. And there are people who seem bad, but when you get to know them they aren't really...

To my mind, civil war is useless, stupid, there are no just causes. The key line of the film is the comment made by a character about the battle on the bridge: "I have never seen so many imbeciles die, and so pointlessly." I was inspired by photographs of Union and Confederate prison camps (at Andersonville, for example, 250,000 prisoners died) for the movie's Union prison camp where the cries of the tortured prisoners are drowned out by the orchestra. Of course I also had in mind the Nazi concentration camps and the orchestras of Jews. It is a little in the spirit of one of the greatest films I have ever seen, *Monsieur Verdoux*. That doesn't keep the movie from being able to make you laugh. There is a picaresque spirit in these tragic situations. The picaresque genre is an exclusively Spanish literary tradition that has some equivalents even in Italy in works like *Fra Diavolo*[54]. In the picaresque as in the *commedia dell'arte* there are no entirely good or bad characters. Nevertheless in *The Good, the Bad and the Ugly* it was impossible to let the worst of the three survive, who was played by a truly vicious Lee Van Cleef. [*g.b.* 1969]

I wanted Eli Wallach because of a gesture he makes in *How the West Was Won* when he gets off the train and talks to George Peppard[55]. He sees a child, Peppard's son, and suddenly turns and shoots him with a finger making a raspberry. That made me realize he was a comic actor of the Chaplin school, a Neapolitan Jew; you could ask him to do anything. In fact we had a very good time working together. He always wanted me to show him the movements he was to make, but just for kicks. [*o.d.f* 1983]

Once Upon a Time in the West

In all my films one of the dominant themes, as you can see, is male friendship, which may be the only sentiment that is still left. And the Western for me is the virility of the individual, and therefore also vengeance. In *Once Upon a Time in the West* vengeance exists, it is precise, it is Bronson's obsession. But after he obtains it he says: "I am finished. I don't know where to go. My life ends here." He has lost his interest in life.

So vengeance is part of life. In *For a Few Dollars More* there is one character who, having gotten his revenge, gives up all his work saying: "Kid, the West is all yours. I've done my job and maybe I'll do like Cincinnatus and go back to tilling my fields." [*m.m.* 1978]

Why do I begin with the great boredom of the three killers? Why, because killers are bored when not playing at the game of life and death! In fact the first of them duels with a fly, the second with a drop of water, the third with his hands – until the man to be killed shows up and then the fly is eliminated while the other one "drinks this rusty water like a holy chalice" and thus they take care of the next guy and make an end of it, and die, because it is right and logical that they should die. [*m.m.* 1978]

---

[54] Actually *Fra' Diavolo* takes place in Italy but it was written by the French composer Daniel Auber.

[55] Actually the sequence Leone describes doesn't happen when Eli Wallach gets off the train, but a little later.

135

All About **Sergio Leone**

If I use so many close-ups in my movies (while in American Westerns the characters are more or less set against the landscape) it's because I give so much importance to the eyes. That is where you can read everything: courage, threat, fear, uncertainty, death, etc. When Fonda has killed his enemies in the street with the help of Bronson on the balcony and he looks up at him, his whole character, his whole problem is in that look and also a presentiment of his end, because all that counts for him now is to understand what Bronson wants. I constructed the film like a jig-saw puzzle, like a mosaic where if you move one piece it ruins everything. Because none of the characters talks about himself, it is always someone else who judges him, reads him. You will have noticed that I always set the finales of my films inside a circle: that is where Lee kills Volonté, where Clint, Eli and Lee duel, where Bronson kills Fonda. It is the arena of life, the moment of truth, and that is why I framed the shot to take in the landscape behind Bronson and Fonda. [*g.b.* 1969]

Fonda had my three films shown to him one after the other in Los Angeles, and when he came out he said: "Where's the contract?".

He showed up on the set with sideburns, a beard and dark contact lenses. I didn't say anything to him, but I didn't shoot his scenes, and day after day I removed one bit at a time: first the sideburns, then the beard, the moustache and finally the contact lenses. When he saw that I had focused the camera at the nape of his neck for his first appearance, he exclaimed: "Jesus Christ, now I understand." I wanted the public to recognize in this villain the same Fonda who had played all the good American presidents. And anyway, it's the truth. The vice presidents of the companies I have dealt with have all had baby-blue eyes and honest faces and what sons of bitches they were! Furthermore he's no saint himself. He had five wives. The last one fell out the window while trying to murder him. He stepped over her and went to act his part in *Mr. Roberts* as if nothing had happened.

He had some problems with the love scenes, but Claudia helped a lot. She behaved as if she had a man of twenty-five on top of her instead of sixty-five. And he played the scene with his usual classic sobriety. [*o.d.f.* 1983]

Bronson was just the actor I wanted. By the time I went to America looking for him I was very well known and so I had a mob of agents offering me all the biggest names. And when I asked for Charles Bronson they asked astonished: "Who?" The rumor even began circulating that I was mad. And yet Bronson was the most important for me because that face of his could stop a train. He was the executioner who even if you went to Greenland would follow you there and find you. He was exactly the archetype that I was seeking and whom I found in him alone. As an actor he is good, as American actors are, the ones who study themselves in a mirror controlling almost every facial muscle, who know everything. [*m.m.* 1978]

My first films were a bit tatty, partly because of the meager funds that I had available. Some of the costumes I would like to redo, improve, bring up to the level of the last films. In *A Fistful of Dollars,* for example, there were some things that weren't right just because I couldn't go and rummage – as I did for the later films – in the Western Costume warehouses in Hollywood among Ford and his friend's old things. Western Costume is a kind of *Rinascente* (an Italian department store, *Ed.*) of costumes which has been financed for at least forty years by the major American studios who have 20% of the stock. All the costumes used by Paramount, Fox, Metro, Universal and Columbia end up in this immense building, from collars, to shoes, to cuffs. In short, everything that has been made, ends up there. Naturally when I went there they showed me all the very newest things, beautiful things, that I had already seen in television films. But I explained that I was an Italian director with a very limited budget, and was wondering if they didn't have any warehouse leftovers. And they told me that they had a lot of stuff in the basements, but that they were practically rags. The search was extremely easy just because the costumes were all piled up in a huge room and after a month of hunting there with my costume designer I found everything I wanted. Things turned

136

up which were later used in a lot of other American movies. Beginning with movies like *Butch Cassidy* certain directors demanded these kinds of costumes. For this reason the cost of renting them went up from five to a hundred dollars and nobody wanted the new costumes anymore... I brought over dust from Monument Valley because I wanted that kind of color. The interiors of *Once Upon a Time in the West* were clearly shot at Cinecittà, but I still demanded dust of that color (and not only because the interiors had to correspond to the exteriors). When Bronson and Fonda came on that set they were astonished at the atmosphere which was so totally different; the actors, psychologically, performed differently. To my mind, when Visconti is attacked for his fussiness it is a mistake. [*m.m.* 1978]

MUSIC

For me the music is fundamental, especially in a Western where the dialogue is purely aphoristic; the films could just as well be silent; one would understand all the same. The music serves to emphasize states of mind, facts and situations more than the dialogue itself does. In a word, for me the music functions as dialogue. I have an almost visceral relationship to Ennio Morricone. I throw as many adjectives at him as I need to, until he gets the idea. At least twelve or thirteen themes are composed for my films and rejected; not because they are ugly (on the contrary they may be the prettiest ones), but because they don't give me the right sensations. This, on the other hand, is what music means to me: on hearing Shostakovich's 7th, a film to make came into my head... Perhaps the fact that I sing so very off pitch is the reason why I am so musical inside. [*m.m.* 1978]

FORD, PECKINPAH AND ME

Ford was an optimist; I am a pessimist. When Ford's characters open a window, what they see, in the end, is a horizon full of hope, while mine are always afraid of getting a bullet between the eyes when they open a window. So for me Ford's best movie was one of his last, *The Man Who Shot Liberty Valance*, where he rediscovered pessimism: he understood that he was wrong, that he had not been a good prophet, so he went back and told things the way they were.

I love Ford very much, but I criticize him even while loving him. I criticize him the way one can criticize Capra, that Italian full of the lust for success. The doors of success open to him, he believes in that beautiful America and, naturally, he makes films of that epoch, tied to that period. [*m.m.* 1978]

Furthermore, in America a certain kind of optimistic rhetoric is obligatory, even Huston told me that. To put *A Fistful of Dollars* on TV they added a preamble where a stand-in for Clint, wearing a poncho like his, speaks to the warden of a prison who promises him a reward and maybe even his freedom, if he sets things straight in that village. They did this without saying a word to me about it, just for the sake of a moral.

Peckinpah once said: "Without Leone I wouldn't have been able to make my movies." Kubrick too said the same thing concerning *A Clockwork Orange*.

A Fistful of Dollars was a trail-blazing film, at least for the way in which it depicted violence. Of Peckinpah's films *Guns in the Afternoon* is the one I liked the most. The later ones, like *Straw Dogs*, I liked less. One feels how alcohol has ruined the idea, everything becomes deformed, excessive. That happens to many. Even Coppola's *Apocalypse Now* strikes me as not having been shot in a state of complete lucidity. [*o.d.f* 1983]

By now I think the Western is everyone's heritage. But one should not confuse the myth of the West with the historical reality of America in the last century. If it is true that Western films are inspired by that period, it is equally true that they shape them at will. I remember one movie: *The Culpepper Co.*, a film about the West which however did not capture the mythical quality that comes from the legend and, above all, from the Hollywood films. Rather it was based on a rigorous historical reconstruction. People wouldn't buy it. Why? Because they did not find in it what they were looking for: the fable. That is the point: the fable, the telling of fables; the myths do not belong to anyone but to everyone. And so the Western too belongs to everyone! [*l.v.* 1979]

When I made Westerns I always had in mind the *pupi,* the Sicilian marionettes. I re-read all the plots that inspired the Sicilian bards' songs: there was a strange affinity between the *pupi* and my Western friends. There adventures were identical. Only the background was changed. There is very little room for invention. [*g.l* 1976]

DUCK*!* YOU SUCKER

I was happy to produce it, but not to direct it. We had to find a director. The Americans suggested a film critic who had directed a film for Roger Corman, *Targets.* His name was Peter Bogdanovich. Everyone spoke well of him. So we had him come to Rome. He arrived at the airport with his sister who was carrying a suitcase. She looked more like his maid than his sister. He made a bad impression and the events that followed only confirmed my fears.

The first week of his stay, Bogdanovich spent the whole time organizing screenings of his film for the entire pseudo-intellectual aristocracy of Rome. And for my fellow directors. We had to wait until the third week before we could begin work on the screenplay. Together with Vincenzoni we made various proposals. Bogdanovich's reply was always a no, "I don't like it!". For an entire week, we had to listen to him repeatedly refusing everything we came up with. I was well and truly peeved. I said to him: "Tomorrow, you do the talking. Because I want to be the one who says "I don't like it!". He turned pale and said: "I want Mamy" , that's what he called his wife. He claimed he could not work without her. I agreed that she could join us. I rented a villa for them. But I demanded they come up with a story within fifteen days.

Two weeks later Bogdanovich and his wife gave me a dozen or so pages in English. I had them translated and freaked out! I got another translator. Same thing: total disaster. That was enough for me. I had Bogdanovich sign every page of the English version and I sent them off to United Artists. Three days later I received a telegram from the States: "Send Mr. and Mrs. Bogdanovich back to New York. IN TOURIST CLASS." I showed Bogdanovich the telegram and said goodbye, but only after advising him not to show *Targets* to many people in America. [*n.s.* 1987]

This is a film that I was only supposed to have produced. But Peter Bogdanovich, with whom I began working, conceived the subject in an old Hollywood style. Then the actors re-fused to work with my assistant. So I proposed it to Sam Peckinpah, but Steiger would only accept his part if I directed it personally.

At first I wanted to have a big difference in age between the two leads who were to have a father-son relationship but in reverse. I had thought of Malcolm McDowell for the part of Sean and Jason Robards for that of Juan. Three months before shooting, Steiger hired at his own expense a Mexican girl to learn the language. And during all the production, up to the post-synchronization phase, he continued to speak Spanish on and off the set. Coburn had spent five weeks in Ireland to perfect his accent. They did these things on their own initiatives out of professional seriousness.

The film is very precise when it comes to certain details such as the armored car (which was the first model the Germans sent to Mexico), the machine guns, the train, the pistols which are of Belgian, German or American manufacture, the motorcycle, the colonial hats. But I do not aim at historical accuracy; I prefer the spirit of the fable. I start out with a historical situation taken as a pretext, and with a genre such as the Western go beyond them.

Words

The corpses in the grotto, the executions in the ditches, the flight of the governor on the train, represent for me (and the Italian public) precise episodes in the fight against Fascism, above all the executions in the Fosse Ardeatine and Mussolini's flight. (The officer who tries to escape disguised as a civilian and is shot in the back is played by an engineer who was a double for Mussolini in his youth.)

I go back to Chaplin for my model whose comedies did more for Socialism than any political leader ever did. The sequence in the bank, with Steiger who finds himself at the head of the liberated prisoners, is taken directly from *Modern Times*. [*g.b.* 1972]

I had some problems with the actors, mostly with Steiger, who, like a good professional, wanted to know right from the start *everything* he had to do. I had a hard time making it clear that I didn't know anything yet, that I would decide from day to day. He kept on insisting: "I want the script!" One day I pointed to my head. For a moment I was afraid he would break it open in order to read the invisible script...

Coburn is a great professional. When he saw Steiger roll his eyes with histrionic dramatics, he tried competing with him. I made him understand that the less he tried to imitate him the better it would be. Coburn is very intelligent and understood at once, so in the film his measured interpretation makes a splendid counterpoint to Steiger. But Steiger acted better than usual. Since he is good only when he is tired, I made him repeat the same scene as many as forty times. He got mad. They calmed him down by saying: "Leone is like a kid at the puppet show. He enjoys seeing you act so much that he makes you repeat the scene." [*g.l.* 1976]

I have little faith in political movies, so just imagine how I feel about these here. One thing that always made me smile was that when I went to Germany (where my movies had great success), no one asked me about Fellini or Visconti but about what Corbucci was doing, maintaining that his films were political. And this made me laugh until I cried.

When *Soldier Blue* was released, everyone cried "miracle" and thought it was a progressive Western. What a lot of nonsense! Like a good craftsman, Ralph Nelson had knocked together what an intelligent producer thought he could sell: "Let's shoot a kind of *mea culpa* because this is the moment for spitting on ourselves." To mistake this for a political film is typical of the European mentality: our false intellectualizing.

As far as "intelligent" Westerns go, I have only seen one of Sollima's films, *The Big Gundown*, whose tide was my suggestion: I got it from a musical theme of Morricone's. A very fine subject by Franco Solinas completely ruined by a banal and stupid movie. In short, I have a very bad opinion of these movies. So much so that when they tell me "you are the father of the Italian Western" I think: "What a lot of sons of bitches." [*m.m.* 1978]

I don't like fake political films, the film as a political rally. I prefer certain indirect political movies such as Wilder's *Front Page* or Forman's *One Flew Over the Cuckoo's Nest* which hit the audience harder than party slogans could do. And then, you cannot be a Communist with a villa. At best you might be able to be a bit of an anarchist. [*o.d.f.* 1983]

ONCE UPON A TIME IN AMERICA

The story of this film started way back in 1967. The late Giuseppe Colizzi, who before making his debut in a Western with *Blood River* did an apprenticeship with me for a year (helping to shoot and edit *The Good, the Bad and the Ugly*), told me about a novel, *The Hoods*, upon which the episode of the robbery at the casino in *Revenge at El Paso* was based. The novel struck me as a modest affair but full of curious details. In New York I contacted Harry Grey, an old Jew from Odessa, who had been a gangster, had been Frank Costello's right-hand man. In fact the novel makes mention of a certain Frank, and Max too was inspired by a real person. At 73 years of age they offered Grey another job, but his wife advised him against it and after two months, they saw him in handcuffs on TV. Grey had written the novel during the fifteen years he spent in Sing Sing. What struck me about it was precisely its similarity to Hollywood films. Fantasy had won out over reality. But you could tell that the episodes about his adolescence were things he had really experienced. [*o.d.f.* 1983]

I was really interested in this loser character, this petty criminal who lives his gangster life in an almost anarchic way. I spoke about it to Warren Beatty in 1967 and told him it was high time someone did a film about gangsters and within a few months he produced *Gangster Story*. In this book I have seized the opportunity to pay a tribute to a certain type of cinema and literature that has influenced us all, and which I believe to be influenced by Dos Passos, Hemingway, Hammett and even a certain part of Hollywood. Among the things I cut was the scene in a theater, where the gangsters, undisturbed, steal the jewellery of Rudolph Valentino fans.

For the screenplay I wanted the best. Arcalli, before he passed away, worked on the film treatment. I considered Medioli, who has a deep understanding of the Thirties, and for the childhood years, Benvenuti and De Bernardi, who wrote *The Woman in the Painting* and *Misunderstood.* Then there was the problem of getting the kids to speak in the most natural way possible and for that I summoned Kaminsky, a Polish Jew and author of crime novels. Ferrini worked with us from the beginning.

For ten weeks we shot in Italy and for twenty abroad (Paris, Montreal, New York). I took my troupe of forty-five people with me to the States and also engaged an American troupe which, to tell the truth, was not of much use to me. But despite this we had problems with the unions and had to return to Italy earlier than we had planned. Among the scenes we couldn't shoot was the one with the opening tides:

Noodles, fleeing from New York in 1933 on a rainy night asks a truck driver for a lift: "Where are you heading?" "Wherever you are." We are in open country near a railroad crossing. A train coming from Detroit passes by transporting cars, hundreds of 1930 Fords. Noodles' eyes rest on the train's wheels. When he raises them the train has become a modern one transporting 1968 models. When all the cars have rolled past a completely changed landscape is revealed, the outskirts of a city with skyscrapers. Beyond the railroad crossing, sitting at the wheel of a car, there is De Niro thirty years older. The barrier crossing goes up and the title appears: *Once Upon a Time in America.* [*o.d.f.* 1983]

The first producer, Grimaldi, wanted to make it a two-part film as he had done for *1900*, but Milchan (of *The King of Comedy*) would not hear of it. I told him: "We are lucky to have De Niro, let's stop and think it over for a moment, let's go over the script again, let's make a single movie, compressed"; but he made me understand that if we did not start at once we would never succeed in making the movie. So during the shooting I cut what I could even while realizing we would end up with a film as long as two.

Among the scenes I regret most having to cut is the scene at the beginning of the film at the theater with the Chinese shadow puppets which Fellini really liked, and the conversation between Noodles and the Jewish chauffeur, where the feeling of mutual ill-will comes over very strongly and where the difference between the Italian and Jewish mafia is explained. The Jews, unlike Italian-Americans, do not love their gangsters. By the way, that chauffeur was played by the producer of the film. The scene where he refuses a tip made all my friends laugh.

For Noodles' three ages I had resigned myself to using different actors (for example, Paul Newman and Tom Berenger, the kid from *Oltre la Porta* [Beyond the Door] who was identical to Newman) when the producer told me he had finally managed to sign De Niro whom I had had in mind from the start. It was as if they had told Collodi, "use a real person for Pinocchio." It was supposed to be more of a mythic film, more a fable, but De Niro's extreme sincerity introduced a more realistic note. It is probably a little different from my other movies where pulling the marionette's strings provided an extra thrill.

For the role of Max I chose a young theater actor, James Woods, and for the final scene the older Max was achieved thanks to the skills of the make-up artists. He has a face that lends itself to ageing, he looks a bit like Leslie Howard. Having already chosen Bob, I had to make sure the accents corresponded, they all had to be from New York. I wasted two months in Hollywood and didn't find anyone, there were only people from Texas and San Francisco. I found the young boys thanks to Cis Corman, a talent scout who does all of Scorsese's films. They all came from the Jewish quarter, but had never acted before. Anyway, even among the adults, Fat Moe had never acted before, Peggy was a comedienne who did shows in coffee bars and Eve was a model.

When I direct I first play everybody's part, then I say "this is what I want, now do it better than me", in this way I don't need an interpreter. The cake scene we did four times, using three cameras. The young lad didn't mind at all because he got to eat four cakes. [*o.d.f.* 1983]

I don't use a storyboard, and in this film it would have been impossible anyway. With Bob you never know what's going to happen, you can't say: he enters, you put him here, because he wants to be free to move in his own way. You have to film him without his knowing.

It was a piece of cake working with Bob, maybe because he does things at my pace, he likes to dissect his movements and actions, something that others, such as Fonda, found hard to do. He is an all-round product of the Actors' Studio. He identifies himself totally with his character, and lives it one thousand percent. When he played the old Noodles, he was an old man who got into his car every evening and drove home. He even said to the producer: "Whatever you do this evening don't flirt with Eve, his girlfriend, because tomorrow we'll be acting together. Flirt with her on Sunday, when I've finished filming." Bob lives with the script, he goes over it a hundred thousand times at home but when he comes on the set he seems spontaneous. For instance, in the film he smiles above all at the people he loves in life. He doesn't smile much at Cockeye or Deborah, because he prefers the others, Eve and Fat Moe, because he has a fondness for them.

I went on the set, I acted his part for him and he replied with a laugh "you're really good", and then he did it much better. For the scene with the coffee cup he said: "It's a tribute to you". He was referring to the fly in *Once Upon a Time in the West.*

He got used to my way of filming with the music playing and in the end preferred to dub himself, rather than record live because he enjoyed having music on the set. Dubbing was necessary anyway because Bob has a very quiet voice. He is probably shy about his acting and this makes him an even greater actor. [*o.d.f.* 1983]

I believe Kubrick adopted this method for *Barry Lyndon*, of composing the music before starting to film. Kubrick called me one day: "I've got every one of Morricone's albums, can you explain why I only like the music from his films?" I replied: "I didn't like Strauss until I saw *2001*."

I think the love theme from *Once Upon a Time in America* was written for a Zeffirelli film that in the end Ennio didn't do. I chose the flute because I'd been captivated by Zamfir, the great Romanian concert performer, and besides the flute is the most magical instrument, it's almost a voice, a whistle. [*o.d.f.* 1983]

This film, born from our love for cinema and American literature, could well be entitled "Once upon a time there was a certain type of cinema". The portrait of America that emerges will be above all nostalgic: America revisited through the Hollywood images that have always fascinated us. Noodles brings with him everything the gangster films of the past have achieved.

It is an intimate film, which follows the memories of one man. It is perhaps the first time a film has ended with a flashback, so Noodles may have dreamed his future under the effect of the opium he smokes, it could all have been a figment of his imagination. On the other hand, I have no right to explore American history other than through a parable. [*o.d.f.* 1983]

My script did not call for that smile at the end. It is clear that having an actor like De Niro, I can end it that way. If I had had Newman or Berenger, they would have elicited a different ending from me.

In America I held seven or eight months of screen tests: everyone was right for his part, even the beginners, that was the amazing thing. They were better than the Neapolitans. Neapolitans have to be good in order to survive; the Americans are good maybe from ignorance. We Europeans have too great a sense of the ridiculous. If I call an attorney to play the part of an attorney, he does not think of what he is like in real life but of Spencer Tracy and tries to imitate him. Nothing could be worse. But James Woods's attorney in *Once Upon a Time in America* was a real lawyer and he behaved as if James Woods were his client. The movie did not win an Oscar because it was not presented for one. By that time it was all over with: things had gone very badly; after ten days they had pulled it to bits.[56] After the failure of the shortened version, Warner Brothers ran the full version in a little movie theater outside Hollywood, just to throw me a bone, where it ran for four consecutive months. And the same thing happened in three other cities: San Francisco, Chicago and New York. They had placed all their bets on *Amadeus* which had cost 50 million dollars.

In video-cassette it came out in both versions. The short one cost half as much. They wanted to prove to the critics that the short version was the one the public liked best. And the first week, with the short one selling for $80 and the long one $160, 2,000 were sold of the short one and 150,000 of the long one.

Then there is the very long one that has never been edited and which lasts fifty minutes longer. Four and a half hours. But we rejected the idea of two parts on TV. It is so intricate that it has to be done in one evening. And besides, let's be honest: this one is my version. The other perhaps explained things more clearly and it could have been done on TV in two or three parts. But the version that I prefer is this one, that bit of reclusiveness is just what I like about it.

And while I made a movie that I thought would please people of my generation – which it did – my greatest surprise was the enthusiasm of young people. Perhaps just because they were lacking a film of that kind... I read letters from these kids that came from all over the world. A Neapolitan youngster Marcello Garofalo, sent me a letter that gave me great pleasure, particularly coming as it did after all the critiques, and saying in part: "The thought that the cinema has you to count on truly makes my life better." A German who saw it 200 times wrote: "For me it is not a movie, it is life." I heard an attorney say the same thing about *Star Wars.* He told me, "If I do not see *Star 'Wars* I can't manage to live. It inspires me, I'm better in court." Robert Hossein phoned me to say that the slogan could be: "A movie that, when you come out of the theater, you can no longer remember the person you came in with."
[*o.d.f.* 1988]

---

[56] In the United States the film appeared shortened by seventy-five minutes and re-edited in chronological order against the director's will.

2. OTHERS ON LEONE

These testimonies were recorded on tape by the author in 1983 and 1984. The text by Peter Bogdanovich is a partial translation of an article published in the November 26, 1973 issues of *The New Yorker*.

DARIO ARGENTO – *The sense of rhythm*

I followed the usual course of so many kids who love the movies, without thinking that movies were something one could actually make. Then I began to work as a critic, and that was how I met Leone.

As a critic I reviewed his first films for *Paese Sera* (a leftist Rome daily, *Ed).* We did a lot of talking and he was struck by my love for cinema. Politics was all the fashion among the kids of my generation and not many of us loved American or French films or knew what a traveling shot was. Leone loved talking movies to me, and I was crazy about talking to him, learning how certain shots had been achieved. And so the desire to be a director took hold of me. Usually at the start of a professional life there is a moment when you cross paths with a certain personality. This does not mean that you necessarily are influenced to the point of becoming a carbon copy, but you are able to learn some secrets, the alchemical secrets of cinema, of rhythm, of narration, of the great machinery. I think this has happened to a lot of my colleagues: it is the fatal encounter that serves to break the ice – the maestro breaks it and you get to see what there is below. If you get your start with mediocre people everything becomes that much harder because you learn the vices, the stupidities of minor films. For my part, I had the good fortune to be at Leone's side. I don't think he intended to be my teacher. He is not someone who surrounds himself with pupils, but his expertise imparted itself.

Leone had a natural instinct for pinpointing talent (even his films which seem to be so highly constructed are actually very instinctive). He goes by impressions, by looks; he understands what goes on inside people. For writing the screenplay of *Once Upon a Time in the West* he had the courage to choose two talents that were still budding, like Bertolucci and me – he, who could have had the world's greatest screenwriters, took two semi-newcomers. He understood that films were changing. There was a need for people who did not tell the usual story in the usual way. In the script we included the images, the sensations. Being virgins for all practical purposes, we had a lot to say stored up, things that had stratified inside us over the years.

The fly inside the pistol was my idea from a film that I was supposed to have made with Duccio Tessari. But when there are three of you writing a film together it is difficult to remember who came up with what ideas. That experience taught me what to do when I start a movie and want to express something inside of me. One talks a lot, one talks vaguely about a story idea, then one brings everything into the discussion – what are movies all about, what is happening right now, what were the last films you saw like. You dive in and stay there, maybe for weeks at a time. You talk about this dolly shot, you remember that old movie, all just to get the motor going.

I learned a lot listening to Leone talk about cinema. Narrate concrete events, as Hitchcock says, for whom even the nightmares had to be realistic. I was still too naive. He brought me down to earth. Leone is no theoretician. He used to say: "No, the public doesn't like that kind of thing." He taught me to keep the audience in mind. We are storytellers, not prophets.

From him I learned that films are time, rhythm – and that thought obsessed me to the point that in my work I time everything with a chronometer, even when it is not necessary. And I learned to use the camera for narration, with continuous interference from the author who behaves like a writer, individualistic even in his punctuation. I understood the character, the meaning of a boom, a dolly shot, of shooting from behind someone's shoulders, the author as one more character, present in every scene and making that presence felt as Godard does.

143

I never saw Sergio on the set. At the time of *The Good, the Bad and the Ugly* I walked into the mixing studio where he was inserting the cries of falcons into the shot of a valley. He tried many, but none of them satisfied him.

Immediately after writing the script of *Once Upon a Time in the West*, gripped by a strange fury, I began my first film, but I don't think it is important to see a director working on the set. A director's ideas do not appear like subtitles and there is no time to give lessons in directing. To learn, I think one must sit by his side while he is preparing the movie at his desk.

When I made my debut with *The Bird With the Crystal Plumage,* I followed Sergio's example and hired many beginners, among them Vittorio Storaro. Everyone told me: "You are a beginner, you must work with seasoned professionals." I thought the opposite. Just because I was a beginner, I didn't want people who would interfere, profiting from my inexperience. But I called on Morricone for the music. To use a lot of music, in every way, make it part of the story, record it before shooting – these are other things I learned from Sergio. But for *Profondo Rosso* [Deep Red] I took the Goblin, four kids who hadn't yet done anything. They had studied *Yes* in England and had made a very beautiful record. The oldest of them was twenty. Such adventures bring their rewards; Sergio was right.

I love him very much, even if we never see each other. There is no need to be together all the time to love someone.

Nino Baragli – *They Called Him "the Pulveriser"*

I call Sergio "the Pulveriser" because he reduces you to a pulp when the editing starts. But working with him is more exciting than with anyone else. When I edit a film of his I don't think about it only when I am in front of the Moviola, but also when I am watching television at night. There is never a sequence that you can shoot in a couple of hours. You need at least a day, and then the next day when you take another look at it, three other solutions present themselves. With him "duplicates" do not exist. You may take one line from one take and one from another which you thought was going to be discarded. Sergio shoots a lot of footage because he has a taste for the shot, because he wants to get the maximum out of the actors, because he wants to cover himself. There are a thousand ways to edit a film of his; certain scenes can become dramatic or ironic according to the editing. Here we have 300,000 meters of footage of which at least 200,000 are edited. Sometimes Sergio bangs the clappers as many as eighteen times. Then when he stops De Niro starts: "Now let's do one for me."

When we have to cut because the movie is too long, we never cut within a scene, we cut out whole blocks, because the rhythm must remain the same. You mustn't confuse rhythm with speed – in that case the editors of TV commercials are the great masters. Instead, you need greater ability to edit slow tempos because it is harder to find the right spot to cut. It's easier to cut a battle scene. Sometimes we try to cut fast, but in general the results are modest. In *Once Upon a Time in America* there are some fast sequences, for example a shoot-out with the gunfire concentrated on an automobile where there are shots eight or ten frames long. But they alternate with slower sequences.

It is hard to keep up a fast rhythm for an entire film. Certainly there are movies with fast editing like *Star Wars* which can be successful, but they are soon forgotten. *Judgment at Nuremberg* lasted three hours and yet I would have been happy if it had been three hours longer.

Leone is a very visual director. The right-hand side of his scripts, is much less full than the left, with sets, situations, states of mind. I'm not crazy about movies that talk too much. My habit is to edit with the sound track and then see the scene again silently and I have to understand everything without the dialogue. That way I am sure I did a good editing job.

One of Leone's best scenes, the one with the opening titles of *Once Upon a Time in the West*, was entirely without dialogue, only effects created during the editing.

It does not matter if sometimes there are some bad cuts: what counts is the feeling and that there should be something in the eyes of the characters. At one time you could not cut from a

For a Few Dollars More.

Once Upon a Time in America.

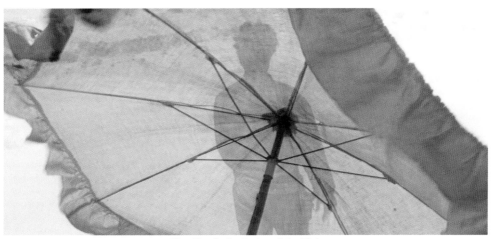

The Good, the Bad and the Ugly.

The Good, the Bad and the Ugly.

The Colossus of Rhodes.

A Fistful of Dollars.

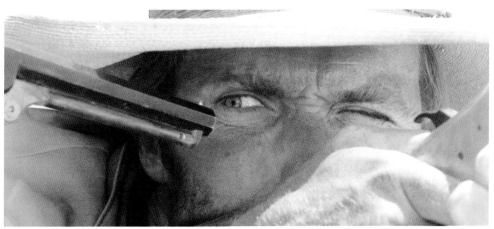

The Good, the Bad and the Ugly.

The Good, the Bad and the Ugly.

Duck! You Sucker.

147

A Fistful of Dollars.

Once Upon a Time in the West.

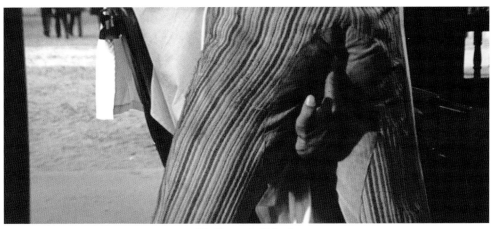

My Name is Nobody.

Once Upon a Time in the West.

Once Upon a Time in America.

149

Once Upon a Time in America.

For a Few Dollars More.

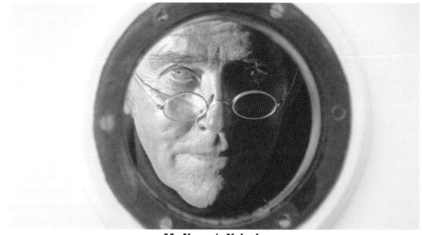

My Name is Nobody.

Once Upon a Time in America.

For a Few Dollars More.

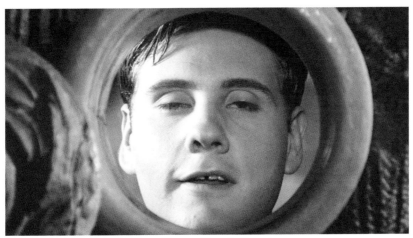

Once Upon a Time in America.

Once Upon a Time in the West.

Once Upon a Time in the West.

The Good, the Bad and the Ugly.

A Fistful of Dollars.

Once Upon a Time in the West.

My Name is Nobody.

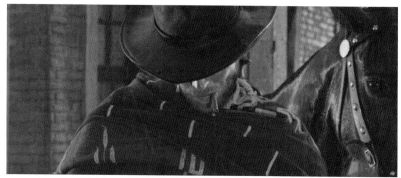

For a Few Dollars More.

*Once Upon a
Time in America.*

Once Upon a Time in the West.

Once Upon a Time in the West.

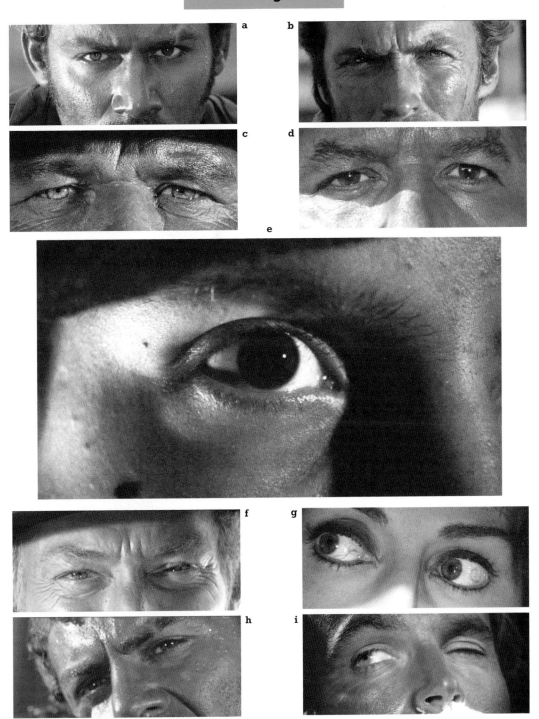

A Fistful of Dollars [a, b, h]; *For a Few Dollars More* [f]; *Once Upon a Time in the West* [c]; *Duck! You Sucker* [d, g]; *My Name is Nobody* [i]; *Once Upon a Time in America* [e].

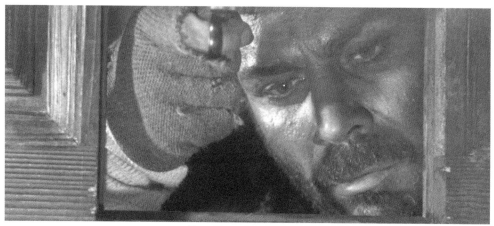

For a Few Dollars More.

Once Upon a Time in the West.

For a Few Dollars More.

Once Upon a Time in the West.

Once Upon a Time in America.

Once Upon a Time in America.

157

Gazes (II)

For a Few Dollars More.

Once Upon a Time in the West.

Duck! You Sucker.

Once Upon a Time in the West.

Once Upon a Time in America.

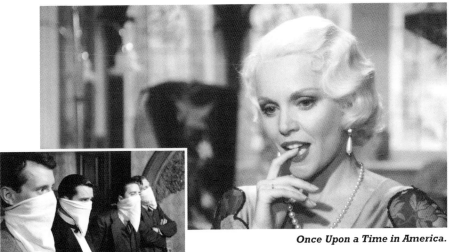

Once Upon a Time in America.

Duck! You Sucker.

Once Upon a Time in America.

Once Upon a Time in America.

Once Upon a Time in America.

long shot to a close-up. With Sergio we do it all the time. When Pasolini made *Accattone* the editor refused to do the job because, according to him, the film could not be edited. Pasolini did not understand the technique of linking-shots. He made a long shot of someone running and then, when he had to change to a close-up, instead of making the linking-shot while he was moving, he let you see him when he was already still. He was a writer who used the camera like paper where you can make corrections and cancellations. And still I managed to edit the film which was successful even if there were some poor cuts.

In general I prefer to do the editing by myself. Directors bring the set with them to the Moviola – they all do. If an actor made them suffer they would gladly cut out everything he did, even if he is excellent. "He was drunk – you weren't there that morning." "I wasn't there and the audience wasn't there. When they see him on the screen they'll like him." I edited *La Notte Brava* [Brave Night] in four days and four nights, sleeping half an hour each night, because the producers, who were young and had no money, had to deliver the edited movie by a certain date in order to get financing from the distributors and finish the shooting. Bolognini saw the edited film and did not change anything. From that day I edited all his movies. I edited *Everybody Goes Home*! while Comencini was still shooting it.

Sometimes while editing you can find solutions that no one thought of during the writing or the shooting. For Comencini's *La Tratta delle Bianche* [White Slave Trade] I got the idea of putting the pelota scene before the credits. And yet editors are never mentioned by critics. No one knows their names except people in the profession. Where does the responsibility of the director end and the editor's begins? All you have to do is come and see us work.

BERNARDO BERTOLUCCI – *Under the Sign of Visconti*

For me Leone has always been the genius among popular film directors. I have found in them a mixture of great vulgarity along with great sophistication, an unprecedented case in the history of Italian cinema. I, coming from the Nouvelle Vague, felt closer to Leone than to other Italian directors.

The first time we met was in a movie theater. I had gone to see one of his films at the first showing on the day it opened and he was in the projection room to supervise. He saw me and after a few days called and we made an appointment. I was going through a very difficult period. Years had passed since I had made *Before the Revolution* and I had not managed to shoot another movie. The prospect of working with a director like Leone excited me very much. I said something that perhaps may have won his heart. I told him I loved the way he shot the horses' asses. Only a very few American directors have an eye for that. And he immediately began to tell me the beginning of a story. Dario Argento was there too. We worked together and developed a long treatment almost without any dialogue. Then I received a proposal to do an episode from *Amore e Rabbia* with the Living Theater. I wanted to shoot something of my own, so I quit that team.

I remember that in *Once Upon a Time in the West* there was a part that was miraculously similar to what I had written. It was when the family is awaiting the arrival of Claudia Cardinale and are preparing the cakes on tables outdoors. I remember several pages I wrote describing in great detail the chirping of the cicadas interrupted by disquieting silences and then the white dust of the bandits who suddenly appear from out of the cornfields. I had written cornfields because I associated the West with my Emilian countryside.

Apropos of geography, looking at a map of the United States for a name to give to the town, I found one I liked very much: Sweetwater. Last year when Michael Cimino showed me the long version of *Heaven's Gate*, influenced a little by Leone and a little by *1900*, he told me: "We shot it at Sweetwater." It is really a strange coincidence. Leone knows American movies very well, and I played around, filling the treatment with allusions (to other films). In those years making allusions had become a cult, and I said to myself: how nice it would be if a director of Leone's talent made unconscious allusions rather than deliberate ones. Maybe I managed that in a few cases.

The hardest part was making Leone accept the presence of a female character. I remember suggesting a scene to him. "The hero enters a kind of whorehouse, throws himself down on the bed and tells the girl: 'Take off my boots.' And she does. 'Massage my feet.' And she begins massaging them." And this should be the beginning of an erotic relationship. Leone interrupted me. "Yes, she massages his feet, slowly, slowly and he falls asleep." His tendency was to neutralize the possibility of sexual relations. He has an extraordinary ability for visualizing his fantasies. For example, the treatment said that Claudia Cardinale appears for the first time getting off the train dressed in the latest New Orleans fashion. Leone says: "The carriage door opens, detail shot from the carriage steps, her feet come into view, then her skirt covers the camera and we note that she isn't wearing underpants." It seemed a very fine idea to me: a character who was immediately identified by her sex.

Leone was always full of ideas, inexhaustible in making transformations, a great perfectionist. I got on very well with him because our relationship with our ideal models was somehow similar. In me, it came from much reading of Bazin and the French; in him it was perhaps more direct; but in any case my way of seeing American Westerns when I was a kid in Parma, going to the movies on my bike, must not have been much different from Leone's way of seeing them in the Trastevere movie houses; the fever in our eyes must have been at the same temperature.

I too used the legendary Hollywood names, Sterling Hayden and Lancaster. I put them rather more in quotation marks. For me moviemaking has always meant making movies that ask just what movies are. So, unfortunately, for me the allusions are more conscious. Both of us were influenced by Visconti, even if my Visconti was more the interior one rather than the Visconti of the fluttering curtains. Mine is the melodramatic Visconti, the one of behavior carried to excess and also of a certain guilty class consciousness. I think that, for Sergio, Visconti is more a point of reference for elegant sets, for example, the carriage at the beginning of *Duck! You Sucker*.

Now I am trying to do a film taken from Hammett's *Red Harvest* which has a plot a bit like that of *A Fistful of Dollars*[57]. I remember proposing it to Leone in 1969, but he was more interested in making *Once Upon a Time in America*. It makes me happy that he is shooting a gangster movie and a movie in two parts like *1900*. It means that our elective affinity continues. I believe that Sergio's movie will be more psychological, while *Red Harvest* will be in the style of an Elizabethan tragedy with music by Kurt Weill – a great gangster carnival.

PETER BOGDANOVICH – *Lost in Translation*

An American actor I know, once had a passionate romance with a Russian ballerina although neither of them spoke the other's language, and it lasted just as long as they didn't know what they were saying to each other; as soon as they did, the affair terminated abruptly. Strangely enough, the language barrier between director Sergio Leone and me didn't have quite the same result, though probably if we'd understood each other from the start, I would have seen less of Rome than I did.

This all happened in late 1969. Leone, the father of the Spaghetti Western (the Clint Eastwood ones beginning with *A Fistful of Dollars*) and the *padrone* of the extreme close-up, had, through United Artists, asked me to direct the first movie he was to produce only, rather than direct and produce. With assurances from U.A. that they would welcome radical changes of the first draft of the Mexican Revolution script I had received, and firm promises that Leone would really function only as producer and therefore leave me to make the film as I saw fit, and taking into consideration that it was a free trip to Italy, where I'd never been, and bearing in mind that I hadn't made a picture for well over a year, that three projects I'd been preparing had fallen

---

[57] In the end, the film Bertolucci is talking about, starring Marlon Brando and Jack Nicholson, wasn't realised.

through, remembering too that a baby had just made us three and that the specter of having to go back to writing articles was hanging over me, I accepted, you might say, reluctantly.

In those days, Sergio didn't have a beard; in fact, he was a rather unimpressive looking guy, medium height, pot belly (usually with a cashmere sweater pulled down tight over it), hardly any chin to speak of but he met me at the airport with the majesty of a Roman emperor expending a bit of largess on a worthy, if nonetheless decidedly inferior, underling.

It was subtle, the feeling behind that first meeting, but the impression was confirmed in the weeks that followed. Actually, Sergio wanted me to believe he was a great director; he didn't believe it, which is perhaps why it was so important that those who worked for him did. I had only just liked a couple of his movies, so it was a difficult act for me to play, though for a while I tried admiring in the way I said things rather than in what I said, most of which I guess was negative. Luciano Vincenzioni, the writer of Leone's two best films (*For a Few Dollars More; The Good, the Bad, and the Ugly*), had been hired to work on this one too, and he and I got on famously right from the start, though his job was the not very appetizing one of being translator, mediator, arbiter, and scenarist all at once. Luciano, by the way, is everyone's ideal Italian – he could be exported as a tourist attraction – charming, gracious, enthusiastic, good-looking, and funny.

For some reason best known to himself, he really wanted me to direct this picture – a lot more than I did – and much of our time alone together was spent in his trying to get me to be more polite with Sergio. Our script conferences were usually at 11 A.M., at which time I would arrive at Luciano's apartment and we would wait for Sergio. Around one o'clock he would call to say he'd be a little late so why didn't we go out and have some lunch. About three o'clock we'd return and Sergio would arrive promptly at 4:30 for two hours of work.

The conferences would usually begin with my complaining about the title of the film, which was *Duck! You Sucker.* Sergio would carefully explain that *"Duck! You Sucker"* was a common American expression, to which I would reply that personally I'd never come across it before. I'm sure he was becoming convinced I wasn't a real American at all.

Most of our time, however, was taken up with plotting. Sergio would begin each new sequence with a rush of English and much acting, all of which he did in the middle of the room accompanied by dramatic gestures. "Two big green eyes!" he would invariably begin, one hand leveled above his eyes, the other below to indicate what we would be seeing on the screen – a shot I could easily picture, as I'd seen at least a score of them in every Leone movie. "Cut!" he would continue. "Foots walk!" And all attention would now focus on his feet as they moved purposefully forward. "Clink, clink," he would say, providing the sound effects for the spurs. "Cut!" he'd yell this time. "Hand on gun!" he'd whisper, grabbing his hip. "Cut!" Hands would zip back to frame his face. "Two big green eyes!" and so on, until a burst of gunfire sent him reeling into an armchair, spent and panting, both from the physical exertion so soon after eating (in Italy, and particularly with Sergio, almost any time of day is soon after eating), and the pure inspiration of the sequence itself.

He and Luciano would look at me for a reaction, which early in these conferences I would attempt to make one of enthusiasm but which inevitably moved into something closer to exasperation.

After all, it had always been my assumption that a director planned out his own sequence of shots, and I had the distinct impression that Sergio expected me to shoot everything just as he was acting it out. The climax of this particular part of our negotiations occurred late one heavy afternoon ar Sergio's home (sometimes to avoid waiting six hours for Sergio, Luciano and I agreed to drive the hour it took to get to his house in the suburbs and work there instead). Sergio had just begun a fresh scene – "Two big green eyes!" – when I interrupted to say that I wished we could just discuss the action instead of the shots and, besides, I didn't like close-ups anyway. When this had been translated, there was an amazed and deflated look on Sergio's face. A long pause followed. If I didn't like close-ups, he finally asked just a bit ominously, what did I like? To which I perversely replied, "'Long shots." Driving back to the city, Luciano shook his head in wonder. "You are crazy," he said. "This man make his whole career on the close-up and you say you don't like the close-up. I think you don't want to do this picture."

But my favorite story-conferences began with Sergio making a dramatic and terribly serious entrance – six hours late – and warning us not to forget that the movie we were making was really about Jesus Christ. I believe this was occasioned by a new set of reviews Sergio had read from France or the American avant-garde which searched out the hidden religious symbolism and significant nuances in his latest film, *Once Upon a Time in the West*. For over an hour, at least once a week, therefore, Luciano and I had to listen to a lecture on how the Irishman in this movie, *Duck! You Sucker*[58], was really a metaphor for Christ. Luciano had to listen, that is, since the lecture was in Italian, and after the first time or two, he spared me the translation. I would usually place my hand on my brow, meditatively, in order to shield my eyes in case they inadvertently closed for too long. Luciano would eventually bring Sergio down to earth and things would liven up.

The best times were spent watching Sergio act out his most cherished moment in the picture, which had to do with the Mexican bandit passing wind while holding a match to his posterior. Sergio particularly relished making the sound both of the initial departure of wind as well as of the subsequent one caused by the meeting of visibile match and invisible gas. After acting it out in splendid detail, Sergio would collapse in sad exhaustion in his chair, shaking his head about the pity of not being able to do this on the screen, at the same time threatening to do it anyway.

If there had been a great deal of this sort of thing one day, it was invariably followed the next by a sobering account of the film's actual religious import.

I had left Los Angeles in October, planning to stay abroad until at least April to make the film. I was home for Christmas. It was a Sergio Leone movie without a doubt, and that's who should be directing it, I told U.A., which is ultimately what happened, though Sergio first found a young Italian director to take my place.[59] To be honest, I think Sergio was about to fire me when I left, having no doubt decided by then I was going to shoot the entire film in long shot. As it turned out, however, after two weeks of Leone's pushing buttons on his Italian surrogate, the stars, Rod Steiger and James Coburn, refused to accept the situation, and so he finally had to direct it personally.

This year, a similar thing happened when Sergio hired an inexperienced Italian fellow to direct another Western, *My Name Is Nobody*, with Henry Fonda. After a while, circumstances again forced Leone to take over, though, finally, I'm afraid that's what Sergio wants; if the picture then turns out to be a bomb, he has the excuse that it was not really his plan to make this one and that he'd been forced to come in and do the best he could, at the same time postponing the major work he was preparing. In other words, exactly that crisis of self-confidence I had suspected four long years ago. When all those critics and people say you're good and you don't really believe it, at some point perhaps the thought of being found out becomes overwhelming and you would rather retire undefeated than face failure.

Actually, if this presumptuous deduction is true, it is a considerable pity, because Leone is often a very good director. My experiences with him prove nothing except that directors should never collaborate. It is, as Mr. Mailer has well described it, a totalitarian job.

And *Duck! You Sucker* after an initial release failed to spark much interest, a quick title switch was made to *A Fistful of Dynamite*, but that didn't help. The French critics loved it, though, as did several American ones. I quite liked it myself- all but the serious parts. I had enjoyed those more when Sergio acted them out himself.

---

[58] In the end the English name of the film didn't change.

[59] It was Giancarlo Santi, Leone's assistant director to *Once Upon a Time in the West*.

CLAUDIA CARDINALE – *A Sweet and Penetrating Look*

I have wonderful memories of *Once Upon a Time in the West*. On the first day of shooting at Cinecittà we began, contrary to custom, with a very delicate scene, the love scene in bed. Our positions were very uncomfortable because we had to hold our faces as the camera work called for (Sergio used several cameras); and the bed was suspended.

Making things more complicated was that I did not know Henry and he had never shot such an audacious love scene before; and on the set that day were all the journalists in the world – it was like being on a theater stage. I had to ask for the reporters all to leave and then we were alone with just Sergio and the cameraman, Tonino Delli Colli, who is a truly lovely person.

Two strangers meet on a set and suddenly find themselves together in bed. It is quite embarrassing, especially because there was Henry's wife sitting right in front of us and watching closely. Later we became very good friends. Henry was a very solitary type. He was always standing around by himself and his relations with people were very precarious, but he was an extraordinary person. You only had to know him to love him. He was always detached, loved silence, painted pictures. He had a beautiful way of moving; I don't think anyone could ride a horse like him; he seemed to be a part of the horse.

Charles Bronson is also a very solitary person. He sat around with his cap pulled down over his eyes just so as not to see anyone and not to have to greet anyone. He always had a rubber ball in his hand which he bounced continuously. It is hard to get a smile from him. He got along well with me, maybe because I am introverted too.

It is very easy working with Sergio. We communicated with looks without having to say anything. His look is both sweet and penetrating. He betrays the tension he feels when he directs by always playing with something in his hands, a pack of cigarettes or matches. Sometimes I came up behind him and blocked his hands!

Sergio has a great love of actors and knows how to help them. He has a wonderful way of telling the story of the movie and has the music written before starting to shoot. Before beginning each scene he played the Jill theme and this helped me to concentrate, to remove myself from reality. It was like a magical way of becoming the character. Sergio shoots a lot of close-ups and it is much easier to act with the camera very close. After many films it has become like a friend to me: the way it hums is familiar to me, and I can feel at once if it is set up well or not.

Sergio is very demanding on the set, and it is right that he should be. Visconti was another you could never satisfy. At the end of a day's work I have to feel totally exhausted because that means I gave everything necessary otherwise I am not satisfied. On the set everything must be very serene and relaxed; so for me it is important to have good relations with the whole troupe. When it is a serious set the technicians will rarely talk of anything else. There is a religious atmosphere when you shoot, a moment of great silence, great concentration, and everyone is involved with the movie. We actors are very sensitive, very receptive. To act you have to be in a state of grace and feel yourself surrounded with great love, great affection. I could never act with a director whom I did not esteem, who did not speak sweetly to me. Sergio is very sweet, very understanding with the actors, but he is very demanding with people on the set: the production, the assistants. He rehearses the camera movements for a long time, because the camera and the actors must become one; the movements must be very smooth, then the acting comes by itself I don't remember ever repeating the scenes many times.

What I liked about my character, Jill, was her grit, her strength. She knows what she wants and sticks to it and wins. You don't find many women's roles like that in Westerns. With few exceptions the women have very limited roles in American Westerns. But in *Once Upon a Time in the West* Jill was the central character, everything revolved around her.

I like the scene very much when Jill comes home and feels that there is something to discover, turns everything upside down, then stretches out on the bed and is photographed through a net like De Niro at the end of *Once Upon a Time in America*.

We shot in stupendous locations: Almeria, Monument Valley with lots of dust and heat, but it was necessary to get into the part. The movie has become a classic. They are constantly showing it in Paris. I went to see it again two years ago on the boulevards and the theater was full. I often hear the Jill theme being played even in the department stores.

When I met Jason Robards in the jungle on the set of *Fitzcarraldo* (he did half the film then had a nervous breakdown and we reshot everything with Klaus Kinski) we spoke nostalgically about our characters in *Once Upon a Time in the West*: his entrance into that kind of tavern is really stupendous. I remember having talked about it with Bob De Niro too when I saw him again on the set of *Once Upon a Time in America*. It was in Canada where I was shooting a film with Lino Ventura and we spent a lot of time together. I discovered that all the actors loved *Once Upon a Time in the West* and remembered every detail of it.

I often see Sergio; it's a relationship that goes beyond the set. I did several films with Luchino. With Sergio I could have done others because it is easier for a director to work with people he knows well. In *Once Upon a Time in America* I was supposed to play the part of Carol, the nymphomaniac, but then the movie was done in a New York style so the idea was dropped. I spent a lot of time with Fellini, too, before he began *8½*. We took long road trips into the countryside chatting about so many things other than the film itself. It was a good way to get to know each other. On the set there was always a lot of improvisation with him. Even Visconti, who was always considered very difficult to work with, was never anything but extremely indulgent with me. He spoke to me only in French, and he always had a kind word, he even held my hand to make sure I stayed close; he had obviously realized that that was the way I wanted to be treated. Richard Brooks, with whom I worked on *The Professionals,* had a reputation for being grouchy and a misogynist, but he adopted me right from the start. He allowed me to see the daily footage, something he never let anyone else do. The biggest compliment he made to me on that set was: "You don't seem like a woman you seem like a man." Another reason I didn't have any problems is that I adapt to all situations, I love adventure: for me making films is a fantastic adventure.

TONINO DELLI COLLI – *Once Upon a Time Black and White*

I met Sergio when I was working with Bonnard on movies like *Il Voto* [The vow] and *Tradita* [Betrayed]. He was an excellent assistant director: he prepared the sets, chose the supporting actors and was like a son for Bonnard. We met again many years later to make *The Good, the Bad and the Ugly*. Sergio and I understood each other very well; there was no need for a lot of instructions. We shared a point of departure, an aesthetic principle: in a Western you cannot use a lot of color. We kept to subdued shades: black, brown, off-white, since the buildings were wooden and the colors of the landscape rather vivid. In *Once Upon a Time in the West* we gave a sandy color to the whole copy. We like colors like these; we have the same tastes.

In *Once Upon a Time in America* we differentiated between three periods. For 1923, a sepia print that recalls the photos of that period. For 1930 we tried to keep the image as neutral as possible, a kind of metallic black-and-white, cold approach to the gangster films of that epoch. For 1968 no special effect. We used a little R_N, a special bath patented by Technicolor Italiana, which made the blacks more velvety, added brilliance to everything and reinforced the contrasts. At first Sergio thought of shooting in Cinemascope but after the first tests he changed his mind. Unfortunately the theaters are not adequately equipped for Scope. The lenses of the projectors make everything fuzzy and you need to create more contrast, use more incisive lighting, sharper photography, to get higher relief. In America we saw *Once Upon a Time in the Weston* television: decompressed, reprinted, a real mess. So in the end we preferred to turn the television set onto black and white.

No I really am not nostalgic for Cinemascope. If anything I miss black and white a little, maybe because it was harder to use. The half-tones and the relief have to be created with light. I am one of the pioneers of color films in Italy. I shot the first movie in Ferraniacolor: *Totò a Colori* [Color Totò]. It looked a little like a postcard. The public wanted to see full colors, as they were not yet used to it; and we had no experience. Ferraniacolor called for strong lighting because the film was not very sensitive. But I began to experiment with effects and found that the results were good even with a little less lighting. There was a development in the course of the shooting, one can see it easily, because the movie was shot in narrative order. The final scenes use a lighting that is not so flat, more precise.

Since then there has been a lot of progress in the use of color. Even the Americans have discovered natural lighting and often shoot with a light coming from above and the eyes in shadow. These are things that are all right for a single scene, but in the long run become annoying. We too use natural lighting but we also illuminate the face. We keep to a more classical style.

Unlike you journalists and the public, I don't like those mannered and too perfect photographies either, because they don't respect the scenario.

I believe the director of photography should be the main ally of the director, should realize his desires, give form to his ideas, coordinate the effects and the costumes. He should be asked to examine the locations because the director doesn't notice the light conditions, doesn't consider the fact that during the day the sun moves. With Sergio we did little preparation: he chose two or three alternatives for every scene, and then we had a quick look around to decide.

With Pasolini we would agree on a painter to coordinate my work with that of the set and costume designers. Leone sometimes would refer to a movie, but it would be hard to get to see it, and then it might not be much use because situations are different from picture to picture. Pasolini didn't know technique very well; the results you get from the various lenses. He would shoot everything panoramically, then a knee-shot, then a bust shot. He was a bit Chaplinesque. But Leone moves a lot; he shoots in movement. He has very precise feelings. A little movement that someone else might find insignificant says something to him. And when the film is shown you notice. The audience is not aware of it on a technical level, but feels it psychologically. He shoots his films well, that's why the audience accepts certain slow moments.

American actors, like De Niro, are also enthusiastic about his pictures. He works a little slowly, but the results are excellent. Furthermore this movie cost about half what it would have cost the Americans to make. To do what we do with eighty people, they need to use one hundred and fifty.

SERGIO DONATI – *The Western as Religion*

I started out at eighteen as a writer of detective stories. Tinto Brass based his movie *Col Cuore in Gola* [With Your Heart in Your Throat] on one of these: *Il Sepolcro di Carta* [Tomb of Paper]. My first job in the movies was collaborating on the screenplay of Ricardo Freda's *Faite-moi Confiance* [Trust Me] from a novel by James Hadley Chase[60]. Around that time I was approached by a young assistant director who looked hungry and went around in an old Fiat 600: Sergio Leone. He asked me to write a horror film taking place in a hotel in snow country. He had known a hotel proprietor who was curious about the spicy behind-the-scenes life of the movie world. I wrote the subject but it came to nothing. Anyway snow brings bad luck for movies.

My books had been translated into a dozen languages but they didn't make me a living. So when I finished my law studies I went to Milan to work as a producer in advertising and I stayed there six years. I am almost prouder of the work I did in advertising than of the films I have written. Leone phoned me every once in a while from Rome with improbable proposals. In '62 we went to Lebanon together for a few days to inspect a location. I wrote a screenplay, *Rebus,* that Nino Zanchin made into a film years later with the actor Anthony Harvey.

One day Leone phoned me telling me to go see *Yojimbo* because he wanted to make a West-

---

[60] Behind the French title there's Chase's crime novel *You'll Find Him – I'll Fix Him* (1956) published in Italy in 1958 as *Sei Tu Che Pagherai* [You'll Pay for It]. Freda and Donati drew a screenplay from it, but the film – due to the lack of money – was never made.

ern from it. I didn't believe in it and I didn't even bother going to see the movie. That's how I lost the chance to write *A Fistful of Dollars*. Then he asked me to write *Grand Slam*, a movie about a diamond theft he was supposed to direct. He had a contract with the producers Papi and Colombo for ten films at a ridiculous fee. On the eve of his departure for Egypt, Leone and the producers quarreled and the movie was directed by Giuliano Montaldo.

I did a little ghostwriting *For a Few Dollars More.* For example, I worked on the scene of the little old guy who lives alongside the railroad tracks and I came up with Eastwood's last line when he adds up the amount of reward on the heads of the bandits lying dead in the street and notices that there is one missing: a line that got applause. In those days people applauded in the movies like they do in stadiums. In the end Grimaldi convinced me to give up my advertising work and come to Rome.

For *The Good, the Bad and the Ugly* Leone wanted the best screenwriters on the market so he recruited top comedy writers Age and Scarpelli and it was a mistake. They didn't write a Western but a kind of comedy with a Western setting; I think hardly a line they wrote got into the final version. The same misunderstanding recurred when Age and Scarpelli worked with Hitchcock on *Triple A*[61]. He wanted a mystery and they wrote a comedy.

I worked for six months on *The Good, the Bad and the Ugly* and it seems to me that I performed several miracles. The picture was too long. Sergio never made the very common mistake of shortening a sequence by altering the rhythm. He preferred to cut out whole blocks of the story. After having cut out half an hour of story we completely changed the dialogue between Lee Van Cleef and the legless soldier, having them talk about the part that had been cut. And finally we worked hard to find the actor expressions that were suitable to this new dialogue.

We were all rooting hard for this picture. Since it absolutely had to come out before Christmas, Baragli and a few others of us had been sleeping on cots for weeks next to the Moviola. I risked being divorced by my wife.

I noticed a curious metamorphosis in Sergio. Whereas he had always worked happily in previous movies, now he had begun to get neurotic, to fear that he wouldn't be able to live up to his reputation. Since he is not presumptuous and knows his limitations, he is always being assailed by doubts, tries to postpone finishing the film and even becomes personally unpleasant. We did the mixing of the last reel at 5:30 in the morning; so the first copy was ready the next day. We were all exhausted and happy after four months of work. The production inspector arrived with a bottle of *spumante* to celebrate. Leone got up, dodged past him and left with a laconic "good night." This is Leone the man.

For his next film he wanted to get off in high gear, so he completely forgot his promise to let me write the script and began working with Bertolucci and Dario Argento. After many months he phoned me: the two intellectuals had disappointed him. I was very offended and took the job just for the money. I wrote the whole script in twenty days, the second half without even getting up from my chair. I wrote the kind of script he likes with interminable descriptions, allusive dialogues, long biographies of the characters, and lots of suggestions for the direction. He always says, "Please don't forget about the cuts." We always have to suggest three or four different cuts so that he has a choice during the editing.

I fought against things that were kept in the film and which actually work well there, like the interminable scene in the saloon in the desert where nothing happens. With regard to the duel, I managed to get him to keep it shorter than in earlier pictures. I would even have kept it off screen and just showed Claudia Cardinale's reactions.

Then I went to Los Angeles with Sergio for the American edition of *The Good, the Bad and the Ugly*. The Americans are obsessed with invisible dubbing, so to create lip synchronization we changed all the dialogue. If someone says "pipa" they are capable of translating "pepper." So I stayed two weeks to supervise the English dubbing.

Sergio hated Clint Eastwood, I think because he had asked for so much for the last movie; each of them thought he was the reason for the other's success. Eastwood arrived at the dub-

---

[61] The script came to be known (and published) as *R.R.R.R.R.*

bing studio with his old shooting script in hand and, to provoke us, placed it on the book-rest demanding to read that one rather than the new dialogue. A young vice-president of United Artists had to intervene, Chris Mankiewicz, Joe's son, threatening to keep him from ever making another picture in America. The Americans are capable of exchanging the most tremendous threats without blinking an eye.

Then Leone phoned me from Spain where he was shooting *Once Upon a Time in the West*: forty minutes had to be cut. When I got to the set I saw him in a crisis for the first time. He was shooting the scene on the McBain farm and he confessed to me: "I was sure I could shoot it with a different rhythm; I tried and couldn't." So I stayed there and cut the script during the shooting. While he was making the movie, I wrote the script for *Duck! You Sucker.* The role of the Mexican was written for Eli Wallach, but the movie was costly and the producers wanted a famous actor like Steiger, an actor I detest and who had nothing in common with the character. For the Irishman, I would have liked to have gotten Jason Robards. But though Robards was a great theater actor, one whom the cameramen applauded when he finished a scene, when you went and looked at the day's shooting the magic had vanished. He is one of those actors who, as the saying goes, doesn't get past the screen. He hasn't got the eyes. I think that's where the whole problem lies.

I did the first draft of the script which was discussed in a meeting with a whole lot of people and Leone sided with them. To get even, I put in all the changes proposed in that meeting. Leone got annoyed, and we broke off for a year. Meanwhile Vincenzoni arrived who had been working by himself. Then came Bogdanovich and they didn't hit it off. Leone insisted on explaining how to shoot to him: "Here you do a zoom shot." And he replies: "I never use zooms. I hate zooms." So Bogdanovich was fired. A year later he called me and I rewrote the second version of the script; then we had another fight. It is tiring to work in this way. *Duck! You Sucker* is a movie I detest, maybe because it does not resemble my first version of it. It is a movie full of rhetoric, noncommittal; it even contains a quotation from Mao.

I also wrote two political Westerns for Sollima: *The Big Gundown* and *Face to Face.* The first was a good subject by Solinas set in Sardinia, the story of a *carabiniere* who pursues a bandit and in the end, after finding out that he was innocent, gets him in his sights and shoots. The story was moved to the West and given a happy ending, partly on Leone's suggestion. *Face to Face* was too verbose. I hate films that preach, and then I don't think that ideology and Westerns go together. Sollima did too much sloganeering. He is more cultivated than Leone, someone who has done a lot of reading. Leone's culture is exclusively visual: he is a great movie lover; he could reconstruct from memory the scripts of *Vera Cruz* and *The Magnificent Seven*.

Leone is a great instinctive director, a great actors' director. He knows how to get everything out of the actors; he does not try to squeeze the actor into the picture or vice versa. There is an exchange between what the actor can give to the film and what the film can give to the actor. He is one of the few Italian directors who is really worth anything. Vincenzoni and I wrote a film taken from *Orlando Farioso.* If Leone had directed, it would have become a cult movie like *The Raiders of the Lost Ark.* For him the Western was a kind of religion; he invented a rhythm, a world in which he believed. To believe deeply in something always bears its fruit in the movies.

At a certain point Leone became part of movie history and probably he did not feel the desire to make anything more. For a long time he flirted with the project of *Once Upon a Time in America*, but he realized that it meant measuring himself with a completely different narrative style. Gangsters cannot move like cowboys; they cannot take a quarter of an hour getting out of a car. In 1967 I began doing preliminary research for this picture. I went to the archives of the *New York Times* to breathe the air of the thirties and I discovered, for example, that the front pages ran headlines like "Last Night Jack Legs Diamond[62] Dined at 21." It was a little like telling the story of the Ciano family in Italy.

I confided my perplexities to Leone: what did we know about the Jewish East Side? It was as if an American director decided to recount the history of Trastevere in the thirties. There are

---

[62] A famous American gangster in the thirties.

the precedents of *The Secret of Santa Vittoria* or the Sicilian episode in *The Godfather* where everything has an incredibly false ring to it. The risks are enormous. At least Leone could get an American art director.

I read a version of the script. There was one great piece of ingenuousness: a gangster who disappears from Chicago in '33 retires to the provinces to cover his tracks and then resurfaces in New York twenty years later. This was possible in the West in 1833, but in 1933 with the FBI? No. And then, who knows? A film can be splendid and not make a penny or vice versa. But nowadays we are in the hands of a bunch of adolescents who talk loudly at the movies. *The Return of the Jedi* took in $60 million in its first week. And that's nothing. The sad part is that popcorn alone earned $9 million!

FRANCO FERRINI – *The Whole Memory of the Cinema*

In 1971 I was commissioned to write a monograph on Leone for the publications of the Centro Sperimentale di Cinematografia. They knew that I was one of the few madmen, along with Bernardo Bertolucci and Glauber Rocha, who liked Leone's movies. At the time this taste was a little scandalous.

Leone was supervising the editing of *Duck! You Sucker* at that moment. He put me up in a Rome apartment (in those days I lived in a small town, at La Spezia) and gave me a Moviola to see the shots. It was an opportunity to spend some time with him. I had the secret ambition of becoming a screenwriter; unlike many of my contemporaries, I didn't dream of being a director.

One evening, probably I was half-drunk, when Leone was taking me home in his brown Rolls Royce, I found the nerve to ask him to let me collaborate on the script for *Once Upon a Time in America*, and he accepted. That night I didn't close an eye partly because there was an electric blanket which I could not manage to unplug and I was worried about its turning into something like an electric chair.

Leone wanted to use a book of novelized memoirs, *The Hoods*, written in Sing Sing by a Jewish gangster. But the author had sold the option to Dan Curtis, a producer-director of horror films. He did not want to give them up and this delayed things for years. So we started thinking of alternatives. One of them was *Mile High* by Richard Condon, the author of *The Manchurian Candidate*, which John Frankenheimer had filmed. For all practical purposes it was the story of John F. Kennedy's father, a financier who, during Prohibition, seems to have had relations with the underworld. But this writer needed years to write a screenplay and Leone was in a hurry.

I did research, I read many books on Prohibition: novels, gangsters' biographies, studies of the Jews. (One valuable book was *The World of Shalom Alaikem* by Maurice Samuel who reconstructed the life of a Russian village during the time of the pogroms.) European immigrants – Russians, Poles – thrown suddenly into the secularized American life tried to keep their rituals, their mythology; they reacted a bit like Italians. There was nothing at all like the Black Hand, but there were many Jewish names among American gangsters. One example is Monk Eastman who was remembered by Borges in *A Universal History of Infamy*. Leone wanted to do a movie on Jewish gangsters at all costs. Weighing heavily on him was the shadow of the two "godfathers" that had dealt with the world of the Italo-American Mafia from every point of view. In the end Grimaldi, who was supposed to produce a picture, got the rights to *The Hoods*. Norman Mailer was the first one called on for a screenplay. His script had a hallucinatory and fragmentary construction in flashbacks with continuous leaps in time that were almost incomprehensible and kept the story from taking on structure. In the final version all this coming and going becomes more convincing thanks to the part played by memory. It is a rather Proustian structure. In Mailer it seemed a little like Resnais and not very suitable for Leone's rather solemn style of narration.

Medioli and Arcalli did a very coherent treatment that became the skeleton of a script in which Benvenuti and De Bernardi also had a hand. At first I had a complex about making mistakes. It was consoling to discover that these old hands at screenwriting had no such qualms. One could quote that old, banal phrase that the police say to people involved in murder cases: "Tell me anything that comes into your head, even if you think it has nothing to do with solving the case." That's the way a screenplay is written.

From the very beginning the film took on its own physiognomy, even in contrast to the book. The book was written by someone who knows the facts but who lacks a sense of the fabulous. We were all very much aware that we were not writing the history of gangsterism, but its mythology seen through European eyes.

Benvenuti and De Bernardi, besides writing *Amici per la Pelle* [Best Friends], which displays a certain affinity with the childhood scenes of our film, have written various opera films; and *Once Upon a Time in America* also has an operatic construction. At the end, for example, there is a great dramatic scene that distinguishes it from all other gangster movies. When Noodles (Robert De Niro) returns to New York after thirty years of exile, he receives a mysterious invitation to a theater where they are performing *Anthony and Cleopatra*. In the dressing room he encounters Deborah (Elizabeth McGovern) who has become a great actress. As she is taking off her make-up he notices that the ravages of time have not altered her beauty, she really is like Cleopatra. The mask is the face. It was a very complicated scene to shoot because the actress has to take off her theatrical make-up while keeping on her movie make-up. Then the woman becomes the source of a dazzling revelation, on a par with the incest revelation in *Oedipus Rex*.

The film begins in dream terrain, in an opium den disguised as a shadow theater. It begins with the raw material of cinema: shadows on a wall. At the end, in 1968, De Niro leaves the party where all the survivors have met again[63], turns a corner, and with magical editing finds himself back on the last night of Prohibition in the Chinese quarter with a crowd that is going crazy. I remember a phrase of Scott Fitzgerald's where he says that the end of Prohibition was the end of the costliest orgy in history. In the end, Noodles goes and takes refuge in the opium den of the film's beginning. After having started out from a dream, after having gone through reality, New York in 1968, he goes to take refuge in a dream again. This strange itinerary of the movie is also a judgement on reality.

Leone always asked us to link one scene to the next, especially the connection from the present to the past and vice versa. He asked us to do the editing in the script; the links could be associative, traumatic, musical, or false links.

He didn't want arbitrary flashbacks but ones motivated by the action. And in fact they are an innovation: a meeting point for the European memory narrative and the American action and behavior traditions. Maybe the loveliest of the links comes at the end when you pass from the Chinese quarter to a journey of no return, a final journey. In the script there is even a quotation from the final lines of Proust's *Remembrance of Things Past*.

Twelve years ago Leone had thought of a very original prologue to film in a sequence shot. A seaport wharf at night. Two men dragging a corpse with obvious difficulty. A movement of the camera reveals the feet of the corpse embedded in a block of cement. It is a typical execution in the style of the American underworld. The camera follows the shroud as it sinks under water; at the bottom of the sea we find other corpses that have undergone the same treatment: men bound to automobiles and bejeweled women. Then the camera enters the course of a sewer, passes through a tunnel and we find ourselves in another underwater graveyard, a poorer one, with corpses bound to a railroad tie, to a cart and this also reflects the division of New York into boroughs. At last the camera comes to the surface and the Statue of Liberty appears very white in the night; and we see the title: *Once Upon a Time in America*.

Unfortunately this sequence could not be realized because a few years later a film by Frankenheimer was released, *The Forty-Four Per Cent Death*, with Richard Harris and Bradford Dillman, that contained a similar scene. Thus the idea was born for a railroad grade

---

[63] In the end, this scene wasn't shot.

crossing with a train full of cars of that epoch, and then the idea of the Chinese shadow theater which Leone ended by cutting, reluctantly, partly because we had found something very similar in Peter Weir's *The Year of Living Dangerously*.

And here is the prologue that I thought up, a bit as a joke: a dark, slightly rounded object fills the screen. At its center something lighter in color can be glimpsed. The image comes into focus: it is a man's head with a newly-shaved tonsure. His pants are slit in a strange way that show his bare legs. He is eating a succulent meal with great gusto. Two guards watch him through a spy hole. It is the last meal of a condemned man. Under the eyes of other condemned prisoners, he walks stoically down a long corridor without resisting. He is in the electric chair where they attach the electrodes to his head and legs and then proceed to the execution before a small group of spectators. The doctor makes sure that he is dead and announces the length of the death agony, a little more than a minute. It was not painless. As the protocol demands, two prisoners are among the spectators who are quick to spread the news by water pipe tarn-tarn. A revolt breaks out and the prisoners destroy their cells as we have seen in so many American movies. All the cells are opened electrically and their inmates ordered out. One of them is missing from the roll call. A guard stands in the entrance to his cell and sees an old man who is writing with a pencil stub on a toilet roll. "Goldberg, come on out!" (the name of the author of the book upon which the movie is based). But absorbed like a rabbi in his indecipherable writing, he does not obey. The guard pulls him out by force and now the toilet paper falls to the floor and rolls out like a papyrus scroll. On it we read *Once Upon a Time in America*.

In my crazy imagination, all this was to be one very long sequence shot. Leone looked at me with indulgence and said it would have cost half a million dollars.

After many years I think I have finally understood what it was in his films that conquered me: his anti-neorealistic style. Leone is the only director who has never once set up his camera in front of the world in which he lives. He only shot pictures set in ancient Rome or the Far West. The year 1968 of this picture is the closest he ever came to portraying recent times; and it is no accident that 1968 is the most mythical year in recent history. It is this aristocratic rejection of reality that I find seductive.

ENRICO MEDIOLI – *In the Beginning There Was a Novel*

The first time I saw *A Fistful of Dollars* I enjoyed myself tremendously and left the theater full of admiration. No two films of Leone's are exactly alike; there has been a trajectory, a rising to greater maturity. I think if Leone selected me it must have been partly because he wanted someone to contradict him. I had never made an action film. The idea of doing something far from my usual routine seduced me. It was like putting myself to a test.

In the beginning there was a novel, *The Hoods*, which cost a lot of money and little of which remained in the movie. We worked with Norman Mailer and he produced two long treatments which didn't work in film terms. It is one thing to be a writer and something else to be a screenwriter; they are two different professions. There were no new solutions, nothing that one might really have expected from Mailer, who is, himself, a New York Jew of humble origins, from the East Side I think. Afterwards I worked with Kim Arcalli, Bertolucci's writer and editor, who died not long ago. He was a wonderful man. He did not write, he spoke for hours, came up with precious ideas; the crux of the film is his.

Franco Ferrini also participated in this work from the start. Then Benvenuti and De Bernardi did another treatment. It is not the first time a lot of treatments have been done for a picture – I remember the case of *Rocco and His Brothers*. When a long period of time is involved there are things that are written one year and are old by the next.

Cinema is written on water. For example, we had included an episode about a strike with allusions to Jimmy Hoffa, the head of the truckers' union who had been involved in a scandal because he apparently made a loan to some Mafiosi, money coming from the union's pension fund which he put into some bad financial investments. At a certain point Sylvester Stallone's *F.I.S.T.* was released. It looked as if someone had read our script and copied it. But no, certain things are in the air and are ripe for use so that you have to keep up to date. And then maybe it was better that we avoided the historical and sociological aspects. We felt we might be interfering in a world that was not our own. It is already going far when a group of Italian writers make a movie about another country; to make political or sociological judgements would have been a little presumptuous. Certainly in *The Damned* we made judgements, but then that was a hell observed with wide open eyes: it was the classical Visconti theme of a family's personal hell.

And so we reached the definitive script, which was very long and had to be cut. We went to New York to inspect locations. Then there was the translation to be done. Leone wanted an American writer. The two screenwriters who first worked on it tended to make too many changes in our script; so we turned to Stuart Kaminsky, an execptional writer of mystery stories, a New York Jew.

It is the story of a group of boys from the East Side of New York who make up a little neighborhood gang and who as adults become gangsters, but without ever becoming part of a big organized crime ring; they remain independent. Everything is seen through the eyes of one of them, the only survivor, who goes in search of a certain time lost in the past.

Time is another important element of the film and it is played out on three levels: when the heroes are boys of around thirteen, when they are young men, and finally when the survivor, Noodles (Robert De Niro), returns in his private quest. The story has several female characters and a love story in which the time motif again unfolds. It is an American world revisited with European eyes, a black fable told in very realistic terms, but the archetypes are these: the gangsters, the gangsters' girls, Prohibition, cruelty, the great male friendships, and tragedy. These were all things that we knew from films. None of us was American, none of us a Jew, none of us a gangster; but we had gotten all of it, filtered through cinema rather than through literature. The secret thread that winds through the movie is a European one. The sense of certain mistakes made, of deceit, of treachery, of bitterness, of time that is irremediably lost. There is also a side which is fun, overbearing, rash and headstrong which belongs to twenty-year-old boys who are criminals but also heroes.

The book narrates chronologically, whereas we start off in a youthful period and from there branch out into childhood and old age. The things I like best are these transitions from one epoch to another and from one age to another for the characters. I think they contain a certain emotional force. They are resolved very realistically. For example, the old Noodles goes into a bar where, as a boy, he used to hang out; and through a window he sees Deborah dancing as a little girl. He sees her directly, without crossing fade outs; and a moment later we see Noodles, too, as a child.

The book ends in 1933, and contains nothing about old age, while the movie ends in 1968 – for no particular reason, possibly just to let it be understood that afterwards things would be different. Leone stuck quite close to the script; there was a lot of hair splitting over the lines. Visconti gave you more latitude. There were infinite numbers of meetings, when everyone wrote; sometimes even Visconti wrote. Visconti had fine ideas for cuts. It was his idea to end *The Leopard* with the ball scene rather than with the death of the prince, as in the book. Leone did not write, but he followed our work closely: he rejected, accepted, modified. As a screenwriter he was the exact opposite of what he was as a director. In the script he wanted everything to flow, he didn't want pauses, perhaps because he knew that in shooting he would drag out the tempos. Then too, in this movie, besides his slow tempos there are those of Robert De Niro. It is no accident if the original film lasts four hours.

The point of departure for our work was a great love for old American movies. I adored them when I was a kid, but now I do not feel like seeing them again; one might be disappointed. It is part of my culture. My high school professor was Attilio Bertolucci, Bernardo's father. He was an exquisite professor of Italian, but he also spoke to us about Joan Crawford, about John Ford. He could never see *Stagecoach* without becoming excited.

Of course, unlike ours, movies like *Scarface* were made at the time of the events they depicted. Today there is no one who is capable of handling Mafia or Camorra stories with the same punch. Maybe some B-movies have a certain power and realism despite their moralizing. I think that seen again in a few years' time they may render the idea of a particular Italian world.

As models for my work I have the great novels of the 1800s. I like a story that grabs you. Today, unfortunately, everything that is incomprehensible and boring is often considered intelligent.

ENNIO MORRICONE – *Towards an Interior Music*

When Sergio came to my house to commission the music for *A Fistful of Dollars*, I recognized him at once: we had been classmates in third grade and I remembered that we had both been rather lively children.

Little by little we found a way of understanding each other. Sergio did not express himself musically and there are always incomprehensions between a director and a composer. Also, on the piano you cannot always make clear what a piece is going to sound like once it has been orchestrated. Sometimes we spent whole days getting through to each other: we were both seeing the same thing, but in different ways. There were never any serious misunderstandings, however. We had long, lively talks to get our opinions across to each other, and then we reached a compromise. The danger is when there is no discussion and you do not even try to understand the other's point of view. In composing the music for Leone's movies I deliberately ignored the American precedents. In general the Americans use symphonic music even for Westerns, something I never do. I find symphonic language excessive, too rich for films.

For the main theme of *A Fistful of Dollars* I played an old Gypsy piece for Sergio which I had arranged years before for a television program, accompanying it with whip lashes, whistles and anvils… He told me to leave it almost unchanged. Sometimes Sergio takes a devilish pleasure in re-evaluating certain themes that other directors have discarded, knowing that the musical discourse is different from movie to movie. I had written the melody for the trumpet piece of the finale for a black singer in a television version of O'Neill's play. Sergio told me to add the trumpet with a Mexican accompaniment of the "Deguello" type – which I really do not like – because Sergio and Cinquini had edited the images precisely on Tiomkin's "Deguello" in *Rio Bravo*.

In the second picture, I had to use the trumpet again, though with guitar and carillon; in the third picture, with other things; and in the fourth we finally almost freed ourselves of it.

After the first picture I did the music before the shooting began. Sergio generally does not even give me the script: he tells me the story, the way he feels the characters, even the way the shots are composed. And I bring him the music. We talk it over and influence each other, something like a marriage where two become one.

Sometimes he plays the music on the set. In *Once Upon a Time in the West* this was very helpful for the actors' sense of character.

I got the organ in *For a Few Dollars More* because Volonté had his hide-out in a church and, in particular, a Michelangelo-like shot of Volonté. I did not want to use just any organ music, and so I used the opening of Bach's *Fugue in D minor*. The trumpet theme starts by taking the A-G-A of the organ. My carillon is a deformation of the tenuous sound of the music box incorporated in Lee Van Cleef's watch. As in the case of the harmonica of *Once Upon a Time in the West,* we are dealing here, to use Sergio Miceli's words, with interior music, music that is born within the scene.

The voice of Edda dell'Orso had already been used in *For a Few Dollars More*. In *Once Upon a Time in the West* it becomes the protagonist. It is the human voice used like an instrument. The music for *Once Upon a Time in the West was* already composed and recorded before the shooting began. I believe that Sergio regulated the speed of the crane shot when Claudia Cardinale leaves the station, to fit the musical crescendo. The Cheyenne theme came to me almost out of the blue. We were in the recording studio, I sat down to play the piano, Sergio liked it; and so I wrote it.

In *Duck! You Sucker*, the sweet music that accompanies the collapse of the bridge expresses the dynamiter's nostalgia for his youth. The roar puts an end to his Irish memories. For the march of the beggars, since I had injected some rather vulgar things – there was even some belching (the illogical thing was to put full-stomach sounds into a march of starving men) – it seemed only right to add something more refined, like Mozart.

There is a special satisfaction in working with someone like Leone. Not only does he make excellent films, but he respects the work of the composer and the orchestra. Other directors do a bad job of mixing the music, they keep it too soft or cover it with noises. But Sergio always gave full value to what I wrote for him.

Tonino Valerii – *A Pistol for Harlequin*

One afternoon in 1963 Enzo Barboni (the future E.B. Clucher) and Stelvio Massi ran into Sergio Leone as they were leaving the Cinema Arlecchino in Rome. They had just seen Kurosawa's *Yojimbo* and they told him it could be made into a good Western.

Leone, who was preparing the epic *Le Aquile di Roma* [The Eagles of Rome], realized that it was a good suggestion and spoke about it with Franco Palaggi, known as Checco, and he in turn proposed it to Papi and Colombo of Jolly Film. Jolly had a Western of Mario Caiano's in the works, *Le Pistole non Discutono* (with a script by Castellano and Pipolo inspired by *The Fascist* which they had written years before for Luciano Salce). A Western from *Yojimbo* could be produced as a *recupero,* which is to say, using the same sets, costumes, and even perhaps the same actors as the other movie.

To write the script, Palaggi called on Duccio Tessari who was going through a bad financial period. The producers did not want Leone as the director – they had no great esteem for him – but Palaggi managed to convince them.

The set designer was to be the same one as in Caiano's picture, Alberto Roccianti. One day the architect Carlo Simi, who was renovating producer Colombo's apartment, passed by the Jolly offices. He saw a drawing of the set on Leone's desk and said sarcastically: "And this is supposed to be a Mexican interior?" "Why?" Leone replied, "would you be able to do better?" Without bothering to reply, Simi picked up a pencil and immediately sketched a room with a high ceiling supported by enormous wooden beams and robust trusses. Leone was struck dumb and immediately had him taken on in place of Roccianti. Simi was to do the sets for all Leone's films. Another clever move was to replace Franco Lavagnino with Ennio Morricone after hearing two of his motifs that Caiano had rejected for *Le Pistole non Discutono*.

The only one who did not lose his job was Massimo Dallamano, the director of photography. He was the first one to understand that the new P2 (two perforations) Technicolor format required a new kind of close-up that took in the face from the chin to the lower part of the forehead in order not to lose too much detail. Furthermore Dallamano was very good at finding the proper angle quickly.

Another precious collaborator was Franco Giraldi, the underrated second-unit director. He shot the most beautiful sequence in the whole film: the Rio Bravo massacre. (Leone only shot the close-ups of Clint Eastwood.) And to think that Leone complained to me that Giraldi had ruined the movie! Gratitude is not one of his strengths.

Leone wanted James Coburn in the main role, but he was too expensive. The producers wanted to give him Cameron Mitchell, the lead in Caiano's movie, but Leone would not hear of it. One day a beautiful girl, Claudia Sartori, happened to come by. She worked in a casting agency, William Morris, if I remember correctly. She said that she had received a 16mm copy of an episode of the Western series *Rawhide* from America. It seemed to her that there was a young actor in it, tall and loose-limbed, who might be right for Leone.

Leone saw the film and accepted with some reluctance; to the point that he sent Mario Caiano to meet the actor at the airport. Clint Eastwood got off the plane with a small suitcase containing a poncho, hat, leather wristbands and pistol grips. Leone added the Tuscan cigar (*Virginia* actually, but Tuscans made do) and, in the Italian version, the unbearable voice of Enrico Maria Salerno.

The editor was Roberto Cinquini, the excellent editor of Germi's movies. The famous sequence of the massacre of the Baxters with all those close-ups of Mexican faces laughing as they shoot, is his work. Cinquini also had the rejected shots printed and had many good shots duplicated. He was a master in this. He knew how to use the same shots as many as four or five times always starting from a different point.

The dialogue is partly mine. Leone returned from Spain without the shooting script, which he had lost. I used the original script changing many things, also because during the editing, the story was modified. With all of this I don't want to belittle Leone's merits as a director. He had worked a long time with the Americans, learning precious secrets. First shoot a master of every scene, then the details from every camera angle and with various lenses. Move from one scene to another with an indirect linking shot. Make up for the insufficiencies in the acting by characterizing the personages by their style of dressing, their ties, and using extreme close-ups, details of eyes and other parts of the anatomy. A good editor will always be able to make something decent out of all this. It is the principle of the silent film directors who at the end of a scene left it to the cameraman to shoot a curtain blowing in the breeze, a grandfather clock ticking away, the remains of a banquet table, footsteps in the sand...

The movie premiered in Florence on a Friday in August without much publicity. For the first few days the theater was almost empty. The commercial manager of Jolly Unidis Pictures, Renato Bozza, bought dozens of tickets every day to keep the theater manager from discontinuing the run. On Monday the miracle occurred: the theater magically filled up with spectators. It was the beginning of success. A detail that should not be forgotten is that this theater, situated near the train station, had a great many traveling salesman among its customers.

But the picture also ran into some unpleasant episodes during its career – for example, a trial for plagiarism. Leone's lawyers advised a defence based on the fact that the double-crossing hero had been inspired by a figure in a Western literary work and so, if anything, Kurosawa was the plagiarist. I was given the job of discovering this work. I happened to see the announcement of a performance of *Harlequin, Servant of Two Masters* by Carlo Goldoni. I phoned Gastaldi, the fortunate owner of the *Dizionario Bompiani delle Opere e dei Personaggi* [Bompiani Dictionary of Literary Works and Characters], and asked him to read me the plot. That same afternoon I took the idea to Papi, feeling a little ashamed for the irreverent juxtaposition. It was passed on to the lawyers who were enthusiastic. I was given a bonus of 300,000 *lire*. And so it was that Goldoni became the inspiration of the Italian Western.

Leone's relations with the producers turned sour due to the success of the picture. Papi and Colombo refused to pay him his established percentage because the Spanish co-producer, whom Leone had recommended, had not even paid for the rental of the village where the movie was shot: Pedrizia di Colmenar Viejo (the stone quarry of the old beehive) fifty kilometers outside Madrid. So, for his next movie Leone was on the outlook for a producer. He found one in the person of the attorney Alberto Grimaldi who until then had only produced a few Spanish Westerns and was looking for his big break. Grimaldi offered Leone a blank check – so, at least, the legend goes – but he refused it in gentlemanly fashion, making do with a percentage.

A subject had to be found. A story written by Enzo dell'Aquila and another young unknown found its way onto Grimaldi's desk. It was bought at a relatively high price on the condition that the two youths renounce appearing in the credits. Maybe Leone was too much of a snob to shoot a movie whose subject had been written by two unknowns. Leone and Vincenzoni wrote the script.

The part of the bounty hunter was meant for Clint Eastwood, but Papi and Colombo were plotting to get him away from Leone. It was necessary to fly to the United States and thwart the competition. But Leone, who hadn't yet gotten rich, did not know that money bestows immortality. He was afraid of flying! I remember the atmosphere of last goodbyes that hovered in the air at that departure from Fiumicino. Furthermore, I too for a long time had been afraid of flying. And I hadn't become either rich nor immortal.

Work on the film proceeded with enthusiasm. It was one of the best troupes that Leone had ever had. I was assistant director with the job of supervising the choice of the supporting actors and preparing the sets. This was a delicate business considering that the shooting made the rounds of Rome, Madrid, Guadix, Almeria and Pedrizia di Colmenar Viejo. For example, the prison in which Volonté was kept had its exterior at Almeria, several interiors in Rome, and some in other locations. Regarding Volonté, the character he played was my invention. In the subject there was a baddie, Tombstone, but he was not on as high a level as the other two heroes. Leone asked me to come up with some ideas to develop this character and I suggested making him a drugged half-breed who killed under the effects of marijuana.

The following year I made my directorial debut with *Per il Gusto di Uccidere* [For the Taste to Kill], after which I made various other films, some Westerns and some not. In 1972 I was working for Leone again on *My Name Is Nobody,* which he produced and I directed.

Leone had particular reasons for wanting to produce it. Enzo Barboni's movies (*They Call Me Trinity* and *Trinity Is Still My Name*) had had unexpected international success, pushing Leone off his throne as the master of the Italian Western. Furthermore they were tongue-in-cheek parodies on the cliches of this genre. So Leone was planning artistic vengeance. Terence Hill, having ridiculed the Italian Western, would have to pay with an eye for an eye by playing straight man to one of the Western's most mythical interpreters, Henry Fonda, and so learn to recognize his own insignificance (thus the meaning of the title – *My Name Is Nobody* – which was originally supposed to be the name of a Western inspired by Ulysses' adventure with Polyphemus). In short, it was supposed to be a kind of execution of the figure of Trinity. But to get Terence Hill, Leone had to introduce many comic scenes of the kind used in the Trinity films.

I was called in after he had rejected several other directors. Perhaps he chose me because, having been his assistant, he thought I would make the movie his way.

At first I refused. I had liked the script, but I was convinced that the true hero of the picture had to be Henry Fonda and not Terence Hill, as Leone maintained. In the end, several months later, I accepted, to make Fulvio Morsella, Leone's brother-in-law, happy. Leone behaved magnificently. He accepted my version and renounced all vindictive feelings towards Trinity, who became a good kid dreaming of meeting his childhood hero. When he finally meets him, he is in trouble and Trinity helps to bring his career to a good end. I made endless on-the-spot inspections of locations in Arizona, New Mexico, Louisiana and New England. Meticulous care was taken in choosing sets, actors and the team. The nine weeks of shooting in the United States went as smooth as silk if you ignore some friction between me and the cameraman, Nannuzzi, who tried to influence the directing.

During the last five days of our stay in the United States, as we were shooting the finale, Leone arrived to tell me that in Madrid I would find a different cameraman and troupe. He watched the shooting and then left again. In Madrid the sets weren't ready and the costumes hadn't arrived. We had to interrupt our work for a week, and since Fonda was due to begin shooting *Ash Wednesday* immediately afterwards, Leone offered to direct the second unit with Terence Hill – who was literally dying to be directed by the master – in the sequence of the duel of the glasses in the saloon and in the village fiesta.

Mancini, the organizer, warned me: "If you let Leone shoot just one frame, everyone will say he directed the picture." I did not take him seriously. Most particularly, I did not want to involve Leone in the financial damages of a delay in completing the shooting. In the end it went just the way Mancini had predicted. When the film came out many critics said Leone was the true director and I only a kind of amanuensis. And Steven Spielberg called *My Name Is Nobody* Sergio Leone's masterpiece!

Luciano Vincenzoni – *Twenty Years Later*

I have known Sergio since my first jobs in the field of motion pictures. The first subject I ever sold, in 1954 when I was twenty-five, was *Hanno Rubato un Tram* [They've Stolen a Streetcar]. Aldo Fabrizi bought it, and it was directed by Mario Bonnard. Leone was the assistant director; and since Bonnard was old and ill, I got the impression that Leone directed half the movie. I remember him at Gigi Fazi's restaurant, seated at a table, silent and attentive, with Bonnard, Fabrizi and the screenwriter Maccari. Possibly, bored in the company of these old men, he would have preferred to have been out with a girl, but he stayed there since it was his job. As a young man he must have suffered boredom and humiliations, but they helped build his character, his capacity to get what he was after.

I got along well with Sergio because the Western was also my private mythology. I had only just been to see *A Fistful of Dollars* and was thinking how much I would like to write a Western when Sergio came and asked me to write the script of *For a Few Dollars More*. The subject and treatment were by Leone and his brother-in-law Fulvio Morsella. The first scene he told me about in order to work up my appetite for doing the script was the duel between Clint Eastwood and Lee Van Cleef when they stomp on each other's feet and riddle each other's hats with holes. I felt at a loss: okay, it was clearly meant to be ironic, but I couldn't imagine John Wayne stepping on Henry Fonda's foot; it would not make me laugh and would strike me as infantile. But when Sergio described the scene to me, I was convinced. After all, it was a game between aggressive children and could easily be applied to such instinctive characters. He maintained that the Western owed its success to the fact that the swaggering of the Western hero, Richard Widmark or John Wayne, was identical to that of the Roman slum kid or Trastevere roughneck. He had grown up in Trastevere and had played with arrogant bullies who stomp on your foot to challenge you, and he transferred these adolescent memories to the West. This ironic quality was what most struck Americans.

The film was a tremendous success. The ticket sales broke box-office records three times at the Supercinema theater. I personally handled the sales abroad. I phoned my friend, Ilya Lopert, the vice-president of United Artists in Paris, who came to Rome with his whole staff. I took them to the Supercinema. Fortunately it was one of the record-breaking days and there were three thousand people in the theater. They saw the film in a joyous uproar of laughs and applause and they wanted to go straight to the Grand Hotel to sign the contract. They paid a guaranteed minimum that was three times the amount of the producers' rosiest hopes. In the way Americans do, as soon as the contract was signed they said: "And now let's "cross-collateralize," counterbalance profits and losses with the next picture; what is the next one going to be?".

We had no project. With the tacit consent of Leone and Grimaldi I began to improvise: "A picture about three rogues running after a treasure in the midst of the Civil War, a little in the spirit of films you distribute in the United States." And they immediately replied: "We'll buy it – what will it cost?" without a written script, just on our word. In the United States even today, *For a Few Dollars More* and *The Good, the Bad and the Ugly* are shown by at least four hundred television stations a month. Leone's movies are practically the only Italian Westerns that have been successful in America. No one has seen the others; they have been handed over to television where they are broadcast maybe at night just to have something to justify showing the commercials. If Leone's films fly at 90,000 feet attitude, the others are moles that travel underground.

Then there was a cooling off in my relations with Leone and I accepted offers for two other movies, Corbucci's *A Professional Gun* and Petroni's *Death Rides a Horse*, because I earned twice as much and didn't have to argue with the directors. But it was a mistake; I would have done better to write the script for *Once Upon a Time in the West*. If I won a certain popularity in America it was not for the films of Monicelli, or Germi, or Lizzani, but precisely for Leone's Westerns; for Spielberg, Lucas, Coppola, all hold him in great esteem. Unfortunately they are less familiar with Germi.

Later we were reunited for *Duck! You Sucker*. The subject was not terribly original, but Leone managed to endow it with a certain magnitude. The difference between this film and *A Professional Gun* was also a question of the means and actors at our disposal. It is one thing to have Tony Musante and Franco Nero and quite another to work with James Coburn and Rod Steiger. The carriage that appears at the beginning of the picture was a masterpiece of carpentry with original Louis Vuitton suitcases from the end of the 1800s and a toilet in a sleeping car. Leone wanted it to be extremely luxurious in order to emphasize all the more the humiliation of the peon. And to satisfy him they had it made. It took twelve horses to pull it and cost a fortune. But he was right, because on the screen this carriage is important.

The idea of Rod Steiger peeing at the beginning of the movie was Sergio's. It was a game he played as a kid. In the spring he and his friends went beneath the trees where there were termite colonies and played at who could hit more of them by peeing. *Viale Glorioso* [Glorioso Street], a film subject that was never made, begins like that, with children who go to the top of some steps, pee and then run to the bottom to see which one's pee gets there first.

Another bit that Sergio was very set on was the scene where Rod Steiger slips into the cattle car, seats himself under a birdcage and then at a certain point the little bird craps on his head. He looks up at it and comments: "And to think that for gentlemen it sings."

Sergio can be heavy-handed and exaggerated as in some fight scenes and executions, but he is never dreary. Others are dreary because they are so by nature or because they bow to the demands of the producer. If a producer says he can only allow two days for a scene and Sergio knows it will take six, he asks for eight. Another director would accept doing it in a day and a half. Leone is capable of running over the work schedule by as many as twenty weeks, which means six billion *lire*, and of shooting a million and a half feet of film when what is seen on the screen is only 13,500 feet. Anyone who is capable of getting away with all of that, is very good indeed. And then he finds himself with all this beautiful footage and doesn't want to throw anything away; each frame is like a child. In fact, with *Once Upon a Time in America* he started out making one film and ended up with two: this may be the producer's salvation. If poor Michelangelo had been given a block of stone and told to sculpt the *Pietà* and a pair of Siamese Madonnas was produced, he had gotten it all wrong. But in the cinema they are cut and sold separately.

Leone's charisma allows him to make the film when and how he wants. He is a man capable of waiting eleven years before making *Once Upon a Time in America*, a man who will not compromise – this is his strength. And he is absolutely right in this: six months later it will not interest anyone to know how many feet of film were shot, but the picture will remain in the film libraries. What counts is the result.

Leone is a trained professional with few peers; someone who personally involves himself in everything from the narrative line to the face of the least important extra being photographed in long shot. He even knows the little differences made in the Colt Navys year by year, and set great store in these things even if no viewer would ever notice them. During the story conferences he put on a cartridge belt and spun a pistol on his finger like a cowboy. You needed to see how lovingly he touched these arms, as if they were jewels. He is a man who loves objects, someone who collects eighteenth century Roman silver, furniture, pictures. He has great knowledge of visual things. He is one of those rare directors for whom you may write a scene with a potential of ten and you get it back from him with a potential of a hundred. And when you see the picture, you ask yourself: "By God, did I really write that?" In *The Good, the Bad and the Ugly* there is an amusing exchange of quips between the two leads sitting around a fire. Sergio had postponed shooting this scene for several days while his assistants were looking for a location along a mountain path with a majestic background that would give the dialogue its full impact.

Let's take the opening of *Once Upon a Time in the West*: here, Leone's memory for movies came into play. He recalled *High Noon* with the three killers dying of boredom in the station; and he added his grandiose eye for a scene. He had hundreds – thousands – of railroad ties brought over to construct the platform where Bronson confronts the three killers. It is a great visual idea. Another director would have said: "We already have the grass, the boulders, isn't it the same thing?" Or then, that immense drugstore situated in the midst of the desert. Leone did not care if it was believable, he cared about the depth it gave to the scene.

There was already talk of the sets for *Once Upon a Time in America*. He had an opium den made as big as a train station with clouds of smoke and bunk beds. It was an exaggeration because real opium dens in the Chinese quarter are rather pathetic little places. But the little man seated below the gigantic screen in a movie theater looks up at a head measuring twelve by six feet. These images overwhelm him and when he leaves he takes away a lasting impression. For Leone it is necessary to *épater* (amaze) always. After having worked with many directors who were real charlatans, I realized Sergio's great qualities for, he is a person who believes in what he does.

Westerns can make a comeback because a new public is growing up. Those who are tired of Westerns are forty by now and they do not go to the cinema anymore; it is their children who do, and they are eighteen. There are students at UCLA who have seen our movies as many as ten times.

I wrote the treatment for *The Good, the Bad and the Ugly – 2*, and it would only have required Sergio's say-so to make it.

It begins twenty years after the end of the first: one stormy evening in a village on the edge of nowhere a dust-covered horseman arrives. He enters the deserted saloon, the bartender pours him a drink and this sand-bleached spectre – it is Eli Wallach – asks: "Have you seen a blond son-of-a-bitch with a cigar? I've been looking for him for twenty years." The answer is no. He leaves. The wind creates swirls of straw, a page from a newspaper flies up into his face. On it is a photograph of Clint Eastwood graying a little, with the caption: "Next week our mayor is marrying Miss What's-her-name thus culminating a long dream of love." Exulted, Wallach turns to his horse saying: "We've found him!" and the horse dies from the strain of the emotion. Wallach steals another horse and gallops off. Blowing around the town square, the newspaper is trapped by a booted foot and is grasped by a hand: it is Lee Van Cleef's, the twin brother of the villain who died in the first movie, intent on revenge.

We are in Clint Eastwood's town. Black-framed posters mourn the death of the mayor killed in a cowardly ambush. Wallach is terribly disappointed. He goes to the cemetery where he finds the grave with a cross, the poncho, the sombrero and a lighted cigar on an iron brace. Beside the grave stands a tall blond kid, Clint Eastwood's son, talking to the dead man: "As you ordered me to do, I have sold the land and the herds and I've raised $220,000. I am going East to invest it all in the railroads. I'll be back to visit you soon. Someone will come to change your cigar every day." He starts to leave when he hears a voice from the grave: "Watch out, kid, the world is full of sons-of-bitches." Wallach follows the boy and from behind a tombstone Lee Van Cleef's hawk-like nose peeks out.

Great adventures, chases, surprise actions. Lee Van Cleef overtakes Clint Eastwood's son in the desert, steals his money, makes him undress, ties him up, and smears him with honey while columns of ants approach, as in a classic with Wallace Berry. Providentially a strange nun arrives leading a caravan of girls who put on religious shows. He also runs into Eli Wallach, and the two of them go off to hunt down Lee Van Cleef. They happen upon a village surrounded by the army; Lee Van Cleef and his brigands are holed up in a school house with some hostages, including the little nun. The two friends offer themselves as substitute hostages, while in fact they are only thinking of getting the money back.

They succeed in this, kill Lee Van Cleef, and recover the money. Eli Wallach proposes splitting it between them, but the door opens, the soldiers enter and Clint Eastwood's son shows them the notice of the reward on Eli Wallach's head. Wallach is taken into the square to be hanged. His neck is already in the noose when a shot is fired from a nearby hill that cuts the noose down and Wallach manages to escape.

Clint Eastwood has agreed to lend his voice and even to produce the movie. An American producer has come to Rome and offered a million dollars for it. Leone would not even have to direct it – the director would be a young American, Joe Dante – but Leone never gave his okay. Who knows why?

3. LEONE IN THE MENAGERIE (HIS COLLEAGUES AND THEIR FILMS)[64]

Almodovar. There was one film, albeit never a candidate for the Golden Lion award, that gave rise to a heated debate amongst the members of the jury. I am talking about Pedro Almodovar's *Women on the Verge of a Nervous Breakdown*. Lina Wertmüller and I did all we could to find supporters for this film because we were convinced that the Spaniard had brought a breath of fresh air and novelty to the Festival and above all had dealt a decisive blow to the cinema's worst enemy: boredom. Unfortunately, there are some who think that to be artistic a film must necessarily be boring. And so Almodovar had to be content with an Osella for story and screenplay[65].

Amarcord. Whenever I look back on my childhood days, I always get this picture of the members of the Fascist Party, exactly the way Fellini showed them in *Amarcord*: the sequence of the parade is in no way caricatural. They were like those Neapolitan comedians who pretend to be terrifying, but are really scared to death, puppets bursting at the seams with colonialist ambitions.

Antonioni. Antonioni is an exceptional director. But he's not a very good story-teller. Whenever I watch *The Red Desert,* I just can't help laughing at the dialogue: talk about banal! You can't say "I film banalities because in life we are banal". That is far too easy a justification. But don't misunderstand me, he is an exceptional director. Until he started trying to explain incommunicability he made masterpieces like *The Girlfriends*, but even that was better without the soundtrack. I don't like the ending of *Blow-up,* but everything else is on par with Hickcock's best.

Bonnard. I really liked him. There was always a very special feeling on the set of his films. Something really alive. He was often regarded as a "calligrapher" and frequently preferred erstwhile styles and techniques – on the set he enjoyed giving orders in French, he was a conservative, not very cultured and a bit naïve – but he was a man who truly possessed a talent for film-making. I must say that I learned a lot from him about how and where to use the movie camera, and how to manage extras.

Chaplin (1). For me, Chaplin is the greatest genius of the art of film-making, and if it hadn't been for him a lot of us today would be doing a different job.

Chaplin (2). Chaplin's *Monsieur Verdoux* had a big influence on *The Good, the Bad and the Ugly*. In my film there are two killers who have to come to terms with the horrors of war, the war between North and South. One of them says: "I've never seen so many men wasted so badly." In Monsieur Verdoux, the killer defends himself thus: "I am only an amateur killer in comparison with Mr. Roosevelt and Mr. Stalin, who do it on a mass scale. I am just a little amateur".

---

[64] From interviews with Sergio Leone (included in: Noël Simsolo, *Conversations avec Sergio Leone*, Stock, Paris 1987) and his writings (*A John Ford, un suo allievo*, "Corriere della Sera", 20 August 1983).

[65] From an article written by Sergio Leone for "Bianco e Nero" (December 1988) in which he tells about his experience as part of the jury at the Cannes Film Festival.

All About Sergio Leone

Japanese Cinema. In the beginning there was Rashomon. And all the Kurosawas and even *The Burmese Harp*. Japanese films fascinate me for their use of silence. This creates a rhythm that I really like. My entire childhood and adolescence were marked by speed. Later, I realized that all the directors I worked for were just like me in my obsession with speed. Whether they were good or bad directors, they all had this in common. They forced their actors to speed up their lines to the extent that often the last syllables uttered by one actor overlapped with the first syllables of another making the whole thing incoherent. Never a pause, however slight, to allow the speaker a moment's reflection before answering. I did not agree with this system. It seemed artificial. It doesn't happen like this in reality. We listen. We react. We think. And, afterwards, we answer. This reflective approach I found only in Japanese or Asian films. It had an impact on me...though my love of Japanese cinema is less evident in my earlier films: they don't have the same rhythm as *Once Upon a Time in the West*. Not surprising really, when you're a bounty killer, everything depends on how quickly you can get your gun out. In *Once Upon a Time in the West*, the mood is contemplative, because it is a dance of death. You need a slow pace, which is my way of doing things anyway, my style. I had been planning to make this kind of slow-paced film for a long time. Make the camera movements seem like caresses.

Political Cinema. When I first became aware there was a new genre of cinema, political cinema, I did not agree. I didn't believe in it. I argued that militant film-making was of interest only to the activists of some political party. Fortunately, at that time, there were other artistic phenomena emerging. Alas! [The "political" authors] never achieved the weight of such movements as neorealism and Italian-style comedy...Bertolucci became internationally famous, Bellocchio turned out to be a disappointment and never again achieved the intensity of his autobiographical film, *Fists in the Pocket*. The most surprising was Carmelo Bene. Vittorio De Sica and I always defended him. He was a great actor and an intelligent director.

Ford (1). Bearing in mind the job I do, to have won the admiration of John Ford honors me more than any other expression of esteem or friendship. This grand old Irishman is, in fact, one of the few directors worthy of being called a veritable master of their profession, in this case cinema, where the less discerning media gurus and critics shout 'miracle' from the rooftops, usually for the wrong reasons, at least three times a week. He has earned this right, like one of the soldiers in his films who earn medals and glory in battle, in the celluloid civil war and the melancholy encampments of Hollywood. His cinema, so pure and straightforward, so human and dignified, has left an indelible mark on everything that has come afterwards. My work for a start. I have always liked to think, for example, that the cold-hearted Henry Fonda of *Once Upon a Time in the West* was the legitimate offspring, in his monstrosity, of John Ford's brainwave in *Fort Apache*: an arrogant and egocentric officer, who violates every moral principle and every treaty in his conduct towards the Indians, leading his men to their destruction in the Valley of Death.

Ford (2). There is one film John Ford should not be happy with, *A Quiet Man*. It is the absolute opposite of the reality of Ireland. To me it's like *Snow White and the Seven Dwarfs*, there is not the slightest mention of the IRA. He began to amend things with *The Man Who Shot Liberty Valance*...and talking of John Wayne, given the chance, I could have made such a splendid bad guy out of him!

Freda. I don't understand the enthusiasm of the French for Riccardo Freda. It seems almost ridiculous. Freda is a run of the mill director. Mario Bava was much more talented.

Godard. Some of Godard's tricks are admirable. But I don't think he is an all-round director. Just as Bergman uses cinema to make literature, Godard uses it to make musical pictures. Sometimes he makes a masterpiece such as *Pierrot le Fou*. We have one point in common. We pass everything off as the specific language of the cinema, of images and sound.

Words

Hitchcock (and Lang). The second time you see a Hitchcock film you notice all the technical errors of the screenplay. Too many improbabilities. He tries to give priority to the imagination alone. This is not my cup of tea. I want everything to be plausible from a psychological, historical and social point of view. Hitchcock managed this only once, in *Dial M for Murder*. The plot structure is inimitable, logical and believable on all levels. His other films are full of holes. He tries to get away with it by relying on the magic of the imagery and rhythm. I find Lang much more interesting. His imagination never undermines his realism. Moreover, it was he who invented everything. Without Lang, Hitchcock would have never existed.

Kubrick and the Americans. Of the modern directors, I have a high regard for Kubrick, apart from *The Shining*, and I like Scorsese for having taken neorealism to New York. I like Coppola's *The Godfather – Part II* very much, not so much *Cotton Club*; of Cimino, the first part of *The Deer Hunter* and the full-length version of *Heaven's Gate*. Spielberg is a genius behind the movie camera, but a victim of the almighty dollar. *Duel* is his best film, *Indiana Jones* is too vacuous, even the Nazis are phoney! I adore John Boorman, although I have my doubts about *Zardoz* and *The Emerald Forest*. But if you ask me who is the greatest American director, I say John Cassavetes. He is much greater than Altman.

Morricone. Let me just say that Morricone is not my musician, he's my screenwriter.

Neorealism and the like. I was aware of the importance of the neorealist movement. There was nothing else like it in the film industry... they were necessary films. They said the right things. It was a healthy change after twenty years of Fascism. But it wasn't my favorite genre. I think Visconti was a great director, but I never thought of him as an author. You could compare him with Toscanini. He's remarkable but he's not Verdi. True, Visconti's direction is superb, but he really didn't have much to say. I definitely preferred Germi or Rossellini. And above, all De Sica, who was the top for me.

Olmi. In the end, there was only one true candidate worthy of distinction. *The Legend of the Holy Drinker* more or less summed up all of those characteristics that we had been looking for: masterfully directed, brilliantly acted, international in its story line, but above all in its structure, entirely appropriate to the atmosphere and spirit of the famous film festival. In addition to all that has been said and written about the virtues of this film, let us not forget that it has an Italian director telling a story that takes place in Paris, who chooses a Dutch actor for the lead role and has him speak in English. Moreover, the film is just cryptic enough to have satisfied even the Indian jury member, the one with the unpronounceable name [See footnote page 181].

Pasolini. I must confess I prefer Pasolini the writer to Pasolini the filmmaker. The man himself was interesting. He had the courage to take a stand on things he believed in. A moderate anarchist who prized his free spirit. He opposed doctrines. And he was expelled from the Communist Party.

The Russians. I can't really say I'm mad about *Battleship Potemkin*, I prefer *Ivan the Terrible*. I loved *The Cranes Are Flying*, and I loved Tarkovsky. I haven't seen any of Mikhalkov's films. I don't like the work of Konchalovsky. That film of his called *Runaway Train* could have been made by Mario Bava.

Sautet. I admire Claude Sautet, who makes films like Scola, only better.

For a Few Dollars More.

4. WHEN THE MAN WITH A .45...
QUOTES AND DIALOGUES FROM THE FILM

I guess I'm talking like a damn preacher, but it's your fault;
what can you expect of a national monument?

(HENRY FONDA TO TERENCE HILL: *My Name is Nobody*).

WINNERS

You can always tell the winners at the starting gate.
(Assessments at the end of life between two losers: Robert De Niro to Larry Rapp in *Once Upon a Time in America*).

WATER AND WINE

- I would like some water, if it's no trouble.
- Water! Well that word is poison around here ever since the days of the Great Flood.
(Claudia Cardinale and bartender Lionel Stander: *Once Upon a Time in the West*).

- I guess it's better to abstain here in Rhodes.
- Not necessarily, nephew, just don't ever be the first to drink.
(Rory Calhoun to Jorge Rigaud when the servant-taster had collapsed after being poisoned: *The Colossus of Rhodes*).

A TOAST

Boys, let's drink to our last shipment! There's more onboard tonight than just booze. It's ten years of our lives, ten years that were really worth living!
(The last toast, namely James Wood's "Judas kiss" to his two old mates, William Forsythe and James Hayden, whom he's about to betray: *Once Upon a Time in America*).

ANIMALS

- He's feeling real bad.
- Eh?
- My mule. He's got all riled up when you fired that four shot at his feet.
- Hey, you're making some kind of joke?
- You see, I understand you men were just playin' around, but the mule, he just doesn't get it. Course, if you were to all apologize.
- [Men Laugh]
- I don't think it's nice, you laughin'. You see, my mule don't like people laughing. He gets the crazy idea you're laughin' at him. Now if you apologize, like I know you're going to, I might convince him that you really didn't mean it.
(Clint Eastwood to the bandits who shot at the feet of his mule: *A Fistful of Dollars*).

You've made a big mistake, Morton. When you're not on that train, you look like a turtle out of its shell.
(Henry Fonda to the cripple businessman Gabriele Ferzetti: *Once Upon a Time in the West*).

PAID LADIES AND GENTLEMEN

- What's your name?
- Eve.
- I want to call you Deborah.
- I've done more complicated things for much less.
(The prostitute Darlanne Fleugel and a heartbroken Robert De Niro: *Once Upon a Time in America*).

Don't be worried, I'm a woman who's rich enough to appreciate the men that my money can buy.
(Margarite Lozano to Clint Eastwood in: *A Fistful of Dollars*).

You know, Jill, you remind me of my mother. She was the biggest whore in Alameda and the finest woman that ever lived. Whoever my father was — for an hour or for a month — he must have been a happy man.
(Jason Robards to Claudia Cardinale: *Once Upon a Time in the West*).

185

I'm expensive now, I've given myself a raise
(The grown up prostitute Amy Rider to her one-time customer Robert De Niro: *Once Upon a Time in America*).

WOMEN FROM THE SOUTH
You see, Darius, here the women have a special fragrance, they seem to be made of the sun, flower petals and the foam of the sea...
(Jorge Rigaud to Rory Calhoun referring to Lea Massari in: *The Colossus of Rhodes*).

LOVE CONFESSIONS
To keep from going crazy, you have to cut yourself off from the outside world, just not think about it. Yet there were years that went by. It seemed like... no time at all, because you're not doing anything. There were two things I couldn't get out of my mind. One was Dominic, the way he said, "I slipped," just before he died. The other was you. How you used to read me your Song of Songs, remember? "How beautiful are your feet / In sandals, O prince's daughter." I used to read the Bible every night. Every night I used to think about you. "Your navel is a bowl / Well-rounded with no lack of wine / Your belly, a heap of wheat / Surrounded with lilies / Your breasts / Clusters of grapes / Your breath, sweet-scented as apples." Nobody's gonna love you the way I loved you. There were times I couldn't stand it any more. I used to think of you. I'd think, "Deborah lives. She's out there. She exists." And that would get me through it all. You know how important that was to me?
(The late and interrupted love confession of Robert De Niro to Elizabeth McGovern, at night at the beach: *Once Upon a Time in America*).

YOUNG MEN AND OLD MEN
Just look how young they've got, these old men.
(Terence Hill to Henry Fonda who has just told him he doesn't want to avenge his brother's torture and death because, all things considered, he was a brute anyway: *My Name Is Nobody*).

One can be young in years and old in hours,

like you.
(From Henry Fonda's final letter to Terence Hill: *My Name is Nobody*).

OLD AGE
Back in my day, it was quite hard to become a grandpa.
(Henry Fonda to Terence Hill: *My Name is Nobody*).

At your age you suffer only for women, at my age you suffer because women no longer make you suffer.
(Old Jorge Rigaud to young Rory Calhoun: *The Colossus of Rhodes*).

We're both getting old. All that we have left now are our memories. If you go to that party on Saturday night, you won't have those anymore.
(After a long time the two old missed lovers get to meet again Elizabeth McGovern to Robert De Niro in *Once Upon a Time in America*).

Anyhow, I was getting to be one more old-timer, and the years don't make wisdom, they just make old age.
(From Henry Fonda's final letter to Terence Hill: *My Name is Nobody*).

WEAPONS
YOUR STRONGEST, YOUNGEST MEN WILL
FALL TO THE SWORD
(Epitaph at the cemetery: *Once Upon a Time in America*).

Every gun makes its own tune and I know that one.
(Clint Eastwood recognizes from afar and from a shot, Eli Wallach's gun: *The Good, the Bad and the Ugly*).

When a man with a .45 meets a man with a rifle, the man with a pistol's a dead man.
(Gian Maria Volonté to Clint Eastwood: *A Fistful of Dollars*).

- Well, you'd better get used to the idea, pal. This country is still growing up. Certain diseases it's better to have when you're still young.
- You boys ain't a mild case of the measles. You're the plague.
(The gangster James Woods explains his social and

historical role to the union rep Treat Williams: *Once Upon a Time in America*).

NUMBERS
- You can count all the way up to two.
- All the way up to six if I have to...and maybe faster than you.
(Charles Bronson and Jason Robards: *Once Upon a Time in the West*).

- One, two, three, four, five, six. Six. Perfect number.
- Huh. Isn't three the perfect number?
- Mm... yeah. But I've got six more bullets in my gun.
(Clint Eastwood, Lee Van Cleef and a Colt ready to shoot: *The Good, the Bad and the Ugly*).

FATE
We're better than fate. Some we give the good life, others we give it up the ass.
(James Woods to Robert De Niro & co. after the newborns swap: *Once Upon a Time in America*).

You often meet your fate on precisely the road you'd taken to avoid it.
(Terence Hill to Henry Fonda, unaware he is quoting from the Babylonian Talmud, Cocteau [Le Grand Écart] and Roberto Vecchioni [Samarcanda]: *My Name is Nobody*).

THE LITTLE BIRD'S STORY
1 Do you know the little bird's story? My grandpa used to tell it to me all the time. There was a little bird who didn't know how to fly; on a freezing cold night he falls out of his nest, lands on the ground and starts calling "pee-pee pee-pee" like crazy 'cause he's dying. Luckly for him along comes this cow, sees him and feels sorry, so she lifts her tail and "splash!" drops this big hot cowpie right on him. This little bird feels warm right now but he's still unhappy, he keeps going "pee-pee pee-pee" louder than ever. A coyote hears someone and comes around, he reaches out a paw, pulls him out of the cowpie. He brushes the dirt off and swallows the bird down in one gulp. Grandpa said there's a moral there, but you have to figure it out for yourself.
(Terence Hill to Henry Fonda: *My Name is Nobody*).

2 I figured out the moral to your grandpa's story, the one about the cow that covered the little bird in cowpie to keep it warm, and then the coyote hauled it out and ate it. It's the moral of these new times of yours: Folks that throw dirt on you aren't always trying to hurt you, and folks who pull you out of a jam aren't always trying to help you. But the main point is, when you're up to your nose in shit, keep your mouth shut. This is why people like me gotta' go, and this is why you faked that gunfight to get me out of the West clean.
(From Henry Fonda's final letter to Terence Hill: *My Name is Nobody*).

QUESTIONS AND ANSWERS
- The future don't matter to us. Nothing matters now - not the land, not the money, not the woman. I came here to see you, 'cause I know that now you'll tell me what you're after.
- Only at the point of dyin'.
- I know it.
(Henry Fonda and Charles Bronson just before the final duel: *Once Upon a Time in the West*).

- Or is the question indiscreet?
- No. No, the question isn't indiscreet. But the answer could be.
(Clint Eastwood and Lee Van Cleef: *For a Few Dollars More*).

What about me?
(Rod Steiger's unanswered question at the end of *Duck! You Sucker*).

SLEEP
Well, if there's gonna be any shooting, I gotta get my rest.
(Clint Eastwood to Gian Maria Volonté: *For a Few Dollars More*).

- What have you been doing all these years?
- I've been going to bed early.
(The meeting between the two old friends after a long time, Larry Rapp and Robert De Niro: *Once Upon a Time in America*).

THE TIME LEFT

People go around wasting days, weeks and years, and all of a sudden there's only thirty seconds to go.

(Henry Fonda, sarcastically, before blowing up the three men who wanted to kill him: *My Name is Nobody*).

THE GOOD ONES, THE BAD ONES AND THE IDIOT ONES

- Well... Remember me, *amigo*?
- M-Mm.
- Course you do. El Paso...
- It's a small world.
- Yes, and very, very bad. Now come on, you light another match.
- I generally smoke just after I eat. Why don't you come back in about ten minutes?
- Ten minutes you'll be smoking in hell.

(The hunchbaked Klaus Kinski and col. Lee Van Cleef who previously lit a match on his hump: *For a Few Dollars More*).

- Lee! LEE! Ha ha! God is with us because he hates the Yanks too. HURRAH!
- God's not on our side. He hates idiots.

(Eli Wallach who mistook Yankees for Confederates because of their dusty uniforms, and Clint Eastwood: *The Good, the Bad and the Ugly*).

THE BIG DREAM

You don't sell the dream of a lifetime.

(Charles Bronson to Jason Robards on Frank Wolff: *Once Upon a Time in the West*).

- You still believe in fairytales, don't you?
- Damn right!

(Henry Fonda to Terence Hill: *My Name is Nobody*).

A WOMAN'S DREAMS

- Noodles... you're the only person that I have ever...
- Ever what? Go ahead, ever what?
- ...that I ever cared about. But you'd lock me up and throw away the key, wouldn't you?
- Yeah. Yeah, I guess so.
- Yeah... and the thing is, I probably wouldn't even mind.

(Elizabeth McGovern and Robert De Niro at the restaurant in 1933: *Once Upon a Time in America*).

- You wake up one morning and say "World, I know you. From now on there are no more surprises," and then you happen to meet a man like this, who looked like a good man - clear eyes, strong hands - and he wants to marry you, which doesn't happen often, and he says he's rich, too, which doesn't hurt.
- *(looking at McBain's photo)* This man, he'd have put his money somewhere.
- If you can find them, I'll giv'em to you. Mrs. McBain goes back to civilization. Minus a husband and plus a great future.
- You deserve better.
- The last man who told me that is buried out there.

(The new-widow Claudia Cardinale tells about her marriage with Frank Wolff [McBain] to Jason Robards: *Once Upon a Time in the West*).

THE DEAD

I saw three of these dusters a short time ago, they were waiting for a train. Inside the dusters there were three men. Inside the men there were three bullets.

(Charles Bronson to Jason Robards: *Once Upon a Time in the West*).

- Tell me, was it necessary that you kill all of them? I only told you to scare them!
- People scare better when they're dyin'.

(The Railroad baron, Gabriele Ferzetti, and the killer hired by him, Henry Fonda: *Once Upon a Time in the West*).

The dead can be very useful sometimes. They've helped me out of tough spots more than once. First they don't talk. Second, they can be made to look alive if I manage it right. And, third...well third if you kill them there's no worry, 'cause they're already dead.

(Clint Eastwood a José Calvo: *For a Fistful of Dollars*).

- Who are you?
- Jim Cooper, Chuck Youngblood...
- More dead men.
- They were all alive until they met you, Frank.

(The killer Henry Fonda and the avenger of the dead ones, Charles Bronson: *Oncer Upon a Time in the West*).

Dear Nobody, dying is not the worst thing that can happen to a man. Look at me...

I've been dead for three days now, and have finally found my peace.

(From Henry Fonda's final letter to Terence Hill: *My Name is Nobody*).

THE BRAVERY OF THE OTHERS

Have you ever been tortured? Are you sure you wouldn't talk? I was sure. And yet I talked. Some men died because of me. What should I do? Kill myself? Why? The dead remain dead but me, I have not changed. I still believe in the same things.

(Romolo Valli, who betrayed the cause under torture, talks to the bold James Coburn: *Duck! You Sucker*).

THE ART OF WAR

Whoever has the most liquor to get the soldiers drunk and send them to be slaughtered... he's the winner. Rebs and us have only one thing in common: the smell of booze.

(The Union Captain Aldo Giuffré explains the American Civil War to Eli Wallach and Clint Eastwood: *The Good, the Bad and the Evil*).

I've never seen so many men wasted so badly.

(Killer Eli Wallach on the massacre caused by the war: *The Good, the Bad and Ugly*).

PROFESSIONS

You think you're better than I am? Where we came from, if one did not want to die in poverty, one became a priest or a bandit! You chose your way, I chose mine. Mine was harder!

(The Mexican outlaw Eli Wallach to his priest brother Luigi Pistilli: *The Good, the Bad and the Ugly*).

Look, between being a bandit and being a revolutionary, I choose the job I know better.

(James Coburn the revolutionary to Rod Steiger the bandit: *Duck! You Sucker*).

ETIQUETTE

I'll kill anything, but never a kid. Be like killin' a priest. Catholic priest, that is.

(Jason Robards to Claudia Cardinale: *Once Upon a Time in the West*).

That's enough for today. Sooner or late he'll talk. It's just a matter of time. Watch out he doesn't escape or die. Otherwise do as you like.

(Gian Maria Volonté to one of his men about Clint Eastwood who's been caught and tortured: *A Fistful of Dollars*).

It's true I have killed people, Mr. Bailey. Sometimes to defend myself, sometimes for money. And many people used to come to us. Business partners, rivals, lovers. Some of the jobs we took, and some we didn't. Yours is one we would never touch, Mr Bailey.

(Robert De Niro to James Woods in the studio of his villa in 1968: *Once Upon a Time in America*).

FRIENDS AND ENEMIES

Fact is, you saved my life today. But I'd rather it was my fault I got shot than your fault I didn't.

(Henry Fonda to Terence Hill: *My name is Nobody*).

Those two, rather than have them behind you, it's better to have them in front of you, horizontal, and possibily cold.

(Gian Maria Volonté to Luigi Pistilli: *For a Few Dollars More*).

Your friends have a high mortality rate, Frank.

(Charles Bronson to Henry Fonda: *Once Upon a Time in the West*).

Son, let me give you a little advice. You start admiring someone, pretty soon you're envious so you start showing off, taking chances. Before you know it, you're dead.

(Henry Fonda to Terence Hill: *My name is Nobody*).

I sleep soundly, because I know my worst enemy is watching over me.

(Clint Eastwood to Eli Wallach: *The Good, the Bad and the Ugly*).

FACES

I'm looking for the owner of that horse. He's tall, blonde, he smokes a cigar, and he's a pig!

(Eli Wallach describes Clint Eastwood to the Hotel Owner: *The Good, the Bad and the Ugly*).

- Hey, amigo! You know you got a face beautiful enough to be worth $2000?
- Yeah, but you don't look like the one who'll collect it.
(Eli Wallach and Clint Eastwood: *The Good, the Bad and the Ugly*).

- (*to a cohort, pointing at Terence Hill*) Hey, get him to pay first.
- Why?
- (*to Terence Hill*) Because you look like you ain't got long to live.
(One of the three killers and Terence Hill: *My Name is Nobody*).

THOSE WHO...

- It's always the best who are the first to go.
- Which means you ain't going nowhere..
(Terence Hill and Henry Fonda: *My Name is Nobody*).

You see, in this world there's two kinds of people, my friend: Those with loaded guns and those who dig. You dig.
(Clint Eastwood to Eli Wallach: *The Good, the Bad and the Ugly*).

- Just think of it. You'll be written up in all the history books.
- You'll be down on Earth reading them while I'm up there playing on a harp.
(Terence Hill suggests to the old gunman Henry Fonda a crazy and unforgettable venture: *My Name is Nobody*).

TOWN MICE AND COUNTRY MICE

I don't think I'd get along in a big city, it's too full of fast men and lose women, begging your pardon, ma'am. I'm too used to a quiet, simple country life.
(Bartender Lionel Stander to "lose woman" Claudia Cardinale: *Once Upon a Time in the West*).

- You'll be carrying the stink of the streets with you for the rest of your life!
- I like the stink of the streets. It makes me feel good. And I like the smell of it, it opens up my lungs. And it gives me a hard-on.
(Different opinions between the parlor gangster and the street gangster: James Woods and Robert De Niro in *Once Upon a Time in America*).

- Now I gotta go. Gonna be a beautiful town, Sweetwater.
- I hope you'll come back someday.
- Someday.
(Charles' Bronson last goodbye, maybe, to Claudia Cardinale: *Once Upon a Time in West*).

HOME, COUNTRY AND FAMILY

- This is Chico, one of the most trusted of my men. Follow him, he will bring you to your room. I would like you to feel at home.
- Well, I've never found home that great, but let's go.
(Antonio Prieto to Clint Eastwood: *A Fistful of Dollars*).

Not my country. My country is me and my family.
(Rod Steiger to James Coburn: *Duck! You Sucker*).

AMERICA

America...America...By God, if it's really as big as they say, with all those banks packed full of dreams.
(James Coburn dreams of America, in Mexico with Rod Steiger: *Duck! You Sucker*).

[...] the country ain't the same anymore, and I'm already feeling a stranger myself. It's grown, and got organized, and a good pistol don't mean a damn thing anymore.
(From Henry Fonda's letter to Terence Hill: *My Name is Nobody*).

Somebody has to run the place, every town has a boss.
(Clint Eastwood to José Calvo: *For a Fistful of Dollars*).

Take it easy! The difference is, they're always gonna win. And you're gonna keep gettin' it up the ass.
(Gangster Robert De Niro speaks about American politicians to the union rep Treat Williams: *One Upon a Time in America*).

- You'll pay for this, you bastards! I'm a citizen of the United States of America!
- To me, you are just a naked son of a bitch. Understand, Yankee?
(The yankee and the peone: *Duck! You Sucker*).

190

CRIMINAL RECORDS

...wanted in 14 counties of this state, the condemned is found guilty of the crimes of murder, armed robbery of citizens, state banks and post offices, the theft of sacred objects, arson in a state prison, perjury, bigamy, deserting his wife and children, inciting prostitution, kidnapping, extortion, receiving stolen goods, selling stolen goods, passing counterfeit money, and, contrary to the laws of this state, the condemned is guilty of using marked cards.

(Death sentence for Eli Wallach, namely Tuco Benedic to Pacifico Juan Maria Ramirez: *The Good, the Bad and the Ugly*).

PRISONS

I'll send you to Yuma, Cheyenne. There's a much more modern prison there: with more walls, more bars, more guards. After the first twenty years you'll like it there, you'll see.

(Sheriff Keenan Wynn to bandit Jason Robards: *Once Upon a time in the West*).

CONSUMER ADVICE

Why carry on living when we can bury you for $ 49.50?

(Advert for James Woods' funeral parlour: *Once Upon a Time in America*).

THE RICH

You want to get rich, huh? Well for that you have come to the right place, if you use your head that is, because everyone here has become very rich or else they are dead.

(The town's bellringer Ralf Baldassarre tells gunslinger Clint Eastwood: *A Fistful of Dollars*).

THE POWER OF MONEY

Not "a bank." The bank! The most beautiful, wonderful, fantastic, gorgeous, magnificent bank in the whole world! When you stand before the bank and you see it has the gates of gold, like it was the gates of heaven. And when you go inside, everything, everything is gold! Gold spittoons, gold handles, and money, money, money is everywhere. And you know, I know 'cause I saw this when I

was eight years old. I went there with my father. He tried to rob the bank, but they caught him.

(Rod Steiger tells James Coburn about the bank he dreams of robbing: *Duck! You Sucker*).

- What do you suppose they're carrying in that coach?
- It would be easy to find out. Get up close to it and take a good look at what's in it, if they fire at you, you know it's gold:

(Clint Eastwood and José Calvo: *For a Fistful of Dollars*).

I don't want to be a hero! All I want is the money! The money!

(Rod Steiger, hero by accident, complains about his new situation with his pal James Coburn: *Duck! You Sucker*).

- How does it feel sitting behind that desk, Frank?
- It's almost like holding a gun.

(The rich businessman Gabriele Ferzetti and the gunman Henry Fonda at his desk: *Once Upon a Time in the West*).

SONS OF A BITCH

- The reward for this man is 5,000 dollars, is that right?
- Judas was content with 4,970 dollars less.
- There weren't no dollars in them days
- But sons of bitches...yeah.

(The avenger Charles Bronson to his prey Jason Robards: *Once Upon a Time in the West*).

Hey, Blond! You know what you are? Just a dirty son-of-a-b-!

(Eli Wallach shouts, with a rope around his neck, to Clint Eastwood: at the end of *The Good, the Bad and the Ugly*).

ENDANGERED SPECIES

- I've met all kinds in my life. Thieves and killers. Pimps and prostitutes. Con men and preachers. Even a few fellas that told the truth. The kind of man you're talking about, never.
- Maybe you've never met them. Or hardly ever. But they're the only ones who count.

(Henry Fonda to Terence Hill: *My Name is Nobody*).

- So, you found out you're not a businessman after all.
- Just a man.

- An ancient race. Other Mortons will be along, and they'll kill it off.
(The good avenger Charles Bronson and the bad one Henry Fonda meet for the last time after Morton's [Gabriele Ferzetti] death: *Once Upon a Time in the West*).

You don't understand, Jill. People like that have something inside... something to do with death.
(Jason Robards to Claudia Cardinale on Charles Bronson: *Once Upon a Time in the West*).

Yeah, the same fellow you want to see written up in history books, 'cause people need something to believe in, like you say.
(Henry Fonda to Terence Hill: *My name is Nobody*).

NEW MEN
So, you're a guy who follows success, you want people to see you.
(The old gunslinger Henry Fonda to the man of today, Terence Hill: *My Name is Nobody*).

- There's proof!
- Frank's speciality has always been to fabricate proof.
(Man in the laundry, Marco Zuanelli, being grilled by Charles Bronson: *Once Upon a Time in the West*).

Where there's revolution there's confusion, and when there's confusion, a man who knows what he wants stands a good chance of getting it.
(James Coburn to Rod Steiger: *Duck! You Sucker*).

See, there's a whole difference between you and me: I always try to steer away from trouble, while you seem to be looking for it all the time. But I must admit, you've been able to solve your share, even if you like others to take the credit. This way, you can remain a "nobody." You got it all nicely figured out. But you gambled too big this time, and there's too many people who know you're "somebody" after all. And you won't have much time left for playing your funny games. They'll make life harder and harder for you, until you too will meet somebody who wants to put you down in history. And so you'll find out that the only way to become a nobody again is to die.
(From Henry Fonda's last letter to Terence Hill: *My Name is Nobody*).

TRUST
How can you trust a man that wears both a belt and suspenders? Man can't even trust his own pants.
(The killer Henry Fonda speaks to his boss Gabriele Ferzetti about his underling Marco Zuanelli: *Once Upon a Time in the West*).

ADULT GAMES
- I didn't hear what the bet was.
- Your life.
(José Marco and Clint Eastwood, after a game of Poker: *A Fistful of Dollars*).

- Ma'm it seems to me you ain't caught the idea.
- Of course I have: I'm here alone in the hands of a bandit who smelled money. If you want to, you can lay me over the table and amuse yourself, and even call in your men. Well, no woman ever died from that. When you're finished, all I'll need will be a tub of boiling water and I'll be exactly what I was before - with just another filthy memory!
- You make good coffee, at least?
(Jason Robards and Claudia Cardinale make friends: *Once Upon a Time in the West*).

DESIRE
You like being alive...you also like to feel a man's hands all over you, you like it even if they're the hands that killed your husband.
(Henry Fonda to Claudia Cardinale: *Once Upon a Time in the West*).

But we can pray here too. Here or in the Synagogue, for the Lord it's the same. Come here and sit down. *My beloved is white and ruddy. His skin is as the most fine gold. His cheeks are a bed of spices.* Even though he hasn't washed since last December. *His eyes are the eyes of doves. His body is bright ivory. His legs are pillars of marble.* In pants so dirty they stand by themselves. *He is altogether lovable.* But he'll always be a two-bit punk so he'll never be my beloved. What a shame. *(They kiss)*
(Jennifer Connelly [young Deborah] reads to the young Scott Tiler [Noodles] a short piece from the *Song of Songs* with some personal insertions: *Once Upon a Time in America*).

Mothers

A Fistful of Dollars.

For a Few Dollars More.

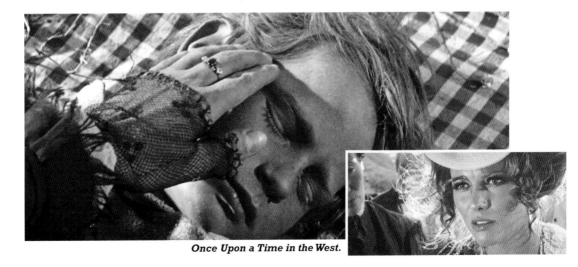

Once Upon a Time in the West.

The Colossus of Rodhes.

Once Upon a Time in America.

Once Upon a Time in America.

Duck! You Sucker.

Once Upon a Time in America.

Once Upon a Time in America.

Once Upon a Time in America.

The Good, the Bad and the Ugly.

My Name is Nobody.

Once Upon a Time in America.

Once Upon a Time in America.

Once Upon a Time in America.

Once Upon a Time in the West.

Duck! You Sucker.

Once Upon a Time in America.

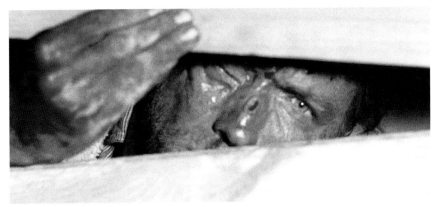

A Fistful of Dollars.

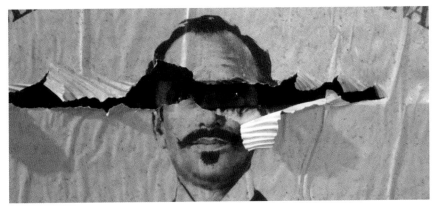

Duck! You Sucker.

Once Upon a Time in America.

199

Profiles

A Fistful of Dollars.

My Name is Nobody.

For a Few Dollars More.

Duck! You Sucker.

Once Upon a Time in the West.

Once Upon a Time in the West.

Once Upon a Time in America.

For a Few Dollars More.

Faces

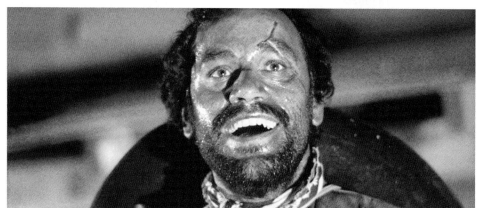

A Fistful of Dollars.

*For a Few
Dollars More.*

The Good, the Bad and the Ugly.

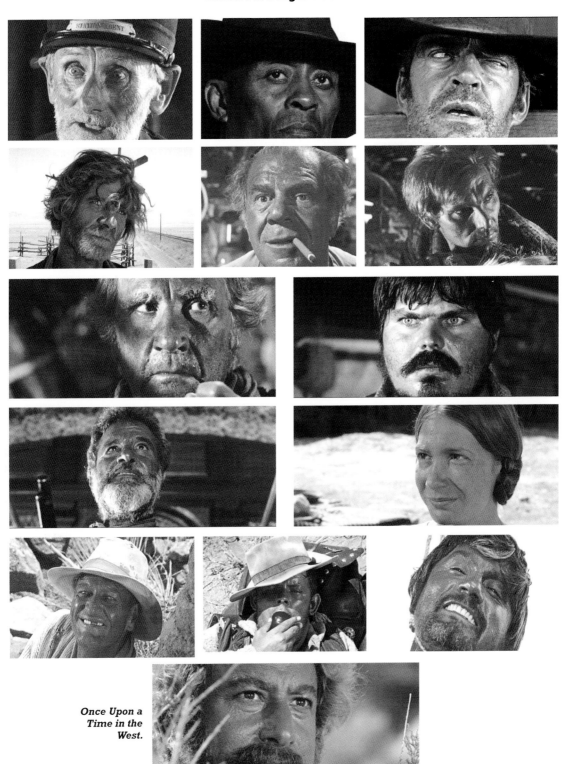

*Once Upon a
Time in the
West.*

205

Duck! You Sucker.

206

My Name is Nobody.

Once Upon a Time in America.

Can't imagine how happy it makes a man to see a woman like you, just to look at her. And if one of them should, uh, pat your behind, just make believe it's nothing. They earned it.
(Jason Robards to Claudia Cardinale: *Once Upon a Time in the West*).

WAITING

- You been waiting for me?
- For a long time
(Henry Fonda and Charles Bronson in the final shootout: *Once Upon a Time in the West*).

- Did you wait for a long time?
- For all my life.
(The grown up Elizabeth McGovern and Robert De Niro on their first date: *Once Upon a Time in America*).

STOLEN LIVES

I took away your whole life from you. I've been living in your place. I took everything. I took your money, I took your girl. All I left for you was 35 years of grief over having killed me. Now why don't you shoot?
(Gangster James Woods, now a congressman, asks for a final favor to the friend he betrayed, Robert De Niro: *Once Upon a Time in America*).

AIMING AT THE HEART

Two things go straight to a man's heart, bullets and gold.
(The leader of the Wild Bunch to the rich Jean Martin: *My Name is Nobody*).

You shoot to kill, you better hit the heart. Your own words, Ramon. The heart, Ramon. Don't forget the heart. Aim for the heart, or you'll never stop me.
(Clint Eastwood to Gian Maria Volonté: *A Fistful of Dollars*).

Hey, Harmonica, when they do you in, pray it's somebody who knows where to shoot.
(The dying Jason Robards to Charles Bronson: *Once Upon a Time in the West*).

WORDS AND MORE WORDS

Instead of talking, he plays. And when he better play, he talks.

(Jason Robards on Charles Bronson "Harmonica": *Once Upon a Time in the West*).

When you have to shoot, shoot. Don't talk.
(Eli Wallach after he shot the killer Al Mulock, from the bathtub: *The Good, the Bad and the Ugly*).

The first thing I learnt working with you is to listen as though I couldn't see and speak as though I couldn't hear.
(Marco Zuanelli to professional killer Henry Fonda: *Once Upon a Time in the West*).

MEN OF FEW WORDS

I get dressed, I kill him and be right back.
(The "ugly" Eli Wallach to the "good" Clint Eastwood on the "bad" Lee Van Cleef: *The Good, the Bad and the Ugly*).

Put your drawers on, and take your gun off.
(Clint Eastwood to Eli Wallach, who's been caught naked with his gun in one hand: *The Good, the Bad and the Ugly*).

IDEAS

- A revolution? Seems to me revolutions are all over the world. You know, they're like the crabs! We had a revolution here. When it started, all the brave people went in it, and what it did to them was terrible. Pancho Villa, the best bandit chief in the world, you know that? This man had two balls like a bull. He went in the revolution as a great bandit. When he came out, he came out as what? Nothing. A general, huh? That, to me, is bullshit! You've come here to join the Revolution?
- No. No, one was enough for me.
(The Mexican Rod Steiger to IRA bomber, James Coburn: *Duck! You Sucker*).

When I started using dynamite I believed in many things, all of it! Now, I believe only in dynamite.
(The rebel bomber James Coburn to his mate Romolo Valli: *Duck! You Sucker*).

LOST INNOCENCE

When I was a child I used to gather flowers, too...
(Lea Massari, dying, to Rory Calhoun: *The Colossus of Rhodes*).

THE GOOD OLD DAYS

- Four shots - one hole. Just like the good old days.
- There was never any "good old days".

(Terence Hill and Henry Fonda: *My Name is Nobody*).

But you can still do one thing: you can preserve a little of that illusion that made my generation tick. Maybe you'll do it in your own funny way, but you'll be grateful just the same. I guess looking back, it seems we were all a bunch of romantic fools. We still believed that a good pistol and a quick showdown could solve everything. But then, the West used to be wide-open spaces with lots of elbow room, and you never ran into the same person twice.

(From the old gunman Henry Fonda's final letter to the young copycat Terence Hill: *My Name is Nobody*).

THE MEANING OF LIFE

Life's stranger than shit. It's crap, it's not worth it.

(Boss Burt Young to James Woods, Robert De Niro and Joe Pesci: *Once Upon a Time in America*).

THE END OF REVOLUTIONS

A revolution? "Little revolution"? Please, don't try to tell me about revolution! I know all about revolutions and how they start! The people that read the books, they go to the people that don't read the books, and say "Ho-ho! The time has come to have a change, eh?" So, the poor people make the change, ah? And then, the people who read the books, they all sit around the big polished tables, and they talk and talk and talk and eat and eat and eat, eh? But what has happened to the poor people? THEY ARE DEAD! That's your revolution! Sh... so, please... don't tell me about revolutions. And what happens afterwards? The same fucking thing starts all over again!

(The accidental revolutionary, Rod Steiger, to the revolution expert, James Coburn: *Duck! You Sucker*).

LAST WORDS

Oh! my friend, I just gave you a royal screw-up!

(Revolutionary James Coburn, dying, to peone/bandit Rod Steiger: *Duck! You Sucker*).

You see? I wanted so many things, and I die having had nothing.

(Lea Massari, dying, to Rory Calhoun: *The Colossus of Rhodes*).

Go away, I don't want you to see me die.

(Jason Robards to Charles Bronson at the end of *Once Upon a Time in the West*).

BOWING OUT

You just need a special act, something that'll make your name a legend.

(Terence Hill to Henry Fonda who told him «You're sure trying hard to make a hero out of me»: *My Name is Nobody*).

Now I gotta go

(Charles Bronson to Claudia Cardinale before bowing out: *Once upon a Time in the West*).

At times, it's harder to stop than to begin.

(Henry Fonda to Terence Hill: *My Name is Nobody*).

Thanks to ... Age & Scarpelli, Franco Arcalli, Dario Argento, Leonardo Benvenuti, Bernardo Bertolucci, Victor A. Catena, Luciano Chitarrini, Piero De Bernardi, Ennio De Concini, Roberto De Leonardis, Sergio Donati, Franco Ferrini, Ernesto Gastaldi, Carlo Gualtieri, Sergio Leone, Luciano Martino, Enrico Medioli, Fulvio Morsella, Aggeo Savioli, Cesare Seccia, G. Schock, Duccio Tessari, Carlo Tritto, Luciano Vincenzoni.

Part Three
MATERIALS

Building a town (and civilization): *Once Upon a Time in the West.*

1. Documents

1a. Western and Melodrama
by Giuseppe Rausa (1984)

Dramatic moments in Leone's two *Once Upon a Time...* films.

The musical scores composed by Ennio Morricone are of penetrating intensity, deliberately exaggerated, constantly in search of patent effects, whether the music is expressing drama, sentiment or mockery, and is in other words totally in keeping with the author's work and its relentlessly pursued intention to reduce every element of the cinematic game to its essence, to abstract stylization. This is true of the way in which characters are designed, in the "compositions" and in the calculated assembly of the episodes of the story. The tendency to use hyperbole is therefore one of the first elements that unite the work of director and composer and indicates the possible link with the other universe which made the hyperbole its core, namely melodrama.

Protagonists Supreme

They are out and out characters every one, the unchallenged gurus of the scene, each with its own precise and unwavering stance. They vary little from film to film and continually reinstate the traditional conflict between good and evil, though with nuanced differences between the first style (Dollars trilogy) and the second (the two ensemble films).

[...] The symbolism, especially in the earlier style, tends to turn everything into a blatant, obvious game, conducted with solemn intonations and in which the predictability of the plot development (similar to the predictability of operatic scenarios) does nothing to hinder our enjoyment.

The conventional, unchanging nature of these characters, together with their protagonism, their domination of the scene, reflects the traditions of Italian melodrama, the importance of three or four figures who impersonate specific character types (the virtuous tenor, in love with the soprano and in conflict with the evil baritone or bass).

The settings in which these characters perform are only loosely defined, a stage that seems to deny the noble deeds of the heroes, a framework of little interest, the importance and quality of which, however, increases from the first to the fifth film, reflecting a tendency to progress from the abstract individualistic Western to the more realistic ensemble films.

Another aspect of the musical theater is the way in which the appearance on the scene of the protagonists is spread over different, successive episodes: each protagonist is introduced in a brief opening chapter that is meant to portray from the outset the relative character type (the equivalent of the opening aria or presentation of each singer in the melodrama). In

Once Upon a Time in the West, in many ways Leone's film-*summa*, the sound track defines each person with a short, incisive motif that will accompany them every time they appear in a scene, a technique typical of melodrama […] A classic illustration of this are Verdi's "recognition themes" as they appear, for example, in *Aida*, where specific motifs remind us of specific characters in the drama. In this same way, Morricone composes for Harmonica a tormented melody full of potential that is brought to a climax in the conclusive flashback; for Cheyenne a teasing tune; for Jill McBain a more complex lyrical refrain that also celebrates the choral, ultimately quintessential, element of the film.

NARRATIVE CONSTRUCTION

The structures with which the stories and their rhythm are organized are both extremely musical and theatrical, and are built into a series of blocks of totally independent sequences, differing in length, each with its own perfectly orchestrated inner symmetry; we might liken them to a series of pictures. Each time, Leone starts with an apparently cool, calm and relaxing situation, then he slowly builds up moments of increasing tension that culminate in a veritable decisive climax (almost always a duel).

The episodes in which the various characters are introduced are good examples of this. These are followed by other segments in which the protagonists are combined in twosomes and threesomes, according to the aforesaid approach. The final pictures are exemplary, where the hostilities are at last resolved in magniloquent, ritualistic duels. The aggressively Baroque soundtrack serves, as in many long-drawn-out climaxes, to cement the various images that follow one another freely and unexpectedly, in a sort of alienating visual delirium that brings long shots and extreme close ups together. It is a moment in which the elapsing of time is suspended in a sort of visual-musical "convergence" where the all-absorbing, all-encompassing sound allows for unreserved creativity in the "composing" of sequences marked by the prospect of the imminent cathartic event. In other words, an arrangement free of narrative and of the need to depict the actions in a specific, established order. (A perfect example is the splendid carillon tune at the end of *For a Few Dollars More*: the suspension of time is achieved through a hypnotically repetitive motif made up of just a handful of notes).

As in melodrama, the conclusions of these pictures are suspended, thanks to a spreading out of the action, substantiated by continual delays in the unravelling of the plot. The more straightforward narrative parts occur at the beginning of each picture (the players who follow through the action in a melodrama) thus permitting the inclusion of purely "lyrical", unconnected segments (the arias or concerted scenes), in which the rituality of the action becomes slow and frustrating, carefully devised in every detail […].

The use of dialogue is original: succinct, often unexpected, pithy, using words and phrases that recur slightly modified on many occasions, "variations on a theme" (verbal) that lay down a connective tissue for the various elements and assume an emblematic significance, similar to what happens in melodrama where certain key phrases, reiterated at different times during the action, represent a sort of manifesto of the entire work (for instance Verdi's *Ernani*, *Othello* and *Falstaff*, but also Wagner's *Lohengrin*). So the dialogue is an integral part of the sound track the purpose of which is to accentuate the manifestly illusory and stylized elements of this cinematic universe, elements that are fundamental in establishing or increasing the tension within the verbal duels or, put more simply, in the unreservedly musical drift of the many duos.

FROM THE INDIVIDUAL TO THE CHORAL STANDPOINT

Both models (from the Dollars trilogy to the choral films) derive from the musical theater tradition. While the former with its playful mocking spirit harks back to Rossini, the latter is undoubtedly more reminiscent of the imposing melodramatic tradition of Verdi.

Morricone's soundtracks develop accordingly: taunting for the earlier Westerns, based on a combination of traditional instruments and specific sound effects (whistles, gun shots, mouth harp, mutterings, carillon, bells), in other words a distinct style of music that has left its mark (interestingly, one of the rare examples of "concrete" music in 19th century melodrama is precisely the overture of Rossini's *Signor Bruschino*). The second style is lyrical and mournful, almost totally void of those special sound effects and the irony, which is merely hinted at, in favor of long melodies of epic proportions relying on female voices evoking agonizing pain and coveted reconciliation. In particular, in *Once Upon a Time in the West* the fusion of the two narrative levels occurs at a musical level too, as the individual themes defining each character intermingle with the choral themes.

[Giuseppe Rausa, *Reciprocal relationships between* the Western *and melodrama in Sergio Leone*, "Segnocinema", May-June 1984]

1b. The Film Leone Didn't Want to Make
by Oreste De Fornari (2008)

The hanging was the best show in town. But they made two mistakes. They hung the wrong man and they didn't finish the job.

CLINT EASTWOOD "HANG 'EM HIGH"

INGER STEVENS · ED BEGLEY · PAT HINGLE as Judge Fenton

I could not resist – for a number of reasons – including this article on Hang 'Em High, *directed by Ted Post, that I wrote for "Cinema e Generi 2008", a magazine edited by film critic Renato Venturelli. The film, the direction of which Clint Eastwood had first proposed to Leone, was, despite the presence of Eastwood himself, far from the spirit of Italian Westerns and thus an interesting subject for comparison. It was not particularly well received by critics in Italy and elsewhere, neither at the time nor later. I have always liked the film. Already in 1968 it topped my list of best films of the year (jointly with Pasolini's* Che Cosa Sono le Nuvole? (What Are Clouds?) *which I compiled for issue number 7-8 of "Cinema e Film". In 1968, there were, of course, many more important films released, but a taste for stirring things up was part of the mischievous spirit of film buffs of that period. I hope this article will convince modern film buffs to take another look at this unfortunate film. [o.d.f.]*

Assuming there are still underrated films, and especially underrated Westerns, then Ted Post's *Hang 'Em High* (1968) is certainly one of them.

It was Clint Eastwood's first film after his return home from Italy, and it is often referred to as an example of the negative influence that Spaghetti Westerns were beginning to have on American productions. More likely, the opposite is true. Ted Post's film shows that American Westerns were already able to deal with European influences.

Let's bear in mind that one of the recurring themes of Italian Westerns is revenge, while one of the cardinal values of the American Western is legality. In this film, the two principles are conflicting.

This is the story. An innocent man survives a lynching after being wrongly accused of stealing a herd of cattle and killing the owner. He vows revenge, but a judge hires him as a U.S. Marshal and warns him not to kill the men who lynched him, but to arrest them and he will see that justice is done.

If, in other Westerns (such as *My Darling Clementine*) where the avenger becomes a sheriff and his personal goal concurs with the law's duty to restore legality, here it is different. The hero's right to revenge is taken away and his hero's status is thus undermined. As sheriff, he must behave like an officer of the law and has no other say in the matter; he cannot even save from the gallows the two teenage rustlers he has arrested. Justice becomes the dominion of the State, a dominion it promotes with a certain ambiguity and an impressive sense of bravado, as shown in the scene of the collective hanging, accompanied by religious singing and with the whole town looking on in morbid wonder. This is the best scene, where the American Western's sense of civil duty stands out.

The following, more conventional part, resolves the act of revenge. The sheriff surrounds the ranch where the rustlers have taken refuge and their leader hangs himself to avoid capture. Not a very satisfactory ending for the avenger. It seems we are a long way from Leone.

The film's originality lies in its "undermined" hero and for its depiction of capital punishment. The judge considers the punishment necessary in order to show people that they must not take justice into their own hands by hanging the rustlers. But the message we get from the film is more complex: neither approval nor indignation, but rather frustration, disillusionment, confusion. Rarely before in a Western had the power of the law been so cold-heartedly and rationally portrayed.

Apart from the presence of Clint Eastwood, shades of the Italian Western are evident in the highlighted violence of some scenes and a certain visual negligence (excessive zooming). There are also Gothic undertones in the music score (which at times seems to evoke the opening of the gallows' trap door), in the set design (the vehicle carrying the prisoners) and even the mournful, lacklustre love story between the sheriff and the widow.

All things considered, this does not make for a masterpiece, nor does it reveal a particular directorial talent. Besides, Ted Post worked mostly for television and only rarely for the cinema. There is little that can be said for his later films that were released in Italy after *Hang 'Em High*. The worst is probably *The Baby*, an erotic horror film about a mentally impaired adult man who is kept in a cot by his mother and sisters. The best is *Go Tell the Spartans* starring Burt Lancaster, a bitter story about Vietnam, but not quite apocalyptic enough to rival Coppola, Cimino and Oliver Stone, who had films released at about the same time. Today, Ted Post is about to celebrate his ninetieth birthday, if he's still with us.

P.S. Ted Post died at the age of 95, on 20 August 2013.

1c. The Hollywood Squadron
by Diego Gabutti (2018)[66]

He did not read comic books. But someone must have told him about *The Black Order Brigade*, a graphic novel by Pierre Christin and Enki Bilal. He asked me to read it and tell me what I thought of it. I had already read it and liked it. It was the story of a group of old-timers from different nations, now in their sixties and seventies, who, some forty years earlier, during the Spanish Civil War, had fought for the Republic in the ranks of the International Brigades. They discover that an old enemy, whom they believed dead or at least out of the picture, is instead alive and kicking and had, during the late seventies, been murdering people in Spain, and they decide to settle things once and for all.

---

[66] Diego Gabutti wrote many books, among which *C'era una Volta in America. Un'avventura al saloon con Sergio Leone* (Milieu, Milano, 2015).

Materials

It was 1984 or 1985. *Once Upon a Time in America* had just been released and the conservative critics, who had never really taken Leone seriously and had snubbed him for years, were still recovering from the shock of his amazing feat (some twenty years earlier, in 1968, *Once Upon a Time in the West* had been something even more prodigious, but the critics had failed to see this at the time, absorbed as they were by the short-lived *cinema engagé* of the Sixties).

While they continued to discuss his *Leningrad*[67] film project, inspired by Harrison E. Salisbury's historical narrative *The 900 Days,* Leone was searching for "stories". He was not looking for stories to make into films, but rather stories to talk about with friends over dinner, or in his garden at the family villa in the EUR neighborhood of Rome. Like Bilal's *Black Order,* the stories were sombre, always a bit *trompe-l'oeil,* something difficult and bizarre that no one had ever attempted before. I imagine all directors, when they are not actually working, conjure up strange ideas that will never reach fruition and Leone was no exception. He day-dreamed of films he would never make. By talking about them, he kept himself on the ball.

He envisaged a New York version of *Filumena Marturano* with Robert De Niro in the role of Domenico Soriano (because he wanted to work with De Niro again, whom he had appreciated on the set of *Once Upon a Time in America,* rather than any true admiration for Eduardo's tear-jerking

melodramas. Though he did give Eduardo credit for having built his artistic persona on strong characters). For a while, he toyed with the idea of Malraux's *Man's Fate*; if I remember correctly, he spoke of it sometimes in interviews, only to bin "the project" once and for all, when someone asked him how it was going, with a curt one-liner: "Can't be done...the Chinese all look the same". He also weighed up the possibility of a film on the *Nun of Monza* with Meryl Streep starring as Marianna de Leyva (he claimed the film was to be particularly brutal, but he spoke of it with a chuckle). Another idea was a less maudlin, indeed positively gruesome, remake of *Gone with the Wind*. He used to mime scenes and was especially captivated by the fire in Atlanta, in which the parabola of all Hollywood's films on the American Civil War would be consumed once and for all in the flames (a kind of *Man's Fate* without all those pigeon-holed Chinese faces). He also considered adapting for the screen Céline's *Journey to the End of the Night*, a rather daunting venture: to give substance to (and create images for) the narrator's voice in *Journey,* and to the author's extensive use of ellipsis and hyperbole would have been no mean task. He was offered one million dollars per episode to front a Western series for television about the journey of a Colt from one owner to another, from the sheriff, to a bank robber, to Tom Mix, during various eras of the Wild West. He discussed the project every now and then, but ditched it in the end, or at least stopped talking about it because, he claimed, he did not wish to put his name to projects he was not going to direct (he knew he would not be able to resist the temptation to have a hand in things and this would have taken up valuable time). It seems that the series is once again on the agenda, though Leone will not, I imagine, have much to do with it. *Colt* is another of his pipe dreams, to chat about over a cup of coffee. I could be wrong, but I think *Leningrad* was one of the projects Leone was especially happy to speak about, but never really wanted to make. Over the years, there have been other directors, such as Giuseppe Tornatore, who have contemplated "taking the baton", and so once in a while the project receives media

---

[67] See his *Leningrado*, published by Sellerio, Palermo 2018.

attention again. Behind every one of these imagined or imaginary films, there was a reason why he nurtured the idea: an actor's gaze, a spot-on snippet of dialogue, a perfect silence, a special shot, something epic in the mood of the story. Blockbuster status was the reason behind *The Black Order Brigade*. He planned to bring to the screen a Brigade of former stars of classical cinema and lead them "once more into the breach", like the charge of the Light Brigade or the battle of Little Big Horn; for these old, some positively decrepit, legends, this was to be their last hurrah. *Once Upon a Time in Hollywood*: this was the idea. Not another *Duck, You Sucker!* with the Spanish Revolution in place of the Irish and Mexican Revolutions. Henry Fonda, whose image had been transfigured by Leone in *Once Upon a Time in the West*, had already been dead two years. But Leone intended to persuade the big names who were still alive. All of them, that is, except Clint Eastwood who, at the time, was doing all in his power, heaven knows why, to forget what he considered one of the big mistakes of his youth: the Dollars Trilogy.

Former Hollywood (and not only Hollywood) old-timers were to fill the ranks of his International Brigade, idols who had shaped the history of cinema over past decades. Alain Delon, Paul Newman, Burt Lancaster, Giuliano Gemma, Vittorio Gassman, Lino Ventura, Charles Bronson, James Coburn, Sidney Poitier, Rod Steiger, Sean Connery, Walter Matthau, Robert De Niro, Mickey Rooney. Name a star or former star and Leone would have found a part for them in his film. There was room for everyone, for the big names and the nickel-and-dimes, because cinema is democratic (or at least Warholian, so there's fifteen minutes of fame for everyone). William Burroughs, in his novels of the sixties, sometimes mentions the Shakespeare Squadron, by which he meant the writers and poets of all time, from Dante to Rimbaud, to Dashiell Hammett and A.E. van Vogt, whose task it was to write a good part for each of us. Leone, just as much, if not more a promoter of the avant-garde, would have pitted his "Hollywood Squadron" of ancient warriors (and antediluvian gadgets) against a formidable enemy: Oblivion, which in the end extinguishes everything, even the best of films, the most beautiful and talented of actresses, the toughest and most handsome of actors and even the most brilliant of directors.

It would have been, like all his other films, a general summary of the history of the cinema, but more explicit than usual. Years later, and on a smaller scale, Sylvester Stallone attempted a similar feat with *The Expendables* franchise, three episodes of which have been released to date, with a fourth (and hopefully last) on the agenda. Stallone, who is nowhere near on the same level, joked about old-timers starring in action films: Bruce Willis, Jean-Claude van Damme, Jet Li, Arnold Schwarznegger, Dolph Lundgren, Antonio Banderas, Mel Gibson, Mickey Rourke, Stallone himself. Leone, even though he enjoyed a joke, would have done things seriously, unlike Stallone.

Mind you, to make a film with stars and about stars, as films were made or even envisaged by the director of *For a Fistful of Dollars*, would be impossible today. Not only because of the cost, but also because the charismatic actors of yesteryear, with their marble-like features and rough and ready charm, faded into obscurity before the anonymous realism of the lacklustre actors of most modern TV serials. Leone, and the actors and directors (and also the audiences) of his generation cared little that the film was "real". It was a film, at best a parable, at worst show business. In film and television today, everything must seem "real", from action movies to sci-fi fantasies. I very much doubt that Leone, who was at the same time an avant-garde and an old-school director, would feel at home in this new Hollywood-style universe, which is becoming less and less big screen and more and more iPhone. He would have turned his nose up at the restrained and sober directorial trends of today (and that which remains of the blockbuster films of the past, whose place has now been taken by the so-called disaster movies, almost always set in Manhattan with masked superheroes wearing underpants over their body stocking who only open their mouths if it is to utter some highfalutin homily). But he would certainly have approved of the straightforward realism of the best television series, especially the noir genre.

In later years (*Once Upon a Time in America* was in this sense a declaration of intent) his interest turned almost exclusively to stories concerning disreputable characters. Assassins, rapists, bad guys in general. He contemplated films about the bad and the ugly, where there was no place for the good.

He would never again have forced his nameless heroes to defend innocent mothers or romantic whores from the lustful cravings of Henry Fonda and Gian Maria Volonté, among the most lacklustre of bad guys by today's standards, above and beyond good and evil. He no longer believed, if he had ever believed, in the saintly causes espoused by bombers and bounty killers. Perhaps Leone, like Clint Eastwood, but for opposite reasons, wanted to write off one of the errors of his youth, which was the same as Eastwood's: the far too temperate Dollars Trilogy. Never satisfied, like all radical artists, he continued to dream of drawing whiskers on the Mona Lisa.

1d. Once Upon a Time in America, in the West... in Cannes
by Franco Ferrini (2013)[68]

Robert De Niro's Last Smile

Since I am one of the scriptwriters of *Once Upon a Time in America*, I have often been asked by a variety of different people what De Niro/Noodle's smile at the end of the film means. To answer this, I must go and get the screenplay, a hefty volume with red binding and a golden-lettered title reading *Once Upon a Time in America*, all on the same line. On the last page it reads:

SCENE 151
OPPIUM DEN 1933 – Indoors sunset

....he is greeted by the old Chinese woman. A moment later Noodles is lying on the mattress puffing on a long pipe. He holds the smoke for several seconds before exhaling it in dense, blueish spirals that rise to the ceiling. A pungent, beneficial, purifying smoke that obliterates memories, conflicts, errors and time.

That is how the screenplay ends, not one word less, not one word more. So, of the Jewish gangster version Mona Lisa smile emerging from the opium fumes, there is no trace in the script. But it's there in the film. And not at just any moment, but in the very last shot, the absolute end, set to remain in the eyes and minds of the spectator leaving the cinema and for a long time after. What does it mean?
First of all let's take a step backwards, because the final shot was filmed on the same day, at the end of the day, as the filming of the first scene, which similarly takes place in the opium den, set up at the Teatro della Cometa in Rome. I know. I was there.

---

[68] Chapters from Franco Ferrini's *C'era una Volta il Cinema* [Once Upon a Time in the Cinema] (Gremese, Rome 2013), reviewed, for the purpose of this book, by the author himself.

SCENE 6
OPIUM DEN ABOVE THE CHINESE THEATRE – Indoors night

(….) Noodles automatically accepts the pipe placed in his hand by the Chinese woman, and takes a deep puff. He stares into the distance with glassy eyes while fumbling for something nearby: a discarded newspaper with a large headline reading: *Bootleggers trapped by feds. Three slain.* And below the headline: "An anonymous tip off has enabled the police…", and below that photos of the three youths killed (….). The scene is interrupted by a sudden, loud sound….

….THE MONOTONE RING OF A TELEPHONE ANNOUNCING AN INCOMING CALL

Noodles, as though hearing it, rouses from his torpor, jerks to a sitting position clearly alarmed.

Lights, Camera, Action!
De Niro is lying on the mattress, pipe in hand, while the other fumbles for the newspaper. The telephone rings, but they are not real rings, an assistant director imitates them with his voice, standing right behind De Niro, so that the sound comes from some invisible point to the rear of the room, catching him by surprise, even though he knows it is hanging in the air. Stop. Let's do another one. Leone always does another one. It's his nickname "Let's do another one". De Niro, however, disagrees. He's got a problem. They have to call an interpreter. The three of them have a chat on the side: Leone, De Niro and Brian, the Irish interpreter. Normally, it is not easy to get a word out of De Niro. Most of the time he expresses himself in monosyllables: yep and nope, just like Gary Cooper in his heyday. On this occasion, however, he becomes extremely loquacious. Okay to repeat the previous shot, okay, sure, but this time, instead of the assistant imitating the ring with his voice he wants something else, anything else, as long as it's different. The voice trick is old hat, he knows it, and waits for it. There would be no surprise. Whereas you don't expect a telephone to ring before it rings, it just rings, that's all. Leone agrees, and calls his chief assistants in order to discuss a solution. De Niro leaves. He wants to be kept in the dark. To improvise. Only in this way can he be real, credible, and authentic. Give someone an electric shock: the first time they don't know what's going to happen, but by the second they'll be waiting for it and the effect will be less powerful. The confab is quickly settled. What's the answer? Italian genius is all you need. De Niro returns, ready to shoot. He's already achieved one effect. The atmosphere is tense. You could cut it with a knife.

Noodles stares into the distance with glassy eyes while fumbling for something nearby, a discarded newspaper with a large headline. The scene is interrupted by a sudden, loud sound…

….the noise of a hammer blow made by a prop man, obviously standing behind De Niro, who is indeed taken by surprise, just as he wanted. BANG!!! Noodles jerks to a sitting position on the mattress, appropriately startled. The Chinaman gives him a friendly reassuring pat on the shoulder to calm him down, and gently encourages him to lie down again, while the prop man continues his hammering, at regular intervals, indicating that the "telephone" is still ringing, even if it is only in Noodle's befuddled mind. Great! The new trick has worked perfectly. Let's do another one. Leone shoots the same scene twelve, sixteen times in a row. He is a perfectionist. He and De Niro are definitely on the same wavelength. And so the scene that everyone now knows by heart is filmed again and again, and then yet again, each time with a different "sound".

Noodles stares into the distance with glassy eyes while fumbling for something nearby, a discarded newspaper….a sudden, loud sound…

…the clapperboard slamming shut, a chain striking a hard object, a loud whistle, etc.

Materials

De Niro acts like he is a man condemned to death, standing on the gallows, the classical black blindfold over his eyes, or hooded like the executioner, his collar bare, waiting for the axe to fall. Every time, brutally aroused by a new trick, the miracle occurs:

Noodles rouses from his torpor, jerks to a sitting position on the bed.

The crew is amazed. But wouldn't it be easier just to act? Sordi, Mastroianni, Gassman, Manfredi and Tognazzi never needed all this business.

Finally, it's time to shoot the last scenes of the film, back in the opium den:

SCENE 150
CHINESE THEATRE 1933 – Indoors sunset

Noodles climbs the steep staircase at the back of the room leading to the opium den, to the accompaniment of the soporifically rhythmic music of the gamelan. A few silent spectators are seated in front of the white curtain on which appear the elegant shadow figures of Rama and Ravana, good and evil engaged in their stylized war…

SCENE 151
OPIUM DEN 1933 – Indoors sunset

…he is greeted by the old Chinese woman.
A moment later Noodles is lying on the mattress, puffing on a long pipe.

Between one shoot and another, during the pause, one of the crew quips:
«Thank goodness there are no telephones this time. Otherwise we'd be here all night.» Chuckles. De Niro, feeling left out, asks the interpreter: «What did he say?» Brian translates. De Niro smiles. Leone sees it. No one knows whose idea it was, the only thing we know for sure is that we saw Leone and De Niro chatting away on the side, as usual with the help of the interpreter, in all probability to decide De Niro's expression in the film's final shot. Then, at the end of his private confab with De Niro, Leone ordered that the movie camera be mounted on a drill press, so as to capture De Niro's face in a close up zooming slowly in through the flimsy net covering on the bed.

Lights, Camera, Action!
Noodles….

….he holds the smoke for several seconds before exhaling it in dense, blueish spirals that rise to the ceiling. And he smiles.

But there are problems with this shot. The first to realize something is wrong, is Claudio Mancini, the executive producer of *Once Upon a Time in America* and a close friend of Leone's. He thinks that De Niro's sad, lonely, final smile is out of place, totally at odds with the rest of the film. If it had been a sentence, it would have been the equivalent of "we were only joking". Everything falls apart. Claudio Mancini, the first to get the message, goes to Leone and poses the million-dollar question: «Is the film subjective or objective?». Leone doesn't understand, or pretends not to understand. Mancini re-phrases the question: De Niro smiles because he's under the effect of the opium, which is for him a balm that sooths his guilt for having caused the death of his friends with his tip-off to the cops, or does he smile because the entire film is *all a dream?* In this last case Noodles is innocent. Nobody got hurt. The tip-off never happened. There is a third possibility. Both ideas are correct. So which of the three? Mancini wanted a clear-cut answer from Leone:
«What do you want? A double, triple interpretation?». Leone thinks a bit, then says: «Everyone can think whatever they like». Later on, during an interview, they asked him the

same question. Is the film subjective or objective? Is it all a dream? Leone replied that it was. But with his finger raised mischievously, half hidden behind his head, he indicated no. His daughter Raffaella, who was present at the time, told me this. So that settles it! Of course, I have my own theory. The real meaning of De Niro's smile is that...no, I'd rather not tell you after all. For the good of the film. The only things people do not forget are unsolved mysteries. Nothing lasts longer.

Robert De Niro Goes to the Bathroom

In *Once Upon a Time in America* Robert De Niro had to play a character who appears in two different ages of his life, the young and the old Noodles. Even though he is quite capable of miraculous physical transformations (for the title role in *Raging Bull* he put on 65 lbs), the idea of having to act made up to look like an old man really worried him. A few years earlier, in *1900*, he played a similar old man part and could not shake off the idea that he had looked ridiculous. A scarecrow with one foot in the grave and a ton of makeup. Luckily, his role in *1900* was very short, but in *Once Upon a Time in America* it was quite a different story. Won't they see that I'm made up? Won't I look ludicrous with wrinkles and a hairpiece?

De Niro was really concerned. In an attempt to allay these fears, and to find an acceptable physical appearance, he patiently endured a countless number of photo shoots (still available today) in which he appeared more or less grey, grizzled and balding, sometimes with a moustache and a couple (just for fun) sporting a *kippah,* the traditional cap worn by Jewish men. So far so good, this is standard practice, but there were those who saw it as an opportunity for some idle chit chat. Even before *Once Upon a Time in America* was released to theatres, Radio Cinema was insinuating that Robert De Niro as an old man looked like Ciriaco De Mita, secretary of the Christian Democrat Party and 47th Prime Minister of Italy, who came from Irpinia (Campania region). By chance, Leone's father, the director Vincenzo Leone, pen name Roberto Roberti, was born in the same area, at Torella dei Lombardi. In the openly cynical and malicious world of cinema, where no one really believes in the reputation of others – especially if they are successful, which in a certain sense is not a bad thing – the opinion, even before release, was that *Once Upon a Time in America* was a rehash of *The Godfather* in kosher sauce and they had nicknamed Leone, Francis Ford *Caccola* (Snotty).

Well, they must have been well and truly miffed when confronted with the dark and endless splendor of the film – not me, but the countless fans of the film saying this – and De Niro's acting, perfect in the role of Noodles, both young and old. Credit is due, of course, to the make-up artists, one of whom was a young hairstylist, Aldo Signoretti. De Niro did not forget him, and brought him to America, thus opening for Aldo the door to a new and successful career, which was to later earn him two Oscars, for *Moulin Rouge* and *Il Divo.*

Going back to De Niro's qualms and misgivings about being made up as an old man, one of the film's scriptwriters, Leo Benvenuti, in an attempt to ease his fears, said: «Don't worry. Play the part of the young Noodles now. You can do the old Noodles later on...in thirty years!». The beauty of it was that De Niro believed him. Or at least it made him think for a moment, the mere idea providing some relief...an instant later he realized, almost with regret, it was just a joke. But this is nothing compared with a similar episode that occurred sometime later in his New York apartment. Apart from us, the Italians, the entire American high command was there, including Cis Corman (*The Deer Hunter, Raging Bull, The Prince of Tides*), a personal friend of De Niro's. As the meeting was about to begin, De Niro turned to his friend and said: "Cis, if anyone calls, you answer and tell them I'm in the bathroom."

Fanatical as always, De Niro wanted to know the shooting schedule well in advance, as the film was particularly complicated and required filming in America, Europe and Canada. Of course, the phone rang.

Cis Corman answered that Bob was in the bathroom. Thus far, nothing out of the ordinary: here's betting every one of us, at some time or another, has pretended to be "out" when the phone rings. But it goes without saying that Robert De Niro's way of being "out" is not the same as ours!...He got up from his chair, where he could have comfortably remained seated while Cis Corman answered the phone as they had agreed, and almost on tiptoe *actually* went off to the bathroom!

Now one might think it was because De Niro couldn't lie, couldn't bear even the most innocent fib, and that consequently he had to turn it into the truth. Cis Corman, who was not so gullible, and knew his man very well, offered a different explanation:

«Take no notice. He's acting. He's an actor, *always*».

We laughed, saying that we'd known all along. After all, we all come from the show biz world.

I do not know if De Niro had ever read that phrase written by the writer and fellow American John Cheever: «The telling of lies is a sort of sleight of hand that displays our deepest feelings about life». But he certainly would have agreed with it.

On the other hand, the Polish sci-fi writer Stanislas Lem could have offered him this advice:

«Do not dramatize your life...they may find a better actor».

To which De Niro would surely have retorted: «I'll dramatize my life as much as I want. Because they'll never find an actor better than me».

That's probably why before leaving the bathroom he flushed the toilet and washed his hands with scented soap.

When he came back, Cis Corman and company duly gave him a round of applause, and he, equally duly, had acknowledged the compliment with a nod and a grin.

At that point, writer and scriptwriter Thomas McGuane, author of *Missouri* and *Atlantic City,* might have reproached him with one of his quotes: «The occupational hazard of making a spectacle of yourself, over the long haul, is that at some point you buy a ticket too».

De Niro's *entre'acte* now over, the meeting resumed. But, shortly after...

Ring-ring ring-ring ring-ring...

Cis Corman again reached for the phone... And De Niro was on his way to the bathroom.

Monument Valley

> *Once having shat*
> *in his new apartment,*
> *he began to feel at home.*
> (W.H. AUDEN, *SHORTS*)

Having doused his senses with valerian to appease his fear of flying, Sergio Leone set off for America to carry out some on-the-spot research for *Once upon a Time in the West.* At last he could shoot in the real Wild West. Where it really happened, instead of going to Spain as he had for the Dollars Trilogy.

Lying on the border between Utah and Arizona is Monument Valley, a mostly flat red-sand desert region, known for the towering sandstone *buttes* or *mesas.* With their reddish colour and flat top, they are a symbol, if not *the* symbol, of the Western.

The Mecca of Western fans, the Scala of horse opera. Who knows how many times he had seen Monument Valley in the Westerns of John Ford when he was a nobody writing screenplays for the mythological films of Ennio De Concini, "my clapperboard guy", was what Mario Soldati had scornfully called him, amazed at the enormous success of *For a Fistful of Dollars.* (The two had bumped into one another now and again, in 1954, on the set of *The River Girl,* directed by Mario Soldati and starring Sophia Loren).

On the lookout for work (clapperboard operator, assistant) Leone used to hang around Cinecittà and other film studios, doing his favourite trick: he would throw open the doors of the editing studio and "fire" at the editors from the doorway with an imaginary Colt, fanning out the shots with his other hand. Then he would shut the door and go and do the same caper at the next studio, fully aware that they would all be laughing behind his back:

"It's Sergio Leone. He's crazy about Westerns. He says sooner or later he's going to make one....an *Italian* one."

Years later, a lifetime later, in Monument Valley, descending the dirt track, Leone felt as though he was in a John Ford cavalry film. More than an inspection, it was a pilgrimage. The day before he had sent his trusted assistant, Claudio Mancini, to the area authorising him – "You're still bright and breezy and you love Westerns" – to personally choose the Monument Valley location.

Claudio Mancini and another Roman had flown there in a small plane, a day before Leone, where they had found two men waiting for them, one dressed as an Indian, the other a cowboy: their guides.

Leone joined them the day after, in a chauffeur-driven car. He had not fancied making the trip in a small plane, the previous flights had been quite enough for him. Awaiting him, on the dusty verge of Highway 163, which cuts the Valley in two, beneath a scorching sun, were Claudio Mancini and the other Roman. There, in the midst of this magic environment, Leone was beside himself with excitement.

At last he had trodden the soil of his dreams, at last he could experience first-hand this majestic and legendary world!

«Hey Serg, it's like being on the moon! We're on the moon!» Claudio Mancini had greeted him with these words, unmistakably enthusiastic over the fantastic locations he had found. «Not even John Ford's been here! What's up? You feel alright? You look pale!»

Pale!... more like ashen! All the excitement... Leone suddenly felt the need. Uncontrollable. He absolutely had to go, but he couldn't go there, in front of everybody (the Indian and the cowboy to boot). A little way off there was an outcrop of rock that made the perfect screen. He nearly didn't make it, but running at the maximum speed possible for a man of his size, he reached the rock and disappeared behind it.

With a super-human effort he managed to hang on for one moment longer, he undid his belt and tore down his trousers and his white pants in a single yank, uncovering his pale and strangely skinny backside, in keeping with his equally skinny legs, and a torso (and arms) cushioned instead with fat.

Crouching down on the naked red soil, he prayed with all his heart that there were no rattlesnakes in the immediate vicinity, and he remembered Lee Van Cleef during the shooting of *For a Few Dollars More*, in Almeria...

They were shooting in the desert. There were no toilets, no caravans, no campers, nada de nada. The hotel was miles away. The crew, the actors, if they had to take a shit they simply wandered off a bit and did it in the sand. No problem. But Lee Van Cleef was different. He was terrified of snakes. He *saw* snakes!

He tried to scare them off by slapping himself all over, but the snakes just didn't want to go and continued to slither after him flicking their forked tongues in and out, twisting and curling as though trying to escape from a gooey, scaly straight jacket, a rehab Laocoonte...a legacy from when Lee was in the last stage of alcoholism and was besieged by all manner of animals: cockroaches, mice, spiders, lizards, snakes. That is why the ophidiophobic Lee Van Cleef had begged, rather than asked for, and obtained from the production team his own personal toilet bowl! He took it with him everywhere, and when he needed to use it he simply sat down and defecated in peace and quiet, his buttocks appropriately raised a tad above the ground. Moreover, he was wearing his colonel's boots, so the snakes couldn't even take a nibble at his ankles. Many a time Leone saw him sitting on his white ceramic throne in the middle of the Spanish desert or behind a wooden building in the phony Main Street, and Lee Van Cleef appeared to him now in the orange light of remembrance.

Sometimes his wife came on the set and provided him with toilet paper. Crouched down amongst the *mesas* and the sandbanks, Leone pictured the "still" of Lee Van Cleef sitting on the cistern-less john and smiled an admiring smile. What a smart-ass!

An appropriate pun if ever there was one!

Lee Van Cleef's profile, with its aquiline nose dissolved in the sun and Leone suddenly stopped smiling, as he remembered that there was no toilet paper here either and he had left his handkerchief in the hotel. There was not a blade of grass to be seen. Just a rolling tumble weed bush, blown by the wind.

The only thing left was to call Claudio Mancini on the walkie-talkie…

«Not even John Ford shat here. Send me some Kleenex!»

No sooner said than done. The second Roman duly delivered the Kleenex to Leone and said: «Gov, y'know, there wasn't nothin' 'ere before, Noth-in'!»

Sergio Leone on the Jury at Cannes

(Idea for a theatrical comedy based on real events: Sergio Leone was in fact a member of the jury at the Cannes Film Festival in 1971; Michèle Morgan was president.)

The Cannes jury is about to meet for the last time, for the final vote, Saturday 26 May 1971. As always, the meeting takes place in the dining room of Villa Domergue, converted into a "courtroom" for the occasion, away from the hubbub of the Croisette, so as to ensure the seven members of the jury and the president, a French actress of international fame, the necessary peace and quiet.

On the wall is a painting by Georgia O'Keeffe entitled *On the Old Santa Fe Road.*

To begin with, though time is short, they engage in idle chatter: funny stories, titillating gossip.

The young American actress swallows some pills to keep herself awake because the night before she had danced till daybreak.

The French film critic – in shirt-sleeves and neckerchief – is telling how Sharon Stone once received the Legion of Honour from the president of the Festival. The event took place at the Café des Palmes, with the festival at its height and half the TV cameras of the world in attendance. The president was supposed to pin the medal of the *Ordre des Artes et des Lettres* on Sharon Stone's dress, but the dress material was so tough that he couldn't pierce it with the pin and Monsieur le President was terrified of pricking the famous bust. It took him fifteen minutes, his shaky fingers palpating the whole time! Sharon was justifiably "heureuse".

Sergio Leone reveals that Clint Eastwood had only two expressions: one with a cigar and one without.

"Ladies and gentlemen, let's get going, we have a job to do." The president calls them to order. The first prize to be determined is the *Palme d'Or*. The president knows there is going to be a battle. According to the rules, the vote is by secret ballot. But there are always those for and those against this or that film on the shortlist. A long discussion ensues. Words, words, words. Blah, blah, blah.

Leone doesn't have a favourite so he soon gets bored. He starts to nod off. He would really love to have a snooze, while his fellow jury members talk and talk.

In comes a gunslinger with a red moustache. He pulls out his gun and begins shooting at everyone, except Leone, from close range, shouting: "BANG! BANG! BANG! BANG!".

Then he spins the gun on his finger and drops it back in its holster. He leaves.

The others are isolated from the scene, dispatched by the gunman, as though locked away in the sleep of death, while Leone, far from being surprised, can now enjoy a nap, or in other words a "dream".

After the gunman, a second vision materialises: four children wearing their school smocks playing with marbles.

The skinny, disconsolate one, Leone as a child, as he goes to roll the marble, artfully moves his hand forward a bit.

His playmates cotton on. "Stop cheating, you! Smart aleck…"

The marbles are put away and the game changes. Question time: what the dads do for a living.

"What does your Dad do?"

"He is...was a film director", replies Leone.

Two other kids join in: "white collar worker"; "pork-butcher" (self-employed).

The fourth, Luzzatti, refuses to answer. The companions keep pressing him, but to no avail. His lips are sealed.

The others have a parley on the side, while Luzzatti plays around with a woodpecker on a pole (a popular pastime in those days, but times have changed). The boys go back to Luzzatti and tell him he can keep his mouth shut as long as he likes, they've guessed what his dad does anyway: he's an undertaker! That's why he didn't want to tell them. They understand. If they were in his shoes, they'd be embarrassed too!

LUZZATTI: "You don't know what you're talking about."

YOUNG LEONE: "Why not? Isn't he an undertaker? What is he then?"

LUZZATTI: "Worse".

SECOND KID: "I got it: a pimp!"

THIRD KID: "A crook".

LUZZATTI: "If only!"

LEONE: "Come on Luzzà, you can tell us. We're pals, aren't we?"

LUZZATTI: (very reluctantly, as though the words almost choked him): "He's...he's...he's a...crit...ic...a film critic!"

There, he's said it! Leone – the man of experience, the Italian juror – bursts out laughing. The president and the other jury members "wake up" and come back to life albeit in a bit of a daze.

Leone mischievously eyes the French critic and says: "Benoit, I was just thinking of you..."

In the meantime, the school kids have disappeared. The spell, the dream, the Amarcord is over.

So, where were we? Ah, that's right, the Jury Prize. Over to the jury, then. Leone, now wide awake and raring to go, nominates a film that up until then has not been taken into consideration, a Swedish film, the only film truly up to snuff!

The Brazilian director confesses that during the screening of the film that morning he had almost fallen asleep because the evening before he, too, had been out on the town.

Leone reminds him: the film tells the story of Joel Hägglund, a native of Sweden who emigrated to America and, taking the name Joe Hill, became a songwriter and labour activist of the IWW (Industrial Workers of the World). He was unjustly accused of the robbery and murder of a grocery store owner and his son in Salt Lake City. Just prior to his execution by firing squad, on 19 November 1915, at the age of 34, he had written to a fellow IWW member: "Don't waste any time in mourning. Organize!"

The scene is next taken over by a young working class girl, dressed in early 20th century labourer's clothes, escorted by a group of strikers. While she sings the popular song "I dreamed I saw Joe Hill last night", the picket engages in a reckless street dance.

The jury members gaze astonished at the dancing, buried once again deep in Leone's mind, in the ballad of his daydream, in the kaleidoscope of his memories and his visions.

The Frenchman pulls a face. In his opinion, the Swedish director, Bo Widerberg, "places too much emphasis on sensation and sentimentality instead of on the psychological complexity of the character".

Leone insists. The American writer backs him up. The Frenchman quips that "it's easy to be an anarchist if you've got millions", alluding to the international success enjoyed by both. *"Chacun dans son domaine; papier ou pellicule."*

Leone bites back: "I don't get involved in politics, but I do touch upon sentiment and I am there where there is suffering, where there is love, where there is enjoyment. The cinema is all about entertainment. I think that's what John Ford said and I agree wholeheartedly."

The Brazilian claps his hands. The Frenchman objects: "What is there to clap about, may I ask? You don't even know what we're talking about."

"Yes I do. I may doze off at the screenings but I'm not stupid. Kindly show more respect. After all, I am the only one here who's won a *Palme d'Or* at Cannes, a few years ago with *O Pagador das Promessas*! And I'm an anarchist, too! *Long live anarchy. Vive l'anarchie! Allons, enfants de la patrie!*"

At this point, back comes the gunslinger with the red moustache, who restores peace and good will with a round of gunshot. Again, the only one left unharmed by the shower of bullets is Leone. Exit the gunslinger. The president and the jury members are isolated from the scene a second time, while Leone takes a cigar from his sand-coloured bush-jacket, removes it from its holder, moistens the tip in his mouth, lights it with his gold Cartier lighter and takes a few puffs as the memories again begin to flow…

Enter a man in evening-dress and a ballerina scantily attired in stage clothes. Music. The two dance. The man is a *danseur mondain*, like Ettore Petrolini's Gastone, while she is a night-club dancer. The duet captivates the *viveurs*, the wealthy ladies and the loafers of 1920s Italy, or thereabouts…

Leone watches the dancers with an expert eye, gradually abandoning his role of Cannes jury member to become instead a film director at Cinecittà. At a certain point, he puts his hands to his mouth like a megaphone and shouts: "Stop!"

The sexy danseur and his partner stop dead in their tracks.

Leone walks up to the girl, appropriately young and beautiful for her role as a cabaret entertainer, and shows her how he wants her to move, touching her body here and there. She says how excited she is:

"It's my first film…my first day *shooting*…that's what you say, isn't it, sir?"

"Don't call me sir. It's my first film, too. I'm only the assistant, the director, the real one, is off sick."

"I was saying…! You're very young…"

"What did you do before?"

"I'm still studying. I'm training at the Rome Opera school of dancing", the girl replies.

"Really! That's great, show me what you can do then! Go for it! Don't let those nerves get the better of you!"

"Okay…*sir*."

Raising his voice, "sir" turns to the invisible troupe:

"Let's do another one!…Lights, Camera, Action!"

The two dancers start again from the beginning. This time it's tops. Leone is happy.

"Perfect! Let's take a break!"

Lights off. Darkness.

When the lights comes on again, the *danseur* in evening dress is nowhere to be seen. But the ballerina is still there (dressed in everyday clothes). She and Leone are seated to the side, as though they were completely alone. He has a towel over his shoulders. The girl is breaking phials one after the other, spreading the liquid contents on his head and gently rubbing it in.

BALLERINA: "Keep still! Still!…That's it, that's better…I said, don't move!"

S.L.: "Whenever we finish shooting a film we seem to pick up all the bugs around: chickenpox, measles, urticaria…"

B: "I know, I know. But your hair has never started falling out before. I think you wore yourself out on this last film."

S.L.: "Dead right, it sure was no picnic. We worked bloody hard, all of us. Especially yours truly."

B.: "I can imagine. All those crowd scenes. Thousands of extras.

S.L.: "And the horses, the elephants. Thank goodness I didn't have to direct the two stars, they were always squabbling, dead drunk. Talk about bathing in milk, more like gin, if you ask me. Rivers of gin."

B.: "Can I ask you something? Who's prettier? Her or me?"

S.L.: "What's that got to do with it? You're my wife."

B.: "Oh really?" (She digs her fingers in.)

S.L.: "Ouch! Not so hard, you're scalping me."

B.: "I asked you a question."

S.L.: You are. Especially in the morning. And you know what? I've decided, I want to be a film director. Stop messing around with those hands! Look at me. I want to discuss it with you."

B.: (lowering her hands) "With me? You decided long ago, sweetie pie, not just now. I was watching you that day on the set. You've got film directing in your DNA. So do it. What are you waiting for?"

Tap tap. There is a gentle knock on the door. The door opens to admit a white-gloved waiter, pushing a two-tiered trolley full of epicurean delights, superior French wines, liqueurs (the fruit is already there, in an elegant basket).

The waiter's arrival breaks the spell. Leone returns to this world and removes the towel from his shoulders, while his wife withdraws discreetly, on tiptoes, like a true ballerina...

Interval

The meeting is about to resume, but the young English director has a camera and wants to immortalise their encounter with a souvenir photo.

The other seven form a group, standing up, while the English director pulls aside the curtains a bit in order to get just the right lighting. He snaps away, one photo after another. He doesn't see that behind him a very tall, very old man has appeared, wearing a black patch over one eye and a shabby cowboy hat on his head.

The president and the jurors become statues. All of them except Leone – who exits the picture and goes towards the old man and the English director, who is cemented in the pose of a photographer taking a shot.

The old man has filled the whole room with smoke from a foul-smelling pipe.

SERGIO LEONE: (incredulous) "Who are you?...John Ford!"...

JOHN FORD: "Jack. I'm Jack to my friends."

S:L.: "Jack!"

F.: "Did you get that autographed photo I sent you?"

S.L.: "I did indeed. I keep it safely in my study. Thank you. Thank you very much, Jack. I was really pleased to get it. No joke. I don't know what else to say."

F.: "What is it you like about my films?"

S.L.: "The mules."

F.: "What? I'm a bit deaf."

S.L.: (louder) "The mules! The Cavalry's mules! The United States Cavalry!"

F.: "The mules?!"

S.L.: "Yes, the mules. What's so funny about that?"

F.: "The mules! That's a good one! (*he laughs and coughs*)."

S.L.: "Jack, you okay? (*he gives him a slap on the back*). Come over here. Sit down (*he helps him to a seat*)."

Six young Cavalry NCOs come marching in, wearing their blue uniforms displaying their ranks and their insignia, the same colour as the stripes on their trousers, and freshly polished boots. The Cavalrymen intone their traditional song, "The Girl I left Behind Me".

F.: (*yelling*) "I can't hear! I can't hear a thing! Louder!"

Materials

They sing at the tops of their lungs. With the last note still hanging in the air six young blond-haired girls dressed to kill enter the scene. They sing the Christian hymn "Shall we Gather at the River?" (Aaron Copeland version). The young men invite the girls to dance. The dance begins, jigs, waltzes, polkas...John Ford beats time on his knee, just as an old timer in a Western might do, while Leone brings out a harmonica and joins the fun with a festive, lively jingle. The couples dance around the juror-statues.

The music stops. The whirlwind stops. John Ford has stopped too, he looks tired. The couples follow suit.

In the silence, the regiment's trumpet can be heard (off-stage). The Cavalrymen and the girls exit. The girls, red-faced from the excitement and hot from the physical effort, fan themselves to cool down.

The two virtuosos of the Western start chatting to one another again. Almost at once Leone looks ill at ease.

S.L.: "Hey, Jack...let me tell you something...y'know Monument Valley...dust and nought else...how many films have you shot among those big red rocks and wind-blown canyons?"

F.: How the hell can I remember? I'm far too old. And as deaf as a post. Speak up, man!"

Leone moves towards the painting by Giorgia O'Keefe depicting a terracotta-coloured mountain, very similar to the *mesas* of Monument Valley. The Old Man joins him.

S.L.: "There I am! (he points at the *mesa*) You see, it was a pilgrimage, not an on-the-spot check for my next film. There I was, in that fantastic, mythical, extraordinary place, where the dust and the rocks were the stuff of my dreams...My producer said: "It's like being on the moon! We're on the moon! Not even John Ford's been here!" And then he added, staring at me closely with a worried look on his face: "What's up? You okay? You look pale!" Pale! I was positively ashen! Well, Jack, you know what too much excitement can do?"

F.: "You tell me!"

S.L.: "A shit behind a rock in Monument Valley with the vultures hovering above and the Indians screaming in my head. That's what it can do...Jack, do you think I defiled the place?"

F.: "Defiled? *(he laughs with gusto)*. I've "nourished" Monument Valley I don't know how many times! And not just me, the whole cast and crew! Do you really think we had time to go back to the caravans?"

S.L.: "And I thought I was the only one...with my pants still down around my ankles I called the producer on the walkie-talkie and I yelled: "Not even John Ford shat here! Bring me some Kleenex!"

Good old John laughs his head off.

S.L.: "It's okay for you to laugh, Jack, maybe you're not scared of rattlesnakes!"

F.: "You must be joking! Damn serpent, but y'know, I got used to them in the end. You know who really hated them? Duke!"

S.L.: "No! John Wayne?"

F.: Yep! You've said it! A born wimp! *(he laughs so hard he almost wets his pants, but quickly becomes serious again)*. I gotta run now. It's late. The nurse will be worried: it's my daughter...See you."

Exit

The president and the other members of the jury "defrost".

There is no time to waste. The golden cavalcade of the competitors wants to know if they can pack their bags and depart, tail between their legs, or stay at Cannes to triumphantly climb the red staircase for the second time. Revamped in hired evening dress, maybe!

Leone gets up, goes over to the telephone in front of the president and takes the receiver off the hook. He places it on the table and says: "I don't want any more calls. Now it's my turn to speak. So far you guys have done all the talking and given me quite a headache."

The president is barely able to control herself for the affront received...how dare he take the phone off the hook! No one has ever had such cheek before! Even if he is one of the jurors and a passionate film buff. Ah, *ces italiens*! What impertinence!

The president picks up the receiver aiming to put it back in its place. Leone blocks her by placing his hand on her dainty wrist. The receiver remains on the table.

The president gets up slowly and moves to one side, facing Leone directly. Leone stubs out his cigar, very deliberately, in the ashtray.

The president takes off her peach coloured jacket and gracefully lets it drop to the floor. She stretches out her hand and picks up a ruler in a very calculated manner, as though it were a rifle...the two rivals back up until they reach the established distance for a dual.

Leone moves aside the flap of his bush jacket and pulls out the Cartier, ready to fire at any moment...

S.L.: (after a pause) "I'm here not for the public, nor for the money, nor even for the prize, Señora."

P.: "I know. You are here only for me. I've been waiting for you...Stranger."

BRAZILIAN: "Well, I'll be damned!".

FRENCHMAN: "Silence. S'il vous-plait, faites silence!."

Leone slowly shifts his position.

The president does the same.

The two face each other. Head on. Leone takes out the harmonica and lifts it to his mouth, playing a few long, heart-rending notes...

The Brazilian reiterates: "Well, I'll be damned!"

The American actress is, by now, wide awake. Even though she still thinks she's dreaming. The sound of the harmonica culminates in a lamentation, almost a dirge. And then strikes up...

A DRAMATIC, MOCKING MELODY, JUST THE THING FOR A WESTERN SHOOT-OUT

The bell tolls twice. The music stops.

The American actress picks up an apple and takes a bite, which sounds like a gun shot. Leone and the president "draw" and "fire".

The president spins round seeming to lose her balance. She drops the ruler as though her hands no longer have the strength to hold it. She is about to fall, but the Frenchman and the Englishman are there to grab her; they hold her upright, as if in a dance. Supporting her under her arms, they take her to a nearby chair. They try to revive her with a drop of brandy. She coughs. The Brazilian pats her on the back. She sends him away with a condescending wave of her hand. The Frenchman retrieves her jacket and hands it to her. The president, once again reinstated in her role, remembers why she is there. In the meantime, someone has put the receiver back on its hook.

"So, gentlemen, shall we get back to work? Where were we?" She notices that Leone is still standing and addresses him, politely: "Maestro, please sit down."

"I have haemorrhoids!"

"Maestro, I've got good news for you. I've decided to create a special prize for "technical quality". And the winner is your favourite, the Swedish film....a film "truly up to snuff"...Am I right?"

"Absolutely".

"It already has my two votes", the president raises her arm. "Anyone else in favour?"

Five hands go up. Those of the Frenchman and the Englishman do not.

The president focuses her gaze on the young English director and says, with a cunning smile:

Materials

"You and the Swedish director are about the same age, more or less. And you young directors are always hostile towards colleagues of your own generation. I can't say I blame you. The competition is tough in this profession."

In the silence, after a moment's hesitation, the English director raises his hand in favour of the Swede. Eight against one, counting the president's two votes. "At this point our duty is done."

The first to get up is the president, quickly followed by the others. Everyone quits the meeting room. The last to leave are Leone and the American writer. The latter brings out a paperback. He says it is the story of four Jewish gangsters during the time of Prohibition, written by a Jewish gangster while he was an inmate at Sing Sing. He suggests Leone read it. It could become a good film.

Leone replies: "I'll think about it." It's his way of saying no.

The other man, to engage his attention, says he is the son of a Rabbi and that his father, like most other Jews, had never recovered from the shock of the Holocaust. For those Jews who survived, the Shoah was a indelible shame, because they gave the world the impression that they were unable to defend themselves, that they were predestined victims, defenceless lambs. And what happens to lambs? They are savaged. Or sent to the slaughter house.

AMERICAN WRITER: "The four Jewish gangsters in the story could demolish this stereotype. And show that I and my family are perfectly capable, if and when we want, to be just as violent, no more, no less, than other people. They will never forgive us for Auschwitz, I know, but this story, partly autobiographical – *parvus sed aptus* – might put things right; tell the world and the latest generation of cutthroats that, come what may, we will not go like lambs to the slaughter house, but like tigers. Of course, that's if you agree to make the story into a film...the way only you know how, under your direction, with your hand, Maestro..."

S.L.: (*takes the book*) "When I was a kid I had a Jewish friend. His name was Luzzatti... Gabriele Luzzatti...We went to primary school together. Then we lost touch. Poor guy. I heard he died at Auschwitz, with the rest of his family."

They leave. After a while, Leone comes back, alone, because he has forgotten his Cartier. Having found it – it was on the table together with the left-overs – he is free at last to leave, but instead he hesitates, lost in thought, staring at the cover of the book the American had given him. Still standing there, he reads a passage from it, a bit here, a bit there. Becoming more and more engrossed, he eventually sits down and begins to read from the beginning.

Enter, surreptitiously and silently, four elegantly dressed young men, their hands gloved, their faces masked by handkerchiefs.

Leone stares at them, but the four good fellows do not notice him. One of them draws a silenced gun, holding it at the ready, while another takes the Georgia O'Keefe painting off the wall to reveal a safe. He starts fingering with the combination watched by his three accomplices. The one with the gun is annoyed by the time it is taking, by the number of unsuccessful attempts. He points the gun at the combination and fires once, then again – PUFF, PUFF, PUFF – smooth and gentle.

The safe springs open. The gunman rummages around inside, scattering papers and documents everywhere. There's nothing else. The fourth gangster refuses to give up. He thrusts his gloved hand into the safe and finds a false bottom, revealing diamond necklaces, jewellery, gold watches, watches encrusted with priceless gems. They fill the pockets of their overcoats and exit in an orderly manner.

Darkness.

When the lights come back on, a man is seated sedately on the couch, while another goes to open the door to someone: "Good evening".

Enter two of the gang who robbed the safe. Only two, the others are nowhere to be seen.

In the meantime, the picture has been put back on the wall, once again concealing the safe. But, as will soon become clear, we are no longer – ideally – in the room where the robbery took place, but in the home of the dealer. The man smoking on the couch is his bodyguard.

The four men, wary and diffident, eye one another up. One of the youths brings out a bag. "The sparklers are in here."

"Let me see", says the dealer.

"Sure". The youth unties the string holding the bag together.

The man on the couch smokes. The youth empties the contents of the bag on the table. The jewels tinkle as they fall: sparkling diamonds, emeralds, rubies, watches, sapphires. The man on the couch stubs out his cigarette and gets up. The dealer puts a magnifying glass to his eye and examines the gems, like an expert.

GANGSTER: "Satisfied? They're not zircons."

DEALER: "Sure they're not. But I don't have the money here right now."

G.: "This wasn't the agreement."

D.: "It's a hell of a lot of money. I can't get it all together just a few hours after the robbery. You'll have to wait until tomorrow. The sparklers are hot stuff. You can leave them here. You can pick them up tomorrow with the money. If you don't like it, the deal's off. Sorry, there's been a set-back. Especially for you. It's dangerous to carry this loot around."

G.: "It's not on."

He puts the jewels back in the bag, while his buddy keeps his eye on things. Too late. The bodyguard has already drawn his gun and is aiming it at the two youths.

D.: (*tries to stop him*) "No! No! Don't do it!"

The two youths stop dead. Silence reigns. One of them throws the bag towards the armed man and at the same time his companion takes out his gun and jumps to the side. Two shots ring out. One misses, the other doesn't. The bodyguard falls to the ground, dead.

D.: (*remorsefully*) "I tried to stop him, you all saw it. But he took things into his own hands. This wasn't meant to happen..."

G.: "That's right, lay it on thick. *Schmuck*!"

2nd GANGSTER: "Shut up. Let's just finish him off."

D: "No, hang on. I can give you a down payment. It's not the whole sum, but my financier will cover the rest tomorrow and you can take the jewels with you. I'll see you tomorrow. Here or somewhere else. Okay, kids?"

As he says this, he reaches for a drawer and takes something out, a "bertha". The other two youths burst in reuniting the foursome and riddle him with bullets from their "berthas". This time the shots are real, booming, deafening and unsilenced.

2nd GANGSTER: "Well done."

There are two bodies on the floor. And two "berthas"

G.: (*picking up the bag with the jewels*) "I've got an idea. Let's sell them to the insurance company."

2nd GANGSTER: That means we'll only get chickenfeed."

3rd GANGSTER: "You been on the opium?"

4th GANGSTER: "I'd rather throw my stake into the Hudson River."

3rd GANGSTER: "I'm with you, brother."

2nd GANGSTER: "Guys, let's get outta here. There's been too much noise."

Materials

3rd GANGSTER: (jokingly) "Really, I haven't heard it. Heard nothing. What was all the noise about, anyway?"

A police siren screeches in the distance.

2nd GANGSTER: Well, the cops have heard it! Let's get out."

The police siren is getting louder and more threatening. They exit in an orderly manner. This is all witnessed by Leone seated in a corner of the room. The siren stops. Leone closes the book, rises to his feet and leaves.

Darkness.
When the light comes back, the two bodies and the two "berthas" have disappeared. Two school children enter dressed in smocks, bows at the neck, back packs on their shoulders. They are Leone as a child and his friend Gabriele Luzzatti.

LUZZATTI: "Gee, these books are heavy! Let's stop a minute."
CHILD DIRECTOR: "Just for a minute, I'll be late home. My dad's a stickler for time."

They take their bags off their shoulders and sit down side by side. The future director takes out a pack of trading cards of film stars and sorts through them while his friend watches.

LUZZATTI.: "Errol Flynn, got it. Clark Gable, got it. Marlene Dietrich, got it. Ronald Colman, don't have it. Bette Davis, got it. I don't like Bette Davis. Melvyn Douglas, got it. He's Jewish. My dad said so. Got it...got it...got it...got it...got it...Damn, John Wayne, don't have it. Want to do a swap? I'll give you five of mine if you give me John Wayne!"
DIRECTOR: "Make it ten."
LUZZATTI: "Eight."
D.: "Seven."
L.: "Six."
D.: "Seven."
L.: "Deal."

Luzzatti gets out his pack of trading cards and the exchange duly takes place: seven for one. But it's not just *any one*, it's John Wayne!

D.: "John Wayne has a nickname: Duke."
L.: "Meaning?"
D.: "No idea. And he's not as brave as he seems. John Wayne's a scaredy-cat. He's afraid of rattlesnakes. He shits himself if he sees one.
L.: "How do you know?"
D.: "They told me. Even your dad doesn't know that."
L.: "Too right! Fancy that! John Wayne. You do know who you're talking about? Jo-hn Wa-y-ne! (showing the cards). Hey, shall we toss a coin for them?"
D.: "Okay, but only one round."

They get up and play *odds or evens* to decide who goes first. The director wins.

D.: "Heads!"
L.: "Don't cheat. I know you."

The future director throws the cards in the air. They wager five cards – the duplicates – each. The cards glide to the ground and the boys pick and choose.

D.: "Mine! Mine! Mine! Mine! Mine! Yours!

L.: "Mine! Mine!

D.: "Mine! Mine!

L.: "Lucky bastard!" Let's play another."

D.: "I can't. They're expecting me home. My dad's got a clock in his head (*he looks at his watch*). Wow, it's late. Bye, Luzzà.*"

L.: "What are you up to today? Meet you at the steps?"

D.: "I'll be there. I've got my toboggan. You bring yours, and we'll go sledding!"

L.: "First of all we'll pee on them, so they slide better and we'll stop at about fifty metres in the middle of the road, so much for the cops!"

D.: "Okay, see you there, at the steps!"

They leave, accompanied by the sorrowful, melancholy notes of the harmonica.

A moment later, pushing a two-tiered trolley, the same imperturbable waiter enters, and begins to slowly clear the table.

Curtain.

2. FILMOGRAPHY AND PRESS REVIEWS

a) Films written and directed by Sergio Leone
b) Films partially directed (but not written)
c) Leone: producer, actor, screenwriter, assistant director, advertiser

a) Films Written and Directed by Sergio Leone

1953
Taxi... Signore?[69]

Director: Sergio Leone; *music:* Tarcisio Fusco; *photography:* Giorgio Orsini; *editor:* Nina Del Sordo; *production:* Auriga Film; *running time:* 10'.

1961
The Colossus of Rhodes
Il Colosso di Rodi
Le Colosse de Rhodes
El Coloso de Rhodas

Director: Sergio Leone; *production*: Cineproduzioni associate (Rome), Procusa (Madrid), Comptoir Franyais, Cine Television (Paris); *acting producer*: Michele Scaglione; *distribution*: Filmar, and (after 1977) Pac, in the USA: MGM; *screenplay*: Luciano Chitarrini, Ennio De Concini, Carlo Gualtieri, Sergio Leone, Luciano Martino, Aggeo Savioli, Cesare Seccia, Duccio Tessari; *photography*: Antonio Ballestreros, Emilio Foriscot (Eastmancolor, Supertotalscope); *sets*: Ramiro Gomez; *costumes*: Vittorio Rossi; *music*: Angelo Francesco Lavagnino; *editing*: Eraldo da Roma; *Special effects*: Vittorio Galliano, Eros Baciucchi; *second-unit director*: Jorge Grau; *àssistant director*: Michele Lupo.

Cast and Characters: Rory Calhoun (Darius), Lea Massari (Diala), Georges Marchal (Peliocles), Mabel Karr (Mirte), Conrado San Martin (Tireus), Ángel Aranda (Koros), Mimmo Palmara (Ares), Roberto Camardiel (Xserses), Jorge Rigaud (Lisippus), Yann Larvor (Mahor), Carlo Tamberlani (Xenon), Alf Randall [Alfio Caltabiano] (Creontes), Félix Fernandez (Caretes), Antonio Casas (Phoenician ambassador), Fernando Calzado (Sirione), José Vilches (Eteocle), Giovanni Pazzafini (gong player), Gustavo Re (a merchant), José Maria Vilches (Eros), José Suarez, Ignazio Dolce, Arturo Cabré, Ángel Menendez, Carlo Gualtieri, Álvaro de Luna, Rafael Hernández.

Origin: Italy / France / Spain.
Executive producer: Michele Scaglione.
Production: Cineproduzioni Associate (Rome), Procusa Film (Madrid), Comptoir Français de Productions Cinématographiques (Paris), Cinéma Télévision International (Paris).

Filming (interiors): Cinecittà (Rome), Istituto Luce (Rome), CEA (Madrid).
Filming (exteriors): Laredo's port, Luarca, Manzanares el Real, Ciudad Encantada, Bay of

---

[69] Belittled by almost all Leone's biographies, *Taxi...Signore?* is a short documentary which «shows taxi daily life, their utility and adventures». Maybe, Leone prepared it while assisting Carmine Gallone make *Taxi di notte* [Taxi at Night], 1950.

Biscay (Spain).
Running time: 142' (Italy), 127' (UK), 128' (Usa).

Distribution: Filmar and, from 1977, P.A.C. (Italy); MGM (Usa).
Release date: 15 June 1961 (Madrid).
Release date France: 11 August 1961.
Release date Italy: 25 August 1961.
Release date USA: 13 December 1961 (New York).

📖 II century B.C. On the island of Rhodes there is a celebration, in the presence of King Xerxes (Roberto Camardiel), for the conclusion of the building of the Colossus, an enormous statue in human form guarding the entrance to the port. The celebration is disturbed by an assassination attempt on Xerxes.

In fact, discontent with the tyrant is spreading on the island. A group of conspirators, including the young Mirte (Mabel Karr), is trying to elicit the help of the Athenian magistrates with the good offices of the Greek hero Darius (Rory Calhoun) who happens to be on the island. But Darius is thinking only of resting and courting the lovely Diala (Lea Masari), the adopted daughter of Carete, the architect who designed the Colossus. One day, as Darius follows her through the underground passages of the palace, he involuntarily comes upon a diplomatic meeting of Xerxes, his treacherous counselor Tireus (Conrado San Martin) and a delegation of Phoenician pirates. Darius is discovered and suspected of spying. For this reason Tireus refuses to allow Darius to depart so that he is forced to accept the help of the rebels and board a ship at night that is about to sail for Athens. But while the vessel is trying to slip past the Colossus, someone pulls a lever that unloads burning pitch onto it. The conspirators, who are now Tireus' prisoners, are cruelly tortured. Meanwhile dozens of Phoenician slaves are brought into the city and gathered at the temple of Baal. It is a trick: they are really Phoenician soldiers, allies of Tireus. He is preparing a coup to overthrow Xerxes and make Rhodes a Phoenician colony. The rebel prisoners are led before Xerxes. Diala tries in vain to convince Darius to collaborate and reveal the names of the other conspirators. When the prisoners are about to be thrown into the flaming mouth of the god, a skirmish erupts which allows them to flee on horseback and take refuge among the rocks. There they prepare to occupy the Colossus and unleash the rebellion. Darius returns to Rhodes by night and enters Diala's room. He wakes her gently and convinces her to accompany him secretly to the Colossus where they are surprised by a group of Tireus' soldiers. Darius defends himself duelling with them and eventually, passing through one of the Colossus' ears, leaps into the sea. In reality Diala and Tireus are co-conspirators for the conquest of power. When her father, who has heard everything, comes forward and threatens to reveal their plans, Tireus has the soldiers kill him as Diala looks impassively on. Meanwhile Darius has reached the rebels'camp, finding it destroyed and strewn with corpses. In the arena, before Xerxes and a great crowd, the rebels are about to be thrown to the lions. Darius arrives and publicly reveals the conspiracy. At that moment a Phoenician arrow kills Xerxes: it is the start of the coup, valiantly parried by the patriots. During the fighting Darius falls prisoner to Tireus and is taken to the Colossus where Diala graciously agrees to delay his execution. The patriots try to break through the entrance to the Colossus with battering rams, but they are repelled by Tireus' soldiers who pour boiling pitch on them. Suddenly an earthquake strikes causing everything to collapse: scenes of panic and despair. Then a tidal wave overwhelms the Colossus. The following day the sun shines again on the ruins of Rhodes. Darius has by now decided to remain on the island together with the honest Mirte.

Critics

When looked at today, *The Colossus of Rhodes* seems like a vaguely progressivist and decidedly spiritless sword-and-sandal epic, especially in the first part where the rhythm is slack and wandering, though this is not really surprising considering that the film had seven different scriptwriters. The whole thing feels ungainly, vague and tentative in purpose, as though the director was unable to decide whether to take the story and its characters seriously or go for a tongue-in-cheek extravaganza. This is well summed-up in the character of Darios (Rory Calhoun), a flirter with a permanent smile stamped on his face. He is a young Greek from Athens visiting his uncle on the island of Rhodes, but very obviously based on the stereotypical American who finds himself accidentally involved in a rebellion in some European dictatorship and who ends up on the side of the oppressed. The trumps are played only in the second half, and there are two of them: the huge machine of the colossus with all its military gadgets and the final earthquake where Leone can at last give utterance to not only his well-seasoned American skills, but also his passion for spectacularly dilating the action, his use of pretentiously melodramatic moments within the general catastrophe, interesting shooting angles and thrilling editing. But, despite the inconsistencies, the Leone touch is visible in everything else; in the magnificent 360° panoramic shots, the astute and symmetrical rendering of crowd and outdoor scenes, the occasional canny axiom ("An ordinary man is not much, a hero is too much", says a stiff Lea Massari who plays an evil enchantress), and the outrageous methods of torture.

[Morando Morandini, "Il Giorno", July 1977]

The Colossus of Rhodes is more than competent, it is a perfect representation of a solid and straightforward type of cinema, with no frills and fancies, that seemed to be the prerogative of the United States. Starting from a delightfully knotty script, with a welcome sense of humour (and yes, we are reminded of Robert Aldrich), Sergio Leone, a former assistant director to Wyler, has managed to do a nice little job. Some scenes remind us of *Vera Cruz*, in particular those that describe the hero's change of heart, thanks to which he ends up on the side of the rebels, and one or two scenes of particular violence. Torture and torment are meted out one after the other; there is, for example, the delightful image of droplets of acid or boiling tar trickling onto the bare skin of the luckless prisoners who take ages to die. And it takes a veritable barrage of blows to finish off the wounded. There is a point when the earth is shaking that we sense a hint of sadism, but this is offset by a strong dose of black humor. For once, there is no sign of sloppiness in the set design and the stunts and certain shots of the statue make it look quite real (no little achievement in the land of plaster and paper mache); and if one might feasibly remark on a certain lack of madness, or delirium, we must also recognize that this tale of classical wisdom has its merits.

[Bertrand Tavernier, "Cinéma 61", October 1961]

1964
A Fistful of Dollars
Per un Pugno di Dollari
Pour une Poignée de Dollars
Por un Puñado de Dólares

Director: Bob Robertson [Sergio Leone]; *script*: inspired by the screenplay of Akira Kurosawa and Ryuzo Kikushima's *Yojimbo,* 1961; *screenplay*: Sergio Leone, Duccio Tessari, Victor A. Catena, G. Schock, Jaime Comas Gil, Fernando Di leo, Tonino Valeri; *dialogue:* Mark Lowell; *music:* Dan Savio/Leo Nichols [Ennio Morricone] (*arrangements*: Alessandro Alessandroni; *trumpet:* Michele Lacerenza; *soprano:* Edda Dell'Orso); *cinematography:* Jack Dalmas [Massimo Dallamano] and Federico Larraya (Technicolor, Techniscope); *camera operator*: Steve Rock [Stelvio Massi]; *special effects*: John Speed [Giovanni Corridori]; *art direction and costumes*: Charles Simons [Carlo Simi]; *editor:* Bob Quintle [Roberto Cinquini]; *second unit director*: Frank Prestland [Franco Giraldi]; *assistant director*: Tonino Valerii.

Cast and Characters: Clint Eastwood (Joe), John Wells [Gian Maria Volonté] (Ramon Rojo), Marianne Koch (Marisol), Wolfgang Lukschy (sheriff John Baxter), Sieghardt Rupp (Esteban Rojo), Antonio Prieto (Benito Rojo), Margarita Lozano (Consuelo Baxter), Joe Edgar [Josef Egger] (Piripero, the undertaker), José "Pepe" alvo (Silvanito, the innkeeper), Daniel Martin (Juliàn), Benny Reeves [Benito Stefanelli] (Rubio), Richard Stuyvesant [Mario Brega] (Chico), Carol Brown [Bruno Carotenuto] (Antonio Baxter), Nino del Arco (little Jesús), Raf Baldassarre (Juan de Dios), José Riesgo (Mexican cavalry captain), Aldo Sambrell, José Canalejas, Alvaro de Luna, Jose Halufi, Nazzareno Natale, Antonio Pica, Enrique Santiago, Fernando Sánchez Polack, Umberto Spadaro (members of the Rojo gang), Lorenzo Robledo (Baxter family's blond gunslinger), Luis Barboo, Frank Braña, Antonio Molino Rojo, Julio Pérez Tabernero (members of the Baxter gang), Johannes Siedel, José Orjas.
*Main dubbers**: Enrico Maria Salerno for Clint Eastwood, Nando Gazzolo for Gian Maria Volonté, Rita Savagnone for Marianne Koch, Mario Pisu for Antonio Prieto, Luigi Pavese for José "Pepe" Calvo.

Origin: Italy/Spain/Germany.
Producers: Harry Colombo [Arrigo Colombo], George Papi [Giorgio Papi].
Production: Jolly Film (Rome), Ocean Film (Madrid), Constantin Film (Munich).

Filming (interiors): Cinecittà (Rome).
Filming (exteriors): Almeria, La Pedrizia di Colmenar Viejo, Aldea del Fresno, Hoyo de Manzanares (Spain).
Running time: 100' (Italy), 96' (France), 95' United Kingdom).

Distribution: Unidis (Italy), United Artists (USA).
Release date: 12 September 1964.
Release date France: 16 March 1966.
Release date USA: 18 January 1967.

   📖 The opening titles are shown against a background of shooting gunmen in silhouette. We are in Mexico. Two isolated huts are visible not far from the village of San Miguel. Joe, the man with the poncho (CLINT EASTWOOD), who is riding a saddled mule, stops to drink at a well and sees a violent attack take place.

   A child approaches the house where his mother, Marisol (MARIANNA KOCH) is confined, when two thugs come out and shoo him away with kicks. One of the two is Chico (MARIO BREGA). The child runs to his father whom they also beat up in turn.

   Joe enters the village. He is welcomed by a peasant with a crazed air, Juan de Dios. In the village square three American hired guns taunt Joe, shooting at the ground to scare the mule and him off. In the tavern in the middle of the square, the proprietor, Silvanito (PEPE CALVO), tells him about the local division of power: on the one hand there are the Baxters, Americans, arms dealers; on the other hand and on the opposite side of the square are the Rojos, Mexicans and liquor dealers.

   From below the windows of the Rojo house, Joe offers his services as a bodyguard. To demonstrate his abilities he commissions three coffins from the undertaker, then challenges the American hired guns who had taunted him and kills them. "I meant to say *four* coffins," he says, turning to the undertaker.

---

* To give to the reader a more complete work, the US edition of this book includes main dubbers chosen by leone in the first edition of the films.

Materials

In the house of the Mexicans, Joe is given a hundred-dollar advance by Don Benito (ANTONIO PRIETO), the eldest of the three Rojo brothers, and then, as Chico takes him to his room, he runs into Marisol. After accidentally overhearing a discussion between Don Benito and his brother Esteban (SIEGHARDT RUPP), who would like to get rid of him, Joe decides to move into the inn.

Some Mexican troops escorting a stagecoach arrive in the village. Joe, curious about who is in the stagecoach, lifts one of the curtains to peep in, but a pistol pointed at him from inside stops him.

The following morning at the inn, Silvanito explains to Joe that Ramon Rojo has taken Marisol from her family and made her his mistress. From the window the two of them watch the soldiers depart and, having become suspicious, decide to follow them.

On the banks of the Rio Bravo near the American border, Joe and Silvanito hide by a low wall and spy on the meeting between the Mexican soldiers and some U.S. Army troops who have met to exchange arms for the gold carried in the stagecoach. But these Yankees are nothing other than Esteban Rojo and his men disguised as blue jackets. The curtain of a cart is lifted and Ramon (GIAN MARIA VOLONTÉ) appears, the third of the Mexican brothers, holding a machine-gun. He does not leave a single survivor. The corpses of the real American troops, killed previously, are strewn on the ground to give the impression of a battle between the two troupes.

At the Rojo house Joe is introduced to Ramon. The latter announces that he has invited the Baxters to dinner to give a peaceful impression to the village since there is to be an inquiry about the Rio Bravo massacre. On hearing this news, Joe, who probably already sees himself losing his job without any more adversaries to be eliminated, decides to quit and give Don Benito back the advance he received.

At the tavern, Joe and Silvanito get ready to leave for the river, equipped with two empty coffins.

It is evening. The Baxters start off for the dinner at their rivals' house feeling suspicious.

At the cemetery, Joe and Silvanito place two cadavers they have removed from the site of the massacre beside a tomb with their backs against the tombstone so that the two dead men look as if they are still alive.

John Baxter comes home with his wife from the dinner at the Rojos which, as the two of them comment, was held in an atmosphere of hypocritical courtesy. Joe is waiting for them. He informs them that two soldiers survived the massacre and can be found wounded at the cemetery. He takes $500 in exchange for the news.

Rojo gives him another $500 for the same information. The two clans, both alarmed by the false news, rush to the cemetery where a gun fight breaks out. The Mexicans get the better of it: besides hitting the two soldiers they thought were alive, they also capture the Baxters' son.

At the same time (the two sequences are shown in parallel action) Joe stuns Chico who is guarding the Rojos' cellar and searches the premises until he finds the gold from the stage-coach hidden in a wine barrel; then he mistakenly gives Marisol a punch and carries her off.

We next see her at the Baxters' who the following day exchange her for their son, held prisoner by the Mexicans.

It is daytime. Seated on the veranda of the tavern in the center of the town, Joe watches the exchange of prisoners take place. The two hostages slowly cross the square on horses to rejoin their respective clans. Everything is going smoothly until Jesus, Marisol's little boy, comes rushing out of the tavern. The woman stops, dismounts and embraces her child. Her husband imprudently runs over to join his family. One of the Rojos' gunmen approaches to kill him, but Silvanito, threatening him with a rifle, stops him. Joe resolves the situation by telling Marisol to go back to the Rojos.

That evening the Mexicans celebrate. Joe practices shooting at a suit of armor; Ramon joins in with his rifle, then sends Marisol away with a rough kiss. She is taken back to her house outside the village. Chico carries Joe around on his shoulders (Joe pretends to be drunk) and drops him on the bed. Left by himself, Joe now goes out through the window and rides his horse to Marisol's house where he breaks in and massacres the guards. One of these, who is only wounded, gets up and is about to shoot him in the back, when the woman screams to warn him. Then our hero throws a dagger at the survivor piercing his chest. He gives Marisol a present of some money so that she can finally get away with her family.

When he goes back to his room, Joe finds Ramon and the others there; they have discovered his trickery.

In the cellar they torture him, but he refuses to reveal Marisol's whereabouts. The Mexicans leave him lying stunned on the floor. When Chico and his companion return, intending to continue beating him up, Joe rolls a demijohn at them on the sloping floor and makes a direct hit. Crawling on all fours he gets out and settles himself around a corner. The others arrive. Joe throws a match onto the flooded floor and causes a fire.

The infuriated Mexicans search for him everywhere and beat up Silvanito just for being his friend. Joe is hidden in the laboratory of the undertaker, who will accompany him out of the village.

The Rojos, believing Joe is hiding out at the Baxters' house, lay siege to the place. They breach the defences with dynamite, roll in some barrels of petroleum and set it afire. The Americans come out one at a time with their hands up and are mowed down by the Rojos, who have placed themselves in front of the entrance. They have no pity even for the mother who is killed as she is leaning over her dead son's body. Joe enjoys the show from his hiding place in a coffin on the undertaker's cart.

We next find him in an abandoned mine, target practicing with a sheet of iron. His wounds are beginning to heal. He begins shooting again against two superimposed sheets of iron and discovers that the bullets do not penetrate the metal.

The undertaker arrives, gives him a stick of dynamite stolen from the Mexicans and informs him that they have taken Silvanito prisoner.

In front of the inn Don Benito, Ramon and two of their men are torturing Silvanito who is hanging from a beam by his hands, when an explosion is heard. Joe appears from out of a cloud of smoke and he advances slowly goading them to shoot at his heart. But Ramon's bursts of fire only throw him to the ground. Every time our hero gets up again, unhurt. When the Mexican's rifle is empty of bullets Joe lifts his poncho revealing the metal shield that stopped the bullets and he throws it away. He pulls out his pistol, kills Don Benito and his two gunmen, cuts the cord holding up Silvanito, and then challenges Ramon to a duel – a pistol against a rifle. The two adversaries must pick their weapons up from the ground, reload and fire. Joe proves to be the fastest. Finally, Silvanito shoots down Esteban Rojo, who had taken up his post in a window.

Joe says goodbye to Silvanito (the gold from the stagecoach will be returned to the Mexican government) and rides off on his horse as the undertaker measures the corpses for coffins.

CRITICS

No complaints whatsoever from a professional point of view. The film is competently made, the Spanish scenery differs little from that of New Mexico and the special effects are on a par with those of Hollywood whizzes. There is, however, something excessive here, marking the fact that this film lies outside the usual standards. We've certainly seen a lot of violent, bloody American Westerns, but *For a Fistful of Dollars* is over the top: the battles are butchery, the torture sadistic and there's blood everywhere. There is no sign of the justice, hope or freedom that are evident in classical Westerns. We have gone from the quixotic adventure of an irreprehensible sheriff to a succession of brutalities that have neither poetical nor narrative justification. Children should not be allowed to see this violence, but even adults would be hard put to find anything other than the promotion of an overwhelming instinct to subjugate others. If there is to be a tradition of Italian Westerns, do we really want it to be distinguished by kicks in the ribs and broken, bloodied noses?

[Tullio Kezich, "Bianco e Nero", November-December 1964]

Let's not spit on the pleasure of others. Here, the overall color is good. The set design is at times striking, and the make-up artists make good use of their gory concoctions. And it's not my intention to dwell on the quality of the dubbing either. All these craftsmen have done their

Little fires

"Flames have fascinated me ever since I was a kid, I must have an arsonist side to me."
(Sergio Leone)

The Colossus of Rhodes.

Once Upon a Time in America.

Once Upon a Time in America.

**When dynamite
is the last resort.**

The Good, the Bad and the Ugly.

For a Few Dollars More.

Duck! You Sucker.

Duck! You Sucker.

My Name is Nobody.

Duck! You Sucker.

For a Few Dollars More.

My Name is Nobody.

Once Upon a Time in the West.

Once Upon a Time in the West.

The Good, the Bad and the Ugly.

The Good, the Bad and the Ugly.

The Colossus of Rhodes.

Once Upon a Time in the West.

My Name is Nobody.

The Good, the Bad and the Ugly.

Once Upon a Time in America.

For a Few Dollars More.

Once Upon a Time in the West.

Once Upon a Time in America.

Once Upon a Time in America.

The Colossus of Rhodes.

Once Upon a Time in America.

My Name is Nobody.

249

A Fistful of Dollars.

For a Few Dollars More.

The Good, the Bad and the Ugly.

Once Upon a Time in the West.

Once Upon a Time in America.

Duck! You Sucker.

251

The Good, the Bad and the Ugly.

Once Upon a Time in the West.

The Good, the Bad and the Ugly.

The Good, the Bad and the Ugly.

Once Upon a Time in the West.

The Good, the Bad and the Ugly.

A Fistful of Dollars.

For a Few Dollars More.

Duck! You Sucker.

A Fistful of Dollars.

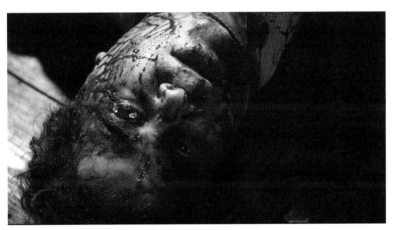

Once Upon a Time in America.

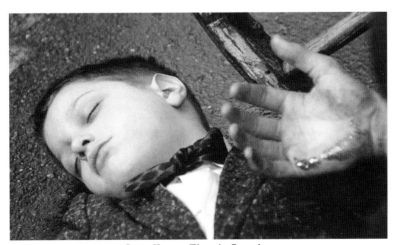

Once Upon a Time in America.

Once Upon a Time in the West.

The Good, the Bad and the Ugly.

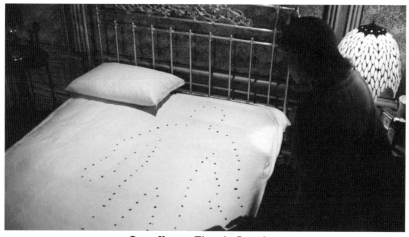

Once Upon a Time in America.

job to the best of their ability and earned the fistful of *lire* that is their due. But, beyond these skills there lies only desolation! A script full of stupidities, amateurish direction, poor acting where the unfortunate Clint Eastwood, a former television cowboy *(Rawhide)*, has little of the dust of his homeland on the soles of his boots. Just for the record: in the main scenes, the *découpage* doesn't know its left from its right, how to judge distance, how to direct movements, orient glances and everywhere, bolsters the action with unnecessary close-ups. Poetical ideas maybe, but that go against our better judgement (with his chest protected by an invisible armour plate, the good guy seems to be invulnerable to the villain, a crack shot who wavers not one instant – he obviously hasn't seen *Johnny Guitar* – before shooting his opponent right between the eyes); a vicious exhibition of violence that makes Samuel Fuller, even in one of his less disciplined moments, seem the epitome of discretion; an irresponsible immorality that exalts torture and treachery. It would not have taken much for this Leone to become the *Leone d'Oro* of Italy, or for this Jacopetti of Westerns to become, even with this ill-devised effort, a worthy Italian *Corniaud*[70] *(The Sucker)*.

[Roger Tailleur, "Positif", summer 1966]

1965
For a Few Dollars More
Per Qualche Dollaro in Più
Et Pour Quelques Dollars de Plus
La Muerte Tenía un Precio

Director: Sergio Leone; *story:* Sergio Leone, Fulvio Morsella (from a story by Fernando Di Leo and Enzo Dell'Aquila); *screenplay:* Sergio Leone, Luciano Vincenzoni, Sergio Donati; *dialogue:* Luciano Vincenzoni; *music:* Ennio Morricone; *conductor:* Bruno Nicolai; *music arrangements for chorus*: Alessandro Alessandroni; *guitar:* Bruno D'Amerio Battisti; *cinematography:* Massimo Dallamano (Technicolor, Techniscope); *camera operators:* Aldo Ricci, Eduardo Noé; *special effects*: Giovanni Corridori: *art direction and costumes*: Carlo Simi; *editors:* Eugenio Alabiso, Giorgio Serralonga; *titles:* Igino Lardani; *first assistant director:* Tonino Valerii; *assistant directors*: Fernando Di Leo, Julio Samperez.

Cast and Characters: Clint Eastwood (Monko), Lee Van Cleef (Colonel Douglas Mortimer), Gian Maria Volonté (El Indio), Luigi Pistilli (Groggy), Klaus Kinski (Wild, the hunchback), Josef Egger (Old Prophet), Mario Brega (el Niño), Mary Krupp (Mary, the tavern keeper's wife), Rosemary Dexter (Mortimer's sister), Benito Stefanelli (Luke), Aldo Sambrell (Cuchillo), Frank Braña [Francisco Braña] (Blackie), Antonio Molino Rojo (Frisco), José Canalejas (Chico), Nazzareno Natale (Paco), Roberto Camardiel (Tucumcari station clerk), Panos Papadopulos (Sancho Perez), Lorenzo Robledo (Tomaso, Indio's traitor), Diana Faenza (his wife), Dante Maggio (in cell with El Indio), Carlo Simi (El Paso bank manager), Ricardo Palacios (saloon keeper), Diana Rabito (woman in the bath), Peter Lee Lawrence [Karl Hirenbach] (Mortimer's brother-in-law), José Marco Davo (Red Baby Cavanagh), Sergio Mendizabel Tucumcari banker), Enrico Navarro (Tucumcari sheriff), Guillermo Mendez (White Rocks sheriff), Kurt Zips (Mary's husband), Jesús Guzmàn (carpetbagger on train), Tomàs Blanco (telegraph operator), Luis Rodriguez (Guy Calloway), Giovanni Tarallo (El Paso guard), Mario Meniconi (train driver), Werner Abrolat (Slim), Antonio Ruiz (child in El Paso), Aldo Ricci, Román Ariznavarreta, Eduardo Garcia, Rafael Lopez Somoza, José Felix Montoya, Enrique Santiago, José Terron, Edmondo Tieghi, Joseph Bradley, Fernando Di Leo (cigar-smoking card player), Francesca Leone (new born baby, Tomaso's daughter).

---

[70] Tailleur refers to Gérard oury's *Le Corniaud* (*The Sucker*), French blockbuster in 1965.

All About **Sergio Leone**

Main dubbers: Enrico Maria Salerno for Clint Eastwood, Nando Gazzolo for Gian maria Volonté, Emilio Cigoli for Lee Van Cleef, Vittorio Sanipoli for Luigi Pistilli.

Origin: Italy/Spain/Germany.
Producer: Alberto Grimaldi.
Production: PEA (Rome), Arturo Gonzales (Madrid), Constantin Film (Munich).

Filming (interiors): Cinecittà (Rome).
Filming (exteriors): Almeria, Guadix, La Calhorra, Granada, Colmenar, Viejo, Hoyo de Manzanares (Spain).

Running time: 130′ (Italy), 128′ (United Kingdom and USA).
Distribution: PEA (Italy), United Artists (USA).
Release date: 18 December 1965 (Turin).
Release date France: 30 September 1966.
Release date USA: 10 May 1967.

  📖 A lone horseman is mowed down by gunfire. The opening titles appear, punctuated by pistol shots.

On a train, Mortimer (Lee Van Cleef) interrupts his Bible reading and announces his intention of getting off at Tucumcari to a petulant traveling companion. The other traveler objects that the train does not stop at that little station, but Mortimer pulls the alarm cord and the engineer stops the train precisely in the desired place.

Mortimer gets off the freight car with his horse. His authoritative appearance, fittingly emphasized by the big pistol sticking out of his belt, is enough to dampen any protests the conductor might want to make. Next to the ticket window a wanted notice is posted with a thousand – dollar reward for the capture of Guy Calloway. Mortimer tears it off and sticks it in his bag.

When Mortimer pushes the wanted notice under a door that the saloon keeper has indicated to him, he is met by a spray of bullets. He breaks into the room to find a woman in a bath tub and Calloway escaping from the balcony. He goes down into the street, deploys the portable arms carrier hanging from his saddle and, with a rifle shot, slaughters the horse of the fugitive who gets up and continues firing unsuccessfully.

Mortimer takes his pistol, approaches calmly, aims and shoots the bandit straight in the forehead.

Mortimer cashes in the reward at the sheriff's office where he sees a wanted notice for Baby "Red" Cavanaugh. The sheriff tells him that another bounty hunter, Monko, is on the bandit's trail at White Rocks.

At White Rocks, Monko (Clint Eastwood) enters a crowded saloon where the sheriff at his request points out "Red" who is playing poker. He breaks into the game and deals cards only to himself and the bandit. Meanwhile the sheriff sends a message to someone at the barber's. Monko wins the poker hand: "What were we playing for?" the other asks. "Our lives" says the bounty hunter disarming his foe and starting to beat him up when three men (one with his face half shaved) appear at the door of the saloon. Monko turns suddenly and shoots them down, then killing "Red" too who, crawling across the floor, had stretched out his hand for a pistol.

He cashes in the reward from the indignant sheriff while seizing the latter's badge which he hands to two passers-by, saying: "Find yourself another one."

One night in Mexico several men attack a prison and free El Indio (Gian Maria Volonté) who, before escaping, shoots his cellmate at close range and kills the prison director while his companions take care of the guards. They leave one of them alive so he can tell the story.

A reward of $10,000 is set on the head of El Indio, dead or alive. The two bounty hunters read the notice attentively at different times and perhaps with different intentions: Monko seems attracted by the amount of money while Mortimer stares at the words "Dead or Alive."

In the brigands den, a deconsecrated church, El Indio wreaks his vengeance on the man who had him arrested. He has his wife and child killed and then makes him fight a duel according to unusual rules: the two men can only shoot after the music box in El Indio's pocket watch has finished playing. After his easy victory, the bandit smokes a marijuana cigarette.

In the Tucumcari bank, Mortimer gets the director to tell him which is the most solid and impregnable bank of the region: it is the El Paso bank which only a madman would dream of trying to attack.

Monko arrives in El Paso. For a small tip a Mexican waif shows him the hotel where Mortimer is lodged. Monko gets a room in the hotel facing Mortimer's by making another guest move out.

In the deconsecrated church, where Groggy's (LUIGI PISTILLI) men have also arrived, El Indio gets into the pulpit to announce that the safe in the El Paso bank is hidden in a piece of furniture in the director's office (which he had learned from his cellmate).

Mortimer presents himself at the bank as a possible new customer and the director shows him the safety measures that make the bank impregnable.

Four of El Indio's men sent out to reconnoitre arrive in town. The same waif brings Monko the news.

In the saloon, Mortimer provokes one of the four (KLAUS KINSKI) by striking a match on his humpback and using his cigar to light his own pipe. But the bandit keeps his rage under control and leaves the saloon with his mates.

The bank employees leave work and a watchman comes in. Lying in wait outside, the outlaws time how long the watchman takes to make his rounds of the building. From his window, Mortimer watches the bandits through binoculars, while he in turn is under the surveillance of Monko's binoculars from a facing window.

Mortimer looks through the archives of the local paper and discovers from a photograph that his mysterious vis-a-vis is a noted bounty hunter.

Monko goes to see an old man, "the prophet," who is obsessed with the passing trains near his house. The prophet informs him of Mortimer's past: he is an ex-officer of the Confederate army reduced to working as a bounty hunter. Hard times.

A Chinese man enters Mortimer's room, picks up his suitcase and carries it downstairs. The ex-colonel follows him with curiosity and in the street discovers the instigator of this strange operation – Monko, who wants to get rid of his rival and orders him to leave town. A half-serious duel starts between the two rivals as the little kids watch admiringly: the men stomp on each other's feet and send bullets whizzing through each other's hair.

Having overcome their mutual mistrust, the two men converse in Mortimer's room. They decide to split the reward money and agree on a common strategy against El Indio: Monko should get himself admitted to El Indio's gang by freeing Sancho Perez, an old outlaw presently incarcerated in the Alamogordo prison. The ex-colonel loves to listen to the music box in his pocket watch, but he refuses to explain the reason for this habit to his partner.

In his hide-out El Indio smokes a marijuana cigarette while listening to the same tune played on an identical watch and remembering the circumstances in which he took possession of the object.

Flashback: A rainy evening and a young couple stretched out on their bed listen to the notes of the same music box; the brigand who has broken into the room kills the husband and rips the wife's nightgown off her.

In the prison of Alamogordo, Monko blows up an outside wall and flees with Sancho Perez.

In the outlaws' den, El Indio welcomes the new recruit to the gang and gives instructions for the following day: Monko and three other men will have to set up a diversion, a robbery at the Santa Cruz bank so as to draw the sheriff's men away from El Paso. During a bivouac, Monko kills his traveling companions. El Indio and his men leave for El Paso.

In the Santa Cruz telegraph office, Monko compels the telegraph clerk to wire off the false news of the bank robbery, then ties him up and gags him.

In El Paso the colonel prepares the weapons and Monko lies in waiting among the houses facing the bank entrance. The employees leave and the watchman enters. He sits down himself in the director's office and bites into a sandwich. The Mexicans arrive in town, some on horseback, others in a covered wagon. Very soon the covered wagon disappears. Suddenly an explosion is heard – a wall of the bank has been blown up. El Indio kills the watchman and then has the piece of furniture containing the safe loaded onto the wagon.

The two partners, astonished, can do nothing but rush in pursuit of him.

During a rest, Monko blames Mortimer for the disgrace and decides that he will continue to hunt down El Indio on his own. The ex-colonel fires on his mate without warning and gives him a flesh wound in the neck so that El Indio will not get suspicious about Monko's being the only survivor of the Santa Cruz expedition; that he has miraculously escaped a vigilantes' attack. He arrives at the bandits' camp where he proves his ability to play his role. He punches Groggy when he dares to insinuate that he is not telling the truth. El Indio, seeing the wound in his neck, believes him.

Near the village of Aguacaliente the bandits decide to test the talents of the new gun-man and make him enter that inhospitable village alone. Suddenly, at the end of the street, three menacing characters take up positions. In a garden, a boy is trying in vain to reach the branches of an apple tree. Monko comes to his aid by shooting down lots of the fruit for him.

Mortimer appears on the balcony of the inn and joins the target practice. Seeing this impressive display of bravura the three disappear.

Inside the saloon, the hunchback recognizes Mortimer and, to avenge the way Mortimer insulted him in El Paso, he challenges him to a duel. The ex-colonel surprises his adversary by pulling a handy Derringer out of his jacket and shoots him straight in the forehead. Then he offers El Indio his services as a safe expert for a large sum of money.

They use sulphuric acid and Mortimer opens the safe without damaging the banknotes. El Indio closes the safe again and hides it in a hut.

At night, Monko climbs into the hut from the roof and finds Mortimer there transferring the banknotes into two sacks. Then he seals the safe in a way to make it appear that it has not been touched. Monko climbs back up through the roof and, when he is about to touch the ground, he feels the shoulders of El Indio under his feet. He just manages to throw the two sacks into the branches of a tree unseen.

The two are beaten bloody by the Mexicans. But during the night, Nino (Mario Brega), El Indio's faithful helper, after knifing another member of the gang, lets them make a getaway. Then El Indio accuses another one of his bunglers of the murder and kills him. He has a di-abolical plan in mind which he confides to Nino alone: arrange for the two bounty hunters and his own helpers to kill each other and to keep the money for himself. Groggy, who has guessed what he is up to, eliminates Nino by a dagger thrust with the intention of taking his place in his chief's confidence. But the two soon are treated to the bitter surprise of finding the safe empty. While a shoot out erupts in the village streets, in which Mortimer and Monka easily come out the winners, El Indio remains seated at a table toying with a cockroach. Then he opens his watch and the music box takes him back to that famous night.

Flashback: El Indio, having shot the husband, rapes the wife. But she, while he is on top of her, gets her hand on his pistol and shoots herself in the side.

From outside Mortimer's cries of challenge can be heard. Groggy rushes out and the ex-colonel shoots him on the run. But Mortimer in turn is struck by a bullet fired by El Indio and is disarmed. El Indio challenges him to the unfair duel ("When the music stops pick up the pistol and try to shoot.").

Monko intervenes and, keeping the bandit covered with his rifle, throws Mortimer a car-tridge belt, thus re-establishing equality between the two duelists. They draw their pistols.

Mortimer is the faster. He goes to take the other pocket watch from the bandit's body: the woman whose picture it contains is his sister. Mortimer renounces the reward and takes leave of his partner who is intent on loading the valuable corpses of the outlaws onto a cart. They do not add up correctly, one is missing. In fact, Groggy, who is only wounded tries to shoot Monko in the back. But the latter quickly turns and fires.

Getting the sacks from the branches of the tree, the bounty hunter moves off driving the cart loaded high with the cadavers.

Materials

What we have here is a successful *pastiche*, more perfect than the earlier *For a Fistful of Dollars*, in that it dispenses with the dross of realism and sentimentality and is stripped to the bone, so to speak, that is to killing of which there is in abundance. Many victims are innocent or at least undeserving and for this reason are, sadistically, all the more credible. This reminds us of another film full of killings: Jean-Luc Godard's *Pierrot le Fou* (1965). But between *Pierrot le Fou* and *For a Few Dollars More* there is a difference: the victims in Godard's film are demoted to insignificant objects and the relationship between killers and killed is broken down, the former laugh, joke, and make love in front of dead bodies as though they were lifeless objects, not lifeless human beings. This shows that the director does "not" participate in the violence, he feels it and condemns it as such, he points it out, but isolates it. In *For a Few Dollars More*, the director is up to his neck in a system the fulcrum of which is murder. There is a relationship between assassin and victim, a relationship based on annihilation, which in the absolute void of the *pastiche,* is promoted to a rule of thumb, a universal concept. The "pop art" absurdity of *Pierrot le Fou* is that of poetry through which we discern the multiplicity of the real world. The bloodthirsty absurdity of *For a Few Dollars More* is that of obsession, which obscures any reality other than violence. The recreation of the Far West is highly accurate, but artificially realistic and totally inanimate, and reminds us rather of a *Trompe l'oeil* painting where even the tears in the canvas are painted. Dusty landscapes, 19th century saloons, lodging houses, train stations, trains, everything Far West, like a cover of the Saturday Evening Post, form the background for huge close-ups of the players staring "guappo-like" into each other's eyes, silently, threateningly, cautiously for what seems like an eternity. And all of this for "a few dollars more".

[Alberto Moravia, "L'Espresso", 16 January 1967]

Invited to write the score for another Sergio Leone film based on the Clint Eastwood character, *For a Few Dollars More*, Ennio Morricone has created one of the craziest, loudest sound tracks of recent years. Perhaps he has totally changed his tune as a sort of challenge to himself, to stimulate his ambition after winning the "Nastro d'Argento" for the score of Leone's earlier film. In any event while the score from last year's film was dominated by a scant melody punctuated by long silences, this time there is not a moment of respite in the succession of ear-splitting musical expedients that seem intent on bringing the audience's nerves ever closer to the breaking point. Not even the silences are restful. This musical overload lasts the entire film, enriched along the way by added orchestral colors and unexpected changes of rhythm, but the volume remains. The killing of the informer for which El Indio, the outlaw, ends up in prison, is accompanied by a Mexican-style guitar, humming and a *fortissimo* organ piece (the outlaw is hiding in a church so there has to be an organ); the outlaws making their way to the bank they are planning to rob in El Paso are accompanied by the main theme (that of the credits, which occurs again and again) played by guitars, then the chorus, then the full orchestra, then the brass, enriched with ringing bells, vocals, whistling, drums and more. In his use of this continual din Morricone seems to scorn the effects (the legitimate ones, that is) that the story offers him on a silver platter, thus betraying his true value as a composer of film music. Let's take the example of the carillon watch that El Indio always carries with him and plays during the shoot-outs with his rivals: only when the watch's tune ends do they pull out their guns and shoot. Here, a true musician of the cinema would have used the gentle carillon alone, the sound of which breaking the silence, would have been, without any help from other musical expedients, pure cinematic poetry, capable of creating an atmosphere loaded with suspense. Morricone, from the initial tinkling to the final notes of the carillon, implements (especially in the final duel with the Colonel, the old gunslinger who has his own personal bone to pick with the outlaw) a veritable musical blitzkrieg, with the orchestra full-on and vocals to boot, that completely ruins this otherwise perfect moment.

[Ermanno Comuzio, "Cineforum", March 1966]

1966
The Good, the Bad and the Ugly / Two Magnificent Rogues
Il Buono, il Brutto, il Cattivo
Le Bon, la Brute et le Truand
El Bueno, el Feo y el Malo

Director: Sergio Leone; *story*: Sergio Leone, Luciano Vincenzoni; *screenplay:* Sergio Leone, Luciano Vincenzoni, Age & Scarpelli, Sergio Donati; *music:* Ennio Morricone; (*director of music*: Bruno Nicolai) *cinematography:* Tonino Delli Colli (Technicolor, Techniscope); *camera operator*: Franco Di Giacomo; *special effects:* Eros Baciucchi; *art direction and costumes*: Carlo Simi; *editor:* Nino Baragli, Eugenio Alabiso; *titles:* Igino Lardani; *first assistant director*: Giancarlo Santi; Fabrizio Gianni.

Cast and Characters: Clint Eastwood (Blondie, the "Good"), Lee Van Cleef (Angel Eyes, the "Bad"), Eli Wallach (Tuco, the "Ugly"), Aldo Giuffré (Captain Clinton), Luigi Pistilli (Father Pablo Ramirez), Rada Rasimov (Maria, the prostitute), Mario Brega (Corporal Wallace), Al Mulock (Elam, the one-armed killer), Angelo Novi (young monk), John Bartha (sheriff), Livio Lorenzon (Baker), Enzo Petito (storekeeper), Antonio Casas (Stevens), Chelo Alonso (his wife), Antonio Ruiz (their son), Antonio Casale (Jackson, alias Bill Carson), Benito Stefanelli, Luigi Ciavarro e Aldo Sambrell (members of Angel Eyes' gang), Lorenzo Robledo (Clem), Romano Puppo (Slim), Antonio Molino Rojo (Captain Harper),Román Ariznavarreta, Saturno Cerra, Frank Braña [Franscisco Braña] and Claudio Scarchilli (bounty hunter), Sergio Mendizábal (blond bounty hunter), Nazzareno Natale (Mexican bountry hunter), Sandro Scarchilli (peon), Jesús Guzmán (Padue, hotel owner), Victor Isreal (Confederate sergeant), William Conroy (Confederate soldier), Axel Darna (wounded Confederate soldier), Franco Tocci (Yankee soldier with cigar), Silvana Bacci (Mexican prostitute), Aysanoa Runachagua (Mexican gunslinger), Antonio Palombi (old sergeant), Joseph Bradley (old soldier), Fortunato Arena, Amerigo Castrighella, Attilio Dottesio e Veriano Ginesi (spectators with sombreros at Tuco's first hanging), Jesús Porras (soldier playing the harmonica), José Terrón (Thomas "Shorty" Larson), Richard Alagicj, Antonio Contreras, Tony Di Mitri, Alberigo Donadeo, Julio Martinez Piernavieja.
Main dubbers: Enrico Maria Salerno for Clint Eastwood, Carlo Romano for Eli Wallach, Nando Gazzolo for Luigi Pistilli, Renato Turi for Mario Brega, Rita Savagnone for Rada Rassimov.

Origin: Italy/Spain/Germany/United States.
Producer: Alberto Grimaldi.
Production: PEA (Rome), United Artists (Hollywood).

Filming (interiors): Elios Film (Rome).
Filming (exteriors): Almeria, Burgos, Granada, La Calahorra, Colmenar Viejo, Guadix, Manzanares el Real (Spain); Durango (Mexico).
Running time: 182' (Italy), 166' (France), 148' (United Kingdom), 161' (United States).

Distribution: PEA (Italy), United Artists (USA).
Release date: 23 December 1966.
Release date USA: 29 December 1967.
Release date France: 8 March 1968.

📖 The opening titles appear superimposed on daguerrotype-style photos. Three killers enter a saloon. Explosions. Tuco (ELI WALLACH) comes tumbling out through a window, shattering the glass: in one hand he holds a pistol, in the other a steak bone. The image freezes and the caption "The Ugly" appears. While Tuco gallops off we see that two of the killers in the saloon are dead. The third, with a wounded arm, tries to shoot at the fugitive, but he cannot manage it and falls to the ground.

Materials

A horseman, Angel Eyes (Lee Van Cleef), enters a lonely farmhouse and sits down to lunch with the head of the family. He asks him for news of Corporal Carson who escaped some time back with the safe of a Confederate regiment. The owner of the house, frightened, gives him the information and begs him to spare his life, offering him double what he is getting to kill him. Angel Eyes takes the money but kills him and his two sons anyway, sparing only the widow. The instigator of the crime, who is in bed with a violent cough, pays off Angel Eyes. The latter explains that the victim had paid him more and so he wipes him out by shooting him in the head through a cushion. The image freezes and the caption appears: "The Bad."

In a rocky place, three bounty hunters are waiting to ambush Tuco who has a reward of $2,000 on his head. Along comes Blondie (Clint Eastwood) and kills them. Now Blondie takes Tuco, tied and mounted backwards on a horse, to the town, delivers him to the sheriff and cashes in the reward. He is about to be hanged in the village square after a clerk has read the list of his many crimes. From a rooftop Blondie shoots the rope and the hats of bystanders to facilitate the bandit's escape.

The two of them meet far from the village and split the reward money. In another town they successfully repeat the trick. Angel Eyes, who is passing through town, watches the scene as a legless Confederate war veteran tells him that if he wants information about Carson he will have to see his woman Maria, a prostitute.

Blondie, abandons his companion tied up in the middle of the desert since the reward on his accomplice's head is not increasing,. The image freezes and the caption appears: ''The Good."

A group of drunken Confederate soldiers let Maria (Rada Rassimov) get off a wagon. Entering her house, the woman finds Angel Eyes lurking in the shadows; he beats her to make her tell him where Carson is.

After an exhausting march in the desert, Tuco reaches a village and quenches his thirst at a horse trough. Then he goes crashing into an emporium and makes the old proprietor show him his entire stock of pistols. After long examination he puts together a weapon composed of three pieces taken from various arms and tries out the new pistol in the courtyard, demonstrating his extraordinary aim. Then he goes off, but not before having emptied the shop's cash register.

The Confederate troops are retreating to a small town. In a hotel three of Tuco's killers sneak up the stairs to Blondie's room where he is cleaning a pistol. But despite the noise of the passing troops, the bounty hunter does not miss the sound of their spurs and he greets the Mexicans with three well-placed shots. All in vain, since Tuco enters from the window at his back, surprising him and ordering him to hang himself from a roofbeam. Blondie already has the rope around his neck when a cannon shot makes the floor give way and Tuco finds himself on the floor below. Above, the rope is still tied to the beam, but Blondie has escaped.

Angel Eyes reaches a half-destroyed fort where some Confederate soldiers have found refuge. At the end of their strength, they are boiling some corn cobs. The bandit questions them on the whereabouts of Bill Carson. They answer that if he is not dead he must have ended up in the Union prison camp at Betterville.

Tuco, who has gone in pursuit of Blondie reaches the bivouac that his rival has shortly abandoned. A cigar stub, still lit, is the sure sign he has been there.

Blondie is about to perform one of his usual last-minute rescues from the gallows with a new partner, Shorty. But Tuco, coming upon him from his back, points his pistol and orders him to leave his accomplice to his fate.

Tuco announces his vendetta: he is going to make Blondie cross the desert on foot, and to make it harder he shoots his hat off and shoots holes in his water bag.

Blondie, exhausted, makes his way among the dunes, his face scorched by the sun, accompanied by Tuco who protects himself under a parasol.

During a rest stop, Tuco washes his feet in a tub. Blondie, dying of thirst, crawls over on all fours, but the other, kicks over the tub with a scornful laugh. Prostrate, Blondie rolls down a dune. He does not have the strength to get up again and the other is just pointing his pistol at him to wipe him out, when the sound of hoofs announces the arrival of a stagecoach without a driver.

Inside are the corpses of some Confederate soldiers from which Tuco pilfers money and valuable objects. One of the dying soldiers is the famous Corporal Carson who, in exchange for a drink of water, reveals the secret that the regiment's cash box is buried in the cemetery at Sad Hill. Before telling him the name on the tomb, Carson demands that Tuco bring him the water bag. The latter goes off for a moment to get it, and on his return discovers that Carson has already died and has given the precious revelation to Blondie. So now it is in Tuco's interests to keep him alive.

Disguised in Corporal Carson's uniform (including his black eye-patch) Tuco drives the stagecoach, looking for a place where Blondie can be given medical treatment. At a Confederate check point they tell him that the only infirmary is in the Mission of San Antonio.

There the monks take Blondie under their care. Tuco, to get the tomb name out of him, deceives him about the condition of his health, insinuating that he is not going to make it. But his old partner is too cagey to fall into the trap and reacts by throwing a coffee cup at him.

Blondie is better by now. Before they leave, Tuco meets a brother of his, a monk (Luigi Pistilli) who reproves him for his sordid career of banditry.

Back on the march, the two, who are dressed in Confederate uniforms, meet up with a cavalry company. Tuco greets them joyously, singing hymns of praise to the Confederacy. Too late he realizes that their gray uniforms are in reality blue ones covered in dust.

They end up in the Union prison camp of Betterville. Tuco, who has assumed the identity of Corporal Carson, is late to answer roll call getting himself a punch in the stomach from the gigantic Corporal Wallace (Mario Brega) and arousing the suspicions of a sergeant who is none other than Angel Eyes.

The commander of the camp, forced by a gangrenous leg to be inactive, reproves him harshly for pilfering from the prisoners. Angel Eyes invites Tuco to lunch in his lodgings. After some initial diffidence, Tuco eats greedily. Seeing that the Mexican is playing dumb concerning the fate of the real Carson, Angel Eyes goes on to more persuasive measures. He crushes his finger in a tobacco box and has the corporal torture him while an orchestra composed of prisoners plays loudly to cover the Mexican's screams. At last, Tuco reveals the name of the cemetery where the treasure is buried.

Now it is Blondie's turn, but Angel Eyes, who despairs of being able to make him talk by torture, leaves with him for the cemetery at Sad Hill. The deal is that they will to split the treasure two ways.

The corporal takes Tuco to the train for the city where he must deliver the outlaw to the authorities and collect the reward.

Blondie and Angel Eyes are sleeping where they have camped for the night. Blondie, awakened by a suspicious rustling sound, shoots and hits a man hidden among the trees. At Angel Eyes' signal, his five stooges pop out of the woods and join the leads in the treasure hunt.

Tuco is traveling in a cattle car hand-cuffed to Corporal Wallace. At a certain point he asks his permission to urinate out of the car and takes advantage of the occasion to leap from the moving train, dragging the soldier with him. Then Tuco knocks his head against a rock, killing him.

To free himself from the handcuffs, he places the corpse between the railroad tracks so that a passing train will cut the chain.

Blondie and Angel Eyes reach a town which has been half destroyed by bombardments while a column of Union soldiers is passing through. Tuco, too, is in town, immersed in a bubble bath in a ruined hotel. An old enemy of his (the guy who lost an arm in the opening shoot-out) comes in to kill him, but the Mexican is faster and shoots him with a pistol hidden among the bubbles.

Blondie recognizes the unmistakable explosion and arrives intending to renew his old partnership with him. Out in the streets the two comrades get the better of Angel Eyes's men

Materials

thanks to their team-work and the smoke raised by the cannonades. But the gang leader manages to escape.

Along a wilderness trail, Blondie and Tuco, stopped by a Union patrol, are taken to the trenches alongside a river: the Confederates are installed on the other side of the river.

A captain who is a whisky lover and a war hater (ALDO GIUFFRÈ) complains about the indifference with which the high military command sends thousands of soldiers to be massacred just for the sake of taking the Langstone Bridge.

One of the daily battles begins in which, under the cover of an artillery barrage, hundreds of soldiers invade the bridge to fight in a bloody hand-to-hand battle. The captain is seriously wounded. The two adventurers, whom only the river separates from the treasure, decide to make short shrift of the situation and, with the captain's blessing take advantage of a cease-fire to mine the bridge. Each of them reveals his secret that is, the name of the cemetery and of the tomb (that of a certain Stanton) and light the fuse. On hearing the explosion, the captain dies in peace.

After spending the night in a ditch, sheltered from the bombardment, Tuco and Blondie wake up to find the whole area evacuated. Only the corpses testify to the previous day's battle. They wade across the river. Among the ruins of a small church Blondie comforts a dying Confederate soldier. He covers him with his cloak and gives him a cigar. Tuco takes advantage of this to go off on horseback, but the other one stops him with a gun shot.

On falling, the Mexican tumbles against a tombstone and finds that he is in the immense Sad Hill cemetery.

After an exhausting search he discovers Stanton's tomb and begins digging with his hands. Blondie is behind him and throws him a shovel. Angel Eyes appears holding a pistol, throws Blondie a shovel and orders him to dig. But in the grave all they find is a skeleton.

Blondie lied. Now he scratches the name of the real grave on a potsherd and places it at the center of a stony circle. The three of them stand on the edge of the circle and prepare to hold a three-way duel. They stare at each other, leer, and challenge each other then draw their pistols in a flash. The Blondie kills Angel Eyes who tumbles into the open grave while Tuco realizes that his pistol is not loaded – his partner unloaded his pistol when he was not looking.

There is nothing scratched on the potsherd at the center of the circle; in fact, the treasure is found in the unmarked grave next to Stanton's. Tuco digs, finds the the bags of gold and exults, but he has a bad surprise in store.

He is standing on a creaky wooden cross with a rope around his neck while Blondie rides off in the horizon after having placed half the loot at the foot of the cross. He reappears, rifle in hand, and shoots through the rope with infallible aim. Tuco falls face-first into the gold. The picture freezes and there appears the caption "the Ugly", followed in turn by "the Good" and "the Bad" (in the grave). It ends with Tuco shouting a colorful insult at his disappearing partner.

PRINCIPAL SCENES CUT OFF IN THE ITALIAN RELEASE VERSION

1. After the hold-up in the armory, Tuco, hidden in a cave, is roasting a potato when suddenly three Mexicans appear and Tuco recruits them to wipe out
Blondie.

2. Tuco, on Blondie's track, reaches a village on the Mexican border where the Confederates are trying to recruit poor peons. Full of pity, Tuco takes up a collection. He enters a saloon and discovers that Blondie is upstairs in bed with a woman. Blondie then makes a spectacular escape, taking the collection money with him.

3. The first scene has been included during the restoration of the film by the Cineteca of Bologna in 2014.

CRITICS

[...] Now, with Sergio Leone's latest film, *The Good, the Bad and the Ugly,* the Italianization of the Western genre could be considered to be over once and for all. The dominant theme is no longer that of a struggle between an intrepid lone hero and the negative forces of nature and society; but that of the greed for money. It is all about petty criminals, who remained firmly in the background of American films, but who in these Spaghetti Westerns step to the forefront and become the heroes. The quality that redeems them, at least in the eyes of Italian viewers, is no longer generosity, but cunning, or rather "ingenuity". These characters are far more like Andreuccio da Perugia[71] than Buffalo Bill. *The Good, the Bad and the Ugly* is hypertrophic and overblown. The interminable silences and long drawn out action sequences are reminiscent of the mafia and go on forever. The sadism is almost grotesque. Moreover, every episode seems forced and dragged out beyond all credibility. Lee Van Cleef's squint and Clint Eastwood's half-smoked cigar cannot hold out for three hours; in the end they are quite without expression.

[Alberto Moravia, "L'Espresso", 8 January 1967]

Ugly/Tuco sums up all the sins and contradictions of the human race: rage and joy, deceit and candor, cowardice and courage, greed and generosity, gaucherie and malice. Clumsy, cunning, scornful, gullible, sarcastic, Ugly is the very spirit of the movie, a scoundrel of little worth, a luckless loser bearing all the troubles of the world on his shoulders, a tormented, unfortunate simpleton who tries to make up for his troubles in the quickest way possible. How can we not like and feel for such a scoundrel? When he is ill-treated or offended we laugh at his wry face and his cussing; when he offends or is cruel to another he does it (or maybe they let him do it) in an unheroic way. (Eli Walach splendidly brings to this character all the aspects, all the nuances of uncouth roguery, of cheeky hypocrisy, of disarming simplicity.) Ugly is a character that lies in every way between the Good and the Bad, between the devil and the deep blue sea; someone we feel sorry for even though he is often little more than a parody. In order to stimulate this feeling of pity in viewers, Leone transforms the sequencing of certain scenes, completely reversing the principles on which this editing technique, pioneered by D.W. Griffith, has been based for the last fifty years: Leone takes a scene of violence and alternates it with another scene that is preparatory to the violence. Ugly is beaten up by one of Bad's thugs and Leone cross cuts it with a scene of Confederate prisoners singing to cover up Ugly's screams. Leone has conferred to the "here comes the cavalry" line of action, which usually makes up the shorter segments in alternated editing, a different value: that of non-violence and compassion. The scenes of the Confederate chorus have become the longer segments, the ones viewers do not want to see because at that point they are on the side of Ugly and are worried about him, while Ugly being beaten up is comprised of the shorter segments, the ones that viewers want to see, not for sadist pleasure (the scene is not sadistic at all) but because they like Ugly and want to see what is happening inside the hut where he is being set upon and because the violence he is suffering is a violence that touches viewers directly.

[Enzo Natta, "Cineforum", January 1967]

This is the code of the West as it might have been interpreted by Machiavelli. Trust no one and turn your back on no on. Some of the torments have a Renaissance ingenuity, like tying a man's hands behind his back, making him stand on the cross of a grave, scattering the coveted gold at his feet, throwing a noose around his neck – and just riding off leaving him to work it out. The overlap between the code of the West and the code of the Borgias is a useful sidelight on the Western myth. The film also comes close to another Latin tradition, that of the picaresque novel, in its succession of episodes, its sense of space and journeying, and its pleasure in the tricks, quick wit and low cunning of a collection of rogues and vagabonds who keep crossing one another's trail. The landscapes reminded my companion of *Planet of*

---

[71] From a tale by Italian poet Giovanni Boccaccio.

the Apes and have something of that real/unreal feeling - partly, perhaps, because they are like the American West, and European at the same time. Also, each situation is an enigma, in one way or another, which becomes a different form of suspense. Although at first the film rigorously abstains from any polarity of morals, it does have a polarity of sympathy (e.g. we prefer underdogs to top dogs, we feel sorry for weak, old, worried faces, we prefer the blustering villain to the steel-cold one). And, very subtly and cautiously, a moral contrast does emerge. But it's never clear enough to weaken our feeling that anything could happen – while enough minor and marginal injustices keep any complacency at bay. The most spectacular is the scene where our dollar-grasping adventurers get involved with a long, futile and bloody battle between North and South over a strategic bridge; and war's wholesale slaughter suddenly reduces the ruthlessness to an almost lovable insignificance.

[Raymond Durgnat, "Films and Filming", November 1968]

Apart from any hint of condemnation of the violence, apart from the implicit denunciation of the absurdity of war, any war, the film is indisputably a powerful, radically constant invitation to an orgy of cruelty, of contempt for human life and natural emotions.

[Centro Cattolico Cinematografico]

1968
Once Upon a Time in the West
C'era una Volta il West
Il Etait une Fois dans l'Ouest
Hasta que Llegò su Hora

Director: Sergio Leone; *story:* Dario Argento, Bernardo Bertolucci, Sergio Leone; *screenplay*: Sergio Donati, Sergio Leone, Luciano Vincenzoni; *music and director of music*: Ennio Morricone (harmonica: Franco De Gemini; voice: Edda Dell'Orso; whistle: Alessandro Alessandroni); *sound*: Claudio Maielli, Elio Pacella, Fausto Ancillai; *cinematography:* Tonino Delli Colli (Technicolor, Techniscope); *camera operator:* Franco Di Giacomo; *special effects*: Eros Baciucchi, Giovanni Corridori; *art direction and costumes*: Carlo Simi; *editing:* Nino Baragli; *first assistant director*: Giancarlo Santi; *assistant director*: Salvo Basile.

Cast and Characters: Claudia Cardinale (Jill McBain), Henry Fonda (Frank), Charles Bronson (Harmonica), Jason Robards (Manuel "Cheyenne" Gutiérrez), Gabriele Ferzetti (Morton), Paolo Stoppa (Sam, the coachman), Woody Strode (Stony, first gunman in the prologue), Jack Elam (Snaky, second gunman who plays with the fly in the prologue), Al Mulock (third gunman who plays with his hands in the prologue), Marco Zuanelli (Wobbles), Keenan Wynn (sheriff of Flagstone), Frank Wolff (Brett McBain), Enzo Santaniello (Timmy McBain), Simonetta Santaniello (Maureen McBain), Lionel Stander (barman), John Frederick (Jim, member of Frank's gang), Fabio Testi and Benito Stefanelli (members of Frank's gang), Spartaco Conversi (member of Frank's gang shot through boot by Cheyenne), Aldo Sambrell (member of Cheyenne's gang), Dino Mele (Harmonica as a boy), Claudio Mancini (Harmonica's older brother), Raffaella e Francesca Leone (girls at Flagstone station), Luana Strode (Indian woman at the station in the prologue), Aldo Berti, Livio Andronico, Salvo Basile, Bruno Corazzari, Conrado Sanmartin, Luigi Ciavarro, Renato Pinciroli, Ivan G. Scratuglia, Paolo Figlia, Stefano Imparato, Frank Leslie, Luigi Magnani, Umberto Marsella, Enrico Morsella, Tullio Palmieri, Sandra Salvatori, Claudio Scarchilli, Michael Harvey, Marilù Carteny.
Main dubbers: Rita Savagnone for Claudia Cardinale, Nando Gazzolo for Henry Fonda, Carlo Romano for Jason Robards, Giuseppe Rinaldi for Charles Bronson.

Origin: Italy/United States
Producer: Bino Cicogna.
Executive producer: Fulvio Morsella.
Production: Rafran Cinematografica, San Marco Films.

Filming (interiors): Cinecittà, Luce (Rome).
Filming (exteriors): Almeria, Guadix, La Calahorra, (Spain); Monument Valley and other locations in Arizona and Utah (USA); Bavispe (Mexico).

Running time: 175' (restored full-length Italian version [director's cut], 167' (original Italian version), 165' (American version), 164' (French version), 144' (English version).

Distribution: Euro International Films (Italy), Paramount (USA).
Release date: 21 December1968.
Release date USA: 28 May 1969.
Release date France: 27August 1969.

📖 As the opening titles appear, three shady types wearing long leather coats who work for a certain Frank are silently waiting for the train to arrive at the tiny desert station of Little Corner. Only one passenger gets off, Harmonica (CHARLES BRONSON) who confronts the three and shoots them down in a flash, but falls himself with a shoulder wound.

On the isolated Sweetwater Farm, Ed McBain (FRANK WOLFF), an Irish widower, and his two children are preparing a banquet to welcome the bride-to-be who is arriving from New Orleans. Suddenly firing is heard and they are shot down one after the other. Five bandits emerge from the bushes led by Frank (HENRY FONDA) who does not even have pity on the lone survivor, a child, and shoots it dead.

At the Flagstone station passengers get off a train, among them Jill (CLAUDIA CARDINALE), McBain's bride-to-be.

We next see her in the wagon of Sam (PAOLO STOPPA), a crusty old man nostalgic for the primitive Old West, riding through the crowded streets of Flagstone. They cross the railway yard, then Monument Valley.

They stop in a tavern. Shortly, Cheyenne (JASON ROBARDS) makes his appearance, a bandit still in handcuffs who has just shot his guards. From a shadowy corner comes the sound of a harmonica: it is Harmonica. Cheyenne provokes him without getting a reaction. The bandit has to make do with scaring a customer and making him cut the chain of his handcuffs with a gunshot as he keeps him covered by his own pistol to avoid any surprises. Cheyenne's men arrive in leather coats. The explanations they give to Harmonica make us realize that this is a kind of uniform for their gang – that is why the three thugs at Little Corner, Frank's henchmen, were wearing them as a trick.

Sam and Jill arrive at the farm where the small group of guests for the wedding feast are gathered in silence around the corpses of the McBains laid out on the tables outside the house. Jill explains that the wedding ceremony has already taken place in New Orleans.

Once the burial is over, a strip of leather coat is found which is immediately taken as evidence of Cheyenne's guilt.

Alone in the house, Jill searches nervously in the drawers and chests and then, fully dressed, stretches out on the large matrimonial bed.

In a Chinese laundry Harmonica manhandles the proprietor, the unctuous Wobbles, who has ordered the three killers, on Frank's behalf, to kill Harmonica at the Little Corner station.

At the farm, Jill has just found several wooden models of public buildings in the drawers when she hears the familiar sound of a harmonica playing outside. She turns out the light, takes a rifle and shoots at a little flame that is shining in the night, but the sound of the harmonica does not stop.

The following morning the ground in front of the house appears to be deserted. Jill opens the door and suddenly Cheyenne appears with his men. He does not appear to be contemplating any harm as he enters alone protesting his innocence for the McBain massacre. But he does not know who was responsible.

In a luxurious private car the owner of the railroad, the paralytic engineer Morton (Gabriele Ferzetti), reproves Frank for having gone far beyond his mandate by killing the McBains while not managing to stop, among other things, the appearance of the McBain widow. The bandit is inclined to violent methods and disdains the businessman. The latter, despite his hurry to reach the Pacific, eliminating all obstacles along his path, does not tire of telling Frank that money is the strongest weapon.

Meanwhile, back on the farm, Jill's condor and her talent as a cook have won Cheyenne's trust. He takes his leave politely.

In the stable Jill is getting ready to load the baggage on the wagon when Harmonica appears and orders her brusquely to stay. He begins to rip off her clothes, then orders her to go to the well. The disarray of Jill's clothes and her routine activities at the well distract two killers on horseback who have probably come to get rid of the widow. Harmonica draws his gun with lightning speed and mows them down while Cheyenne watches with satisfaction from a hilltop.

At the Chinese laundry Jill tells Wobbles she wants to talk to Frank. Wobbles denies knowing him, but then goes out, apparently exhausted. Harmonica follows him from a distance.

Wobbles arrives at Morton's private car and tells Frank of Jill's visit. Frank notices that Harmonica is hiding on the roof of the train and orders the engineer to leave.

The train stops in the middle of the desert as Frank's men arrive on horseback. After killing Wobbles with three pistol shots because he incautiously allowed himself to be followed to the train, Frank stops Harmonica and asks him his name and what he wants. He gets no reply. Harmonica remembers something (in flashback) very vaguely. Frank leaves on horseback for the McBain farm.

On the moving train Cheyenne, hiding out on the roof, eliminates the three bandit bodyguards with some clever maneuvering and frees Harmonica.

At the farm Jill receives a delivery of a large amount of wood that her husband ordered. No one knows what it is to be used for, but the woman remembers a wooden model with the word "station" written on it. She is rummaging around in the storeroom when a hand offers her what she is looking for: it is Frank's hand.

In front of the entrance to a cavern, the bandits' hide-out, Morton advises Frank not to kill the woman prisoner, but the latter seems mainly interested in humiliating his partner, even knocking him to the floor by kicking at his crutches.

At the farm, Harmonica tells Cheyenne about McBain's project of building a station which, according to the terms of the contract, should be operating when the railroad arrives. The two of them begin hammering in stakes so that Jill will find the job completed on her return.

In the bandits' hide-out Frank is in bed with Jill who, with her amorous skills (in New Orleans she worked as a prostitute), probably is hoping to get him to spare her life.

In Flagstone the sheriff is auctioning off the McBain farm with the consent of the widow who is present. Frank's men intimidate the aspiring buyers.

On the train Morton is contemplating a picture of the Pacific Ocean, the supreme goal of all his efforts. Then, joining Frank's men who are playing poker, he distributes banknotes rather than cards.

In the meantime the auction has reached the moment of truth and the farm is about to be sold at a ridiculously low price to Frank's representative. At the top of the stairs Harmonica appears covering Cheyenne with his pistol. The brigand, with a big reward on his head, is Harmonica's bid. A horseman departs from Morton's railway car.

The sheriff and his helpers escort Cheyenne to the train for Yuma where there is a well-known penitentiary. The bandit's henchmen are already casing the site.

In a deserted saloon Jill is reassured by Harmonica who, in fact, is restoring her property to her. While she is going up the stairs, Frank vainly tries to buy the farm from Harmonica and to get him to give his name. The latter has another flashback, a little clearer than the previous one, where he sees Frank in his youth.

On the floor above, where Jill is taking a bath, Harmonica, indifferent to her charms, is on the balcony keeping track of Frank's movements (who is cautiously wandering in the deserted streets shooting at Morton's killers in ambush on the roof tops). Harmonica joins in the action, personally eliminating several killers and sending signals to Frank. This strange behavior puzzles the widow.

Frank reaches the private train stopped in the desert. There is no sign of life. Corpses are strewn inside and outside the train. A little farther off, Morton is dying near a puddle.

The railway construction site has by now reached the vicinity of the McBains' property where the station is almost fully built. Harmonica is leaning against a wooden fence whittling a piece of wood when Frank arrives, determined to discover who he is and challenge him to a duel.

From with in the house Jill and Cheyenne observe the scene. The duellists, about to begin combat, stare long at each other and Frank tries to position the other with the sun in his eyes. Harmonica has a clear recollection.

Flashback. Frank and his henchmen have put a rope around a man's neck, attaching it to a stone arch. To prolong the agony they have balanced him on the shoulders of a boy in whose mouth they haye stuck a harmonica. The boy falls exhausted in the dust and the other, having lost his support, breaks his neck. That adolescent was Harmonica, the hanged man his brother.

Return to the present. The duellists draw and fire, Frank spins round and falls to the ground. Dying, Frank asks: "Who are you?" and Harmonica for an answer sticks the harmonica into his mouth. With that act the bandit before dying may remember the long-forgotten episode.

Harmonica enters the house, takes his things, and departs. Cheyenne too takes his leave – a little bitterly because he would have been glad to stay if Jill had asked him to. But the woman was only attracted by the mysterious harmonica player, who paid no attention to her.

The two adventurers are not far from the house when Cheyenne drops to the ground, thus revealing that Morton had shot him from behind during the shoot-out on the train. He begs his friend not to watch him die.

The credits come up as Harmonica on horseback disappears into the distance, carrying the body of Cheyenne.

PRINCIPAL SCENES CUT OFF IN THE ITALIAN RELEASE VERSION

1. On arriving in Flagstone, Jill offers Sam two banknotes if he will take her to Sweetwater in his wagon.

2. Harmonica is lying on a bed in a room above Wobbles' laundry. The proprietor's wife, a beautiful Mexican woman, enters and offers herself to him. He asks her to massage his feet, which she does. Suddenly the woman's two capable hands are replaced by the two strong hands of a man. Harmonica has no time to react. Three tough guys begin beating him up and push him into a stable where the sheriff is waiting for him. The latter has found a long leather coat under Harmonica's saddle and they are identical to those used by McBain's murderers. Harmonica puts on the coat. It is too short for him. The sheriff is convinced of his innocence; Harmonica beats up the three tough guys and leaves.

3. A bank official in Flagstone shows Jill a certificate that McBain had entrusted to him fifteen years earlier: it is a deed to the Sweetwater property.

4. Harmonica and Cheyenne look admiringly at the facade of the station they have just finished building.

5. The auction scene is preceded by a long prologue in the barbershop where Frank is getting a shave. Silently, Harmonica observes the scene through the shop window. Leaning against the corner of a building he is whittling a piece of wood. He sees Jill arrive in a wagon with one of Frank's men; she turns to the sheriff to set the date of the auction of the Sweetwater property.

Materials

6. After the surprise intervention at the auction by Cheyenne and Harmonica, a man rushes to the barbershop to inform Frank who has just finished his shave.

[Some scenes, cut off in the Italian edition, were put back into the edition restored in 1995 longer by 11', under the direction of Clavier Salizzato, in cooperation with Alessandro Baragli e Fausto Ancillai, with the assistance of Sergio Leone Production, Telepiù, Centro Sperimentale di Cinematografia / Cineteca Nazionale.]

CRITICS

Many aspects of this film are typically Baroque: the sweeping story, the broad interiors, the penchant for details, but also the introduction of one or more fringe stories within the main theme, a scheme dear to the picaresque genre. Like all forms of the Baroque, this film has its own peculiarities, akin to the literary models familiar in France, where "qualities merge into differences, differences into contrasts, and the sensible world is polarized according to the rigorous laws of a sort of material geometry" (Gérard Genette). There is in Leone, together with a predilection for erosion, putrefaction and death, an appreciation for work. The narrative oscillates between the beech tree chosen by McBain for building purposes and the nothing that tempts Cheyenne and the others[72]. Close to the sawmill some men are killed and Harmonica cuts a piece of wood before going off to kill Frank in a final shoot-out, while all around men go about their business as if nothing were wrong. This collective background provides the film with its realistic basis. By choosing as the film's framework the construction of a railroad, Leone renews a tradition that has seen many moments of glory in film history, one among them John Ford's *The Iron Horse*. But these features serve merely to stimulate the imagination. Leone has chosen a sombre tone, punctuated by strokes of humour. But the film's seriousness and lyricism are never an imitation. We are not in the West, but in an imaginary place that exists thanks to the West and its physical reality. From the appearance of Woody Strode to the scene of Claudia Cardinale walking toward the wells, *Once Upon a Time in the West* is the spitting image of a Western, but never actually becomes one. Leone attempts to rekindle suspended time, chasing after the authentic West he knows he will never catch, but in doing so developing his own personal universe. Once again the Baroque is not far off, and thanks to this singular detour, the West is not far off either.

[Michel Ciment, "Positif", November 1969]

The myth of the Western, underpinned by a primitive violence, could not but lead Leone to a serious reflection on human destiny in *Once Upon a Time in the West*. To be tragic, according to a somewhat pretentious tradition that still carries weight, means to be serious and epic. *Once Upon a Time in the West* is indeed serious and epic: protracted pace, but full of suspense (arcane), vast spaces, clever, mellow counter lighting (sunsets provide most of the lighting effects throughout the film), precise transitions from one shot to another, calmly executed except for the canonical killing scenes where the rhythm intensifies, close ups and extreme close ups of both main and secondary characters in equal measure (held for a long time which, on the big screen, makes them look like anatomical scans). The philosophy of the "savage" assumes deviant connotations. Harmonica, Frank, Cheyenne, Morton all go alone to face their destiny, spied on by the attentive eye of a director who loves them as idols of a lost world. They are the last, titanic individualists, who win or lose with neither joy nor human desperation, but because that is what fate has decided. Their actions, their hatred, their vendettas are guided by a god. They can be neither appraised nor judged. The viewers, if they can overcome the tedium of this ritual sombreness, are invited to admire in silence, and to evaluate step by step the chasm that divides them, the insignificant, contemptible

---

[72] The pun referred to Sartre's *Being and Nothingness*. It's based on the homophony between the French words "être = to be" and "hêtre = beech".

271

viewers, from these idols. Apart from the tragic Greeks, Leone is also familiar with Nietzsche and his concept of the Overman. And he loves only the Overman (who leaves as soon as he has finished his fatal task, at which point those petty, insignificant little men involved in the construction of a railroad, take the reins).

[Fernaldo Di Giammatteo, "Bianco e Nero", January-February 1969]

Once Upon a Time in the West is Sergio Leone's most American Western, but it is still dominantly and paradoxically European in spirit, at one and the same time Christian and Marxist, despairing and exultant, nihilistic and regenerative. In the very beginning, Strode, shortly before he is to be gunned down, feels some drops of water falling on his forehead as he is framed in close-ups on the fresco-like wide screen. He places his Stetson on his head so that it will receive the water between its camel-like humps, and shortly thereafter he drinks the water from the Stetson in a gesture so ceremonial as to make the hat seem like a holy chalice. We have been told that Italian and other "furriners" should not meddle in a distinctively American art form. But actually Leone is no further away from the legends of the American West than the Florentine Renaissance painters were from the Crucifixion, and if film is even partly a visual medium, Leone's vision is as valid as anyone else's. Indeed, Leone has succeeded in making what is essentially a silent movie and we would still have been shown all that is essential to know about the obsessive concerns of the characters. We would have come to understand Claudia Cardinale's role as the bearer of water, life, and continuity to the civilization in the New West. We would see that around the edge of the Bronson-Fonda confrontation is the fashionable leftist flourish of the Latino revenging himself on the Anglo, but only around the edges. At the core of the confrontation is not the politics of a revisionist genre, but the mythology of a poetic parable and how fitting it is that the aging prairie liberalism of Ford's features should be foredoomed by a revenge plot of awesomely Freudian dimensions. Even so, Leone takes no chance with his archetypes. Fonda's hubris cannot be curbed merely for past excesses. In the course of the movie itself, he and his long-coated henchmen must be shown exterminating an entire family down to a small child as an expression of big business at work overcoming obstacles at whatever cost to moral values. And we must see again and again (without any dialogue) the dreamlike reenactment of the traumatic experience of Charles Bronson's revenge-seeker with the Harmonica so that all the violence and all the close-ups may finally fit into a harmonic pattern of the feelings of loss we can never forget or even endure until we have transformed them into the poetry of fables and fantasies. The Western is above all fable and fantasy, as desire for revenge is childish and fruitless. Leone has understood fully that in setting out with his hero to learn to kill, he has learned instead that he has come this way only to learn how to die. The gunfights themselves partake of Leone's penchant for the circular staging of the corrida. At one point Bronson actually extends one foot forward as if to execute an intricate maneuver with a cape, but this is the West, and history comes out of the barrel of a gun, a dynamic truth Leone emphasizes with his intercutting of locomotives thrusting out of cavernous gun barrels.

[Andrew Sarris, «The Village Voice», August 1970]

1971
Duck! You Sucker / A Fistful of Dinamite

Giù la Testa
Il Etait une Fois la Révolution
Agàchate, Maldito!

Director: Sergio Leone; *story*: Sergio Donati, Sergio Leone; *screenplay:* Sergio Donati, Sergio Leone, Luciano Vincenzoni (*dialogue adaption*: Roberto De Leonardis, Carlo Tritto); *music and director of music*: Ennio Morricone; *cinematography*: Giuseppe Ruzzolini (Technicolor, Techniscope); *camera operator*: Idelmo Simonelli; *second unit cinematography*: France Delli Colli; *special effects*: Antonio Margheriti; *art direction*: Andrea Crisanti; *set decoration*: Dario Micheli; *stunts:* Benito Stefanelli; *editing:* Nino Baragli; *second unit director*: Martin Herbert [Alberto De Martino], Giancarlo Santi; *assistant director*: Tony Brandt.

Cast and Characters: Rod Steiger (Juan Miranda), James Coburn (John/Sean Mallory), Romolo Valli (Dr. Villega), Franco Graziosi (Governor Huerta), Domingo Antoine [Antoine Saint-John] (Col. Gunther Reza), David Warbeck (Nolan, John's friend), Vivienne Chandler (Coleen, John's girlfriend), Rik Battaglia (Santerna), Maria Monti (Adelita, coach passenger), Jean Rouguel (priest on stagecoach), Roy Bosier (landowner on stagecoach), John Frederick (American on stagecoach), Antonio Casale (notary on stagecoach), Michael Harvey and Conrado San Martin (stagecoach drivers), Goffredo Pistoni (Nino), Corrado Solari (Sebastian), Renato Pontecchi (Pepe), Franco Collace (Napoleone Miranda), Amelio [Memé] Perlini (peon), Biagio La Rocca ("Benito"), Goffredo Pistoni (Juan's father), Vincenzo Norvese (Pancho Miranda), Amato Garbini and Franco Tocci (policemen on the train), Anthony Vernon (passenger on the stagecoach), Giulio Battiferri (Miguel), Nazzareno Natale (member of Juan's family), Fabrizio Moresco (one of Juan's sons), Omar Bonaro, Florencio Amarilla , Sergio Calderon, Luigi Tripodi and Stefano Oppedisano (revolutionaries), Poldo Bendanti and Furio Meniconi (executed revolutionaries), Edmondo Tieghi (member of the firing squad), Benito Stefanelli (guard), Manuel Bermudez (Mexican with dynamite), Saturno Carra and Romano Milani (prisoners in the bank), Alberigo Donadeo (Santerna man), Luis Morris (man who spits at poster), Paolo Figlia (soldier), Aldo Sambrell (Mexican officer), Simon van Collem, Rosita Torosh.
Main dubbers: Carlo Romano for Rod Steiger, Giuseppe Rinaldi for James Coburn, Sergio Tedesco for Dominigo Antoine, Pino Locchi for Rik Battaglia.

Origin: Italy/Spain.
Producers: Sergio Leone, Fulvio Morsella.
Production: Rafran Cinematografica, San Marco Films.

Filming (interiors): Studi Dino De Laurentiis (Rome).
Filming (exteriors): Almeria, Guadix, Burgos, Soria, Granada, La Calahorra (Spain); Dublin, Wicklow County, Howth Castle (Ireland).

Running time: 154' (Italy), 138' (USA, United Kingdom), 150' (France).

Distribution: Euro International Films (Italy), United Artists (USA).
Release date: 29 October 1971.
Release date France: 29 March 1972.
Release date USA: 28 June 1972.

📖 A quotation from Mao: "A Revolution is not a dinner party..." As the opening titles are shown Juan (ROD STEIGER) urinates against a tree and then flags down a stagecoach along a country road. The guards search him carefully, make him pay his passage and let him into the coach.

Inside the sumptuously furnished vehicle, the passengers (a clergyman, an elegant lady, and an American) are eating lunch. To humiliate Juan they make him sit on a foot stool and chat derisively about the promiscuous ways of the peasants.

The stagecoach has to slow down. Some peons slip under the vehicle, block the wheels and massacre the guards in a shoot-out. They are Juan's sons, his old father and some of his men.

One passenger, who tries to get out his pistol, is killed. The woman is dragged by Juan behind the house where in a rather still and passive way she lets him rape her. All the passengers are robbed of their valuables and clothes and are boarded onto a wagon which is pushed downhill and ends up in a watering hole.

Now Juan and his family are traveling in the stagecoach. They stop suddenly because of a landslide brought on by an explosion. It is the work of Sean (JAMES COBURN), an Irish terrorist who is practicing the use of dynamite. He is traveling on a motorcycle and his overalls are lined with explosives. The two now embark in a loud exchange of insults. The Mexican shoots a tire of Sean's motorcycle. The latter, in turn, rips open the roof of the coach with nitroglycerin. After giving them another taste of explosives, he gets them to repair his tire. One of Juan's men tries to use the dynamite by himself but he gets the wrong fuse and is blown up.

The two of them have an outdoor lunch on the elegant seats removed from the stagecoach. Sean lets his mind dwell on memories.

Flashback. An automobile excursion in the Irish country side. In the car Sean, a friend (DAVID WARBECK), and a girl (VIVIENNE CHANDLER). Sean and the girl kiss.

Juan had other things on his mind and proposes an alliance to rob the famous Mesa Verde bank. Sean declines and goes off on his motorcycle. The irate Mexican shoots a hole in his gas tank, and Sean, in turn, blows up the coach. Then he goes off on foot towards a mine where he has been engaged to search of silver.

One night Sean, who happens to find himself near an old, abandoned mission, mistakes some shadows moving among the ruins for Juan and his men. He sets up mines around the area and is preparing to detonate them when Juan appears and presses the detonator with his foot. Inside the fort were the mine owner and some soldiers whom Juan had lured to the spot. Sean, now without a job and with the law on his trail, is obliged to join up with the brigands.

The gang is riding alongside the railroad tracks when a train separates Sean from the Mexicans for a few minutes. Sean seizes the opportunity to escape.

Juan and his sons are riding on a train at night. With them in the compartment is Dr. Villega (ROMOLO VALLI) immersed in a book. A policeman is on the point of recognizing Juan, who stabs him and throws him off the train. Another policeman intervenes and Juan holds up his hands, but very soon the policeman must surrender when Dr. Villega points a pistol in his back. Thus the bandit throws the second guard from the train.

The group gets off at the Mesa Verde station. The streets are full of soldiers. From the announcements put up all over town, the benevolent governor declares he offers bread and justice.

A man who is trying to escape from the soldiers runs towards Juan, is struck by a bullet in the back, and dies in his arms. Next, the bandit happens to witness the execution of three political prisoners. Finally, he meets Sean in a tavern facing the bank.

Flashback. Sean's Irish friend is handing out a revolutionary newspaper in a Dublin pub. Return to the present. John leads the Mexican into the cellar of an inn which serves as a hideout for the conspirators. Villega is finishing up attending to one of them and he reveals the plan for a general rebellion: Juan is to hold up the bank. The rogue is happy to accept the job since he is counting on making off with the loot.

On the day of the insurrection, Sean, installed in the tavern, blows up the entrance door of the bank with a charge of dynamite hidden in the toy train that one of Juan's sons has dragged down under the building. The Mexican leads his men into the bank, but in the safes, instead of gold, he finds dozens of political prisoners who acclaim him as a hero of the revolution. This does not seem to console him for the loss of the booty.

Materials

In a desert area, Gunther Reza (Domingo Antoine), the Teutonic condottiere of Huerta's troops, is traveling in an armored car at the head of some marching soldiers.

Sean and Juan are resting in the rebel's camp. The Mexican rants bitterly and resentfully about the futility of all revolutions.

The rebels shake off their pursuers by doubling back towards the grotto of San Isidro. Sean and Juan, for their part, are lying in wait for the enemy troops from the heights of a hill overlooking a bridge. The Irishman kills time by napping while the Mexican seethes with anger over such a display of phlegm. As soon as Huerta's troops are on the bridge, the two begin to machine-gun them until they take cover under the arcades. Then Sean stops shooting, puts cotton into his ears and, activating the detonator, blows up the bridge. Gunther Reza comes out of it uninjured.

In the San Isidro grotto, Juan, seized by desperation, rips a chain with a crucifix from his neck and, throwing all caution to the winds, grabs a machine gun and goes out to confront the soldiers who quickly take him prisoner. In the meantine Sean discovers the bodies of the massacred rebels. Among them are the Mexican's father and all his sons.

At night, in a courtyard hammered by rain and lit by the lights of military trucks, several conspirators are executed after first having to pass before Gunther Reza's truck. Beside him Dr. Villega is sitting, his face marked with bruises, and identifies the prisoners. Among the small crowd witnessing the scene is Sean who recognizes Villega and recalls a similar occurrence in a Dublin pub.

Flashback. The English police smash their way into a pub and Sean's friend, his face swollen by thrashing, identifies some of the customers. When Sean's turn comes, he turns and shoots with a gun hidden in a newspaper.

Return to the present. The condemned fall under the hail of bullets. An officer gives them the *coup de grace* with his pistol.

The next day Juan is about to face the firing squad in the courtyard of a barracks when the Irishman attacks the platoon with dynamite and escapes on his motorcycle taking the condemned man with him.

Near the railroad a mass execution of political prisoners is taking place. By now Huerta's defeat is judged to be imminent and at the station a great throng is waiting for the train to the United States. But not all of them manage to board it. An officer who has hidden his uniform under an overcoat is shot down together with two prisoners. Juan and Sean, hidden in the cattle car, are looking forward to grandiose hold-ups in the land of the dollar. The last to board is the governor, the one with his picture on all the posters.

As Sean is strangling a wild rooster that is disturbing his sleep by fluttering its wings, a truck on the tracks brings the train to a halt. The rebels begin their assault. The governor tries to flee, enters the cattle car and is captured by John and Juan. The images of his massacred family come into Juan's mind, but when the governor offers him a bag full of valuables in exchange for his life, he stares at the contents and seems tempted. The governor takes advantage of his distraction to open the doors of the car and only then does Juan decide to kill him with two bullets in the back. He wants to reach the border with the loot, but the rebels who have won the day, acclaim him as a hero and carry him around in triumph.

On the moving train, in the car being used by the rebels as a general headquarters, they are thinking about how to block a train Huerta has sent after them. Sean proposes dynamite. To put his plan into action he only needs one man, Dr. Villega.

Gunther Reza is brushing his teeth on the military train. It is night. Villega, alone with Sean on the moving locomotive, realizes that the other knows of his betrayal and asks his pardon.

The Irishman remembers (in flashback) the end of the episode in the pub where he killed not only the policemen but his own friend who had given in to torture.

That act must have cost him a lot and now he declines to inflict the same punishment on the doctor. The locomotive, loaded with dynamite, proceeds towards the military train. Sean lights the fuse and leaps off. Villega decides to redeem himself with a heroic death. The trains collide and blow up. The rebels, hidden behind the irrigators, unleash their attack on the survivors. Sean is hit in the back by Gunther Reza. For vengeance Juan mows him down with his machine gun then vents his fury by blasting away at the corpse. As the Irishman dies, he prophesies that Juan will be named a general and gives him back the chain with the crucifix. Then, as Juan goes off in search of help, he takes his cigar and ignites the arsenal he carries on his person. As the end credits unroll we see Juan's distraught face, "What about me?"

PRINCIPAL SCENES CUT OFF FROM THE ITALIAN RELEASE VERSION

1. At first, Sean and Juan's trip in the desert was much longer. (At a certain point, the boys take the Irishman's motorcycle and completely dismantle it; the father yells at them, and they have to put it back together.)

2. After their victorious battle on the bridge, the rebels reunite in the grottoes. They look worried. In flashback, Sean recalls his past in Ireland. Overcome with rage he throws a bottle at a gramophone.

3. Dr. Villega is tortured by Gunther Reza and his men. Only their shadows on the wall are visible.

4. The epilogue: A flashback with a long panorama of the great green spaces of Ireland. Sean kisses a girl under a tree. So does his friend, without John seeming to be jealous. [This scene, that lasts three minutes and forty seconds was uncut from versions in other European countries and was put back into the 1996 version, restored under the direction of Claver Salizzato, in cooperation with Alessandro Baragli and Fausto Ancillai, with the aid of Sergio Leone Production, Telepiù, and Centro Sperimentale di Cinematografia Cineteca Nazionale].

CRITICS

The first time we are puzzled by this film is immediately after the credits, when a quote by Mao Tse Tung is used as an indirect stanza for the story itself: "A revolution is not a dinner party, or writing an essay, or painting a picture, or doing embroidery; it cannot be so refined, so leisurely and gentle, so temperate, kind, courteous, restrained and magnanimous. A revolution is an insurrection, an act of violence by which one class overthrows another." Additionally, it could be suggested that Leone's current ethic and ideology is well summed up in the words spoken by John Mallory, an Irish Republican revolutionary and explosives expert: "When I started using dynamite...I believed in...many things, all of it! Now, I believe only in dynamite". Given these assertions [...] one cannot but credit Leone with a certain descriptive strength (and we don't mean narrative) in that the film dispenses with a narrative fabric that ties the episodes together, that avoids the use of ploys mechanically exhibited at all costs, or of a historical-informative guide that would make it easier for viewers, who probably know little or nothing about the Mexican Revolution, to understand what is going on. Without this historical panorama, the continual butchery and executions end up being pure spectacle and the victims and oppressors little more than dummies (the non-committal condemnation of violence and the non-sense of it is all too hackneyed). [...] True, Leone tries to make good bringing together in a luxury stage-coach a concentration of the various oppressors (even a cardinal, a wealthy female passenger, a capitalist Yankee, land owners and other affluent "monsters"), but despite the sketchy approach reminiscent of Eisenstein, he soon makes sure the *baddies* are chastised and ridiculed; thus provoking in the viewer a sort of gastro-glandular, as opposed to a rational, catharsis.

[Vice, "Avanti", 1971]

Juan and Sean, the outlaw and the revolutionary. One is driven by a desire to become a different person, the other is tormented by the fear that the past is about to be repeated. Juan dreams of redemption, Sean flees from the ghost of betrayal. Both their journeys come up against the cynicism of the story and its inherent vocation to be no more than an instrument of massacre. For this reason *Duck! You Sucker* is Sergio Leone's most brutal film: the most lucid, the most agnostic, the most radically nihilistic and pessimistic. Everything is on the side of revolution, but pervaded by the bitter realization of its futility, as Juan explains to Sean in one of the most intense and important exchanges of the entire film [...] Anarchistic without anarchy without "mentors" and without sacred scripts, *Duck! You Sucker* begins with water and ends with fire. In the smart camera shot that opens the film, following the lengthy and "fragmented" Mao Tse-tung quote about the revolution, Leone shows a tree trunk covered with ants that are suddenly swamped by a powerful jet of urine as Juan empties his bladder, washing the ants to the ground where they drown in a brownish-yellow froth at the base of the tree. The film ends with the explosion of the dynamite-filled train and the screen is invaded by a wall of fire that annihilates human lives just as Juan's urine had annihilated that of the ants. *Duck! You Sucker*, as someone remarked, is indeed a world where you do not die, you are demolished. There is no alternative: if it's not the fault of nature, it's the fault of history, and life is but a desperate attempt to defy an uninterrupted sequence of carnage. Leone watches the spectacle carefully avoiding both the ironic cynicism of a creator who wants out of the evils of the world, and the resigned pietism of one who in the face of these iniquities finds it easier to plead impotence. The anarchism of his vision, his innate rebellion against the laws of Nature and the mighty of our past, lead Leone to represent the world he sees with an indignation that call to mind the Law of Retaliation of Dante's *Inferno*. Because *Duck! You Sucker* is, in its way, a brutal, melancholy descent into hell.

[Gianni Canova, "Segnocinema", July-August 1994]

If "revolution is not a dinner party" the music of death does not necessarily have to resemble a requiem. Apart from the questionable combination of Western and politics, *Duck, You Sucker!* is perhaps Leone's most genuinely musical film, maybe not the title score which is possibly the best of his filmography, but rather where the presence of the music manages to disrupt the sense of drama and pokes fun at Juan's far from revolutionary ambitions. For instance, where the sense of impending doom is countered by the integration of Mozart's *"Eine Kleine Nachtmusik"* into the score during the bank robbery that turns into a jailbreak, freeing the political prisoners of Mesa Verde, or the ambush at the bridge, aimed at killing as many army troops as possible, where the deadly combination of gunfire, explosions and carnage is mitigated by the gentle theme "Sean, Sean, Sean". But even the impassioned moment of a shootout (fundamental to Leone) is pure music, as shown in the alternation between the flashback to the Irish pub where Coburn defends himself from his friend's betrayal and the execution by firing squad of the Mexican revolutionaries. Those who remain alive have little to be happy about: the Irish hero who is given up for lost several times during the film, in the end decides to blow himself up, leaving the Mexican to reckon with his somewhat vacuous question: *"What about me?"*

[Carlo Avoldola, "Segnocinema", July-August 1994]

1984
Once Upon a Time in America
C'era una Volta in America
Il Était une Fois en Amérique
Érase una Vez en América

Director: Sergio Leone; *story*: from the novel by Harry Grey *The Hoods* 1953; *screenplay:* Leonardo Benvenuti, Piero de Barnardi, Enrico Medioli, Franco Arcalli, Franco Ferrini, Sergio Leone; *additional dialogue*: Stuart Kaminsky; *music and director of music*: Ennio Morricone [additional songs: "God Bless America" (Berlin), "Summertime" (George & Ira Gershwin, Du Bose Heyward), "Night and Day" (Porter) "Yesterday" (Lennon & McCartney), "Amapola" (Lacalle & Morricone), Overture from "The Thieving Magpie (Rossini), directed by Francesco Molinari Pradelli]; *sound engineer*: Jean Pierre Ruhu*; cinematography*: Tonino Delli Colli (Technicolor); *camera operator*: Carlo Tafani; *art direction*: Carlo Simi, James Singelis; *costumes*: Gabriella Pescucci, Richard Bruno; *editing*: Nino Baragli; *casting*: Cis Corman, Joy Todd; *first assistant director*: Fabrizio Sergenti Castellani; *assistant directors*: Luca Morsella, Dennis Benatar, Amy Wells.

Cast and Characters: Rober De Niro (David "Noodles" Aaronson), James Woods (Max Bercovicz), Elizabeth McGovern (Deborah Gelly), Treat Williams (Jimmy Conway O'Donnell), Tuesday Weld (Carol), Burt Young (Joe), Joe Pesci (Frankie Menaldi), Danny Aiello (police chief Vincent Aiello), William Forsythe (Philip "Cockeye" Stein), James Hayden (Partick "Patsy" Goldberg), Darlanne Fluegel (Eve), Larry Rapp (Fat Moe Gelly), Dutch Miller (Van Linden, diamond merchant), Robert Harper (Sharkey, trade union organizer), Richard Bright (Chicken Joe), Gerard Murphy (Crowning, unscrupulous businessman), Amy Ryder ((Peggy), Ray Dittrich ("Trigger", Eve's murderer), Frank Gio ("Beefy", Eve's murderer), Mario Brega "Mandy", Eve's murderer), Karen Shallo (Mrs. Aiello), Angelo Florio (Willie "the Ape"), Scott Tiler (young Noodles), Rusty Jacobs (young Max/David Bailey), Jennifer Connelly (young Deborah), Brian Bloom (young Patsy), Adrian Curren (young Cockeye), Mike Monetti (young Fat Moe), Julie Cohen (young Peggy), Noah Moazezi (Dominic), Rochard Foronjy (officer "Whitey"), James Russo (Bugsy), Frankie Caserta and Joey Marzella (Bugsy's gang), Clem Caserta (Al Capuano), Jerry Strivelli (Johnny Capuano), Marvin Scott (Marvin Brentley, TV interviewer), Mike Gendel (Irving Gold, Bailey's lawyer), Paul Herman ("Monkey" the barman), Olga Karlatos (woman in the puppet theater), Ann Neville (girl in coffin), Joey Faye (old man next to the hearse), Linda Ipanema (nurse Thompson), Tandy Cronic, Richard Zobel and Baxter Harris (reporters), Arnon Milchan (chauffeur), Bruno Iannone (thug), Marty Licata (cemetery caretaker), Louise Fletcher (cemetery director), Marcia Jean Kurtz (Max's mother), Estelle Harris (Peggy's mother), Chuck Low (Deborah's father), Gerrit Debeer (drunk), Alexander Godfrey (newsstand man), Cliff Cudney and Paul Farentino (mounted policemen), Bruce Bahrenburg (Sgt. Halloran), Mort Freeman (street singer), Sandra Solberg (friend of young Deborah), Jay Zeely (foreman), Susan Spafford (nurse), Ron Nummi (waiter), Massimo Liti (young Macrò at the puppet theatre), Claudio Mancini (newsreel assistant), Francesca Leone (Bailey's girlfriend), Margherita Pace (nude stand-in for Jennifer Connelly).
Main Dubbers for the 1984 Italian version: Ferruccio Amendola for Robert De Niro, Sergio Fantoni for James Woods, Rita Savagnone for Elizabeth McGovern, Maria Pia Di Meo for Tuesday Weld, Leo Gullotta for Joe Pesci, Gigi Reder for Burt Young, Carlo Giuffré for Danny Aiello, Cesare Barbetti for Treat Williams, Vittoria Febbi for Darlanne Fluegel, Vittoria Caprioli for Richard Foronjy.

Origin: Italy/USA.
Producer: Arnon Milchan.
Executive producer: Claudio Mancini.
Production: The Ladd Company, Embassy International Pictures, PSO.

Materials

Filming (interiors): Cinecittà (Rome), Hotel Excelsior (Venice).
Filming (exteriors): New York [Williamsburg Bridge, Manhattan Bridge, Brooklyn, Woodlawn Cemetery, Vinegar Hill], New Jersey [Spring Lake, Hoboken Terminal], St. Petersburg Beach Florida [Don Cesar Hotel] (USA); Montréal, Louiseville (Canada); Paris [Gare du Nord] (France); Bellagio, Pietralata (Italy).

Running time: 218' (original version), 139' (Ladd Company version USA), 228' (English version), 145' (version restored by Cineteca di Bologna in 2012).

Distribution: Titanus (Italy), Warner Bros (USA).
Release date: 20 May 1984 (Cannes Film Festival).
Release date USA: 1 June 1984.
Release date Italy: 2 September 1984 (Venice Film Festival).

 📖 *The scenes indicated with brackets, with a total running time of 27 minutes, were cut off from the 1984 Italian commercial edition. They were included in the restored version by the Cineteca of Bologna in 2012.*

[A Chinese shadow play that represents the eternal struggle between good and evil. At the side of the screen, drum, bell and gamelan players. In the theater only a few sleepy spectators.]

Opening titles against a black background. Out of the silence arises the song *God Bless America*.

New York, 1933. A young lady, Eve (DARLANNE FLEUGEL), returns to her room where she is attacked by three gangsters. They want to know where Noodles is hiding. She won't talk. They kill her with two pistol shots.

Fat Moe, the obese proprietor of the bar that bears his name, is beaten up in his bar by the girl's killers and ends up by talking: Noodles is at the Chinese theater.

In an opium den above the theater, Noodles (ROBERT DE NIRO) is in an opium trance. He reads in a newspaper that three whisky smugglers have just been shot by the police.

Flashback (punctuated with twenty-two rings of a telephone). The site of the massacre at dawn. A burnt truck, the cargo of whisky spilled out, the police who are covering the corpses of the three gangsters, Patsy (JAMES HAYDEN), Cockeye (WILLIAM FORSYTHE) and Max (JAMES WOODS), the last with his face burnt beyond recognition. Noodles among the crowd observing the scene; the night before during a goodbye party to Prohibition in the speakeasy below Fat Moe's, Noodles who telephones to the police.

Return to the present. Two of the girl's killers enter the theater looking for Noodles among the audience of a Chinese shadow play. But he manages just in time to vanish and reach Fat Moe's. Here, by an ingenious maneuver, he eliminates one killer who has stayed on guard duty and he has the bar owner give him a key.

In a railway station Noodles opens a locker containing a suitcase. Probably he was expecting it to be full of money and instead he only finds old newspapers. He buys a one-way ticket.

The same station in 1968. Noodles, sixty years old, has just arrived and rents a car.

After stopping near a Jewish cemetery being demolished he goes to visit his old friend Fat Moe at his bar and shows him an anonymous letter he has just received. Someone has discovered where he has been hiding out for thirty-five years. The two friends cannot understand who could have taken the million dollars that represented the gang's joint fund. Noodles, excited by memories, makes the rounds of the bar, looks at the yellowed photographs of his friends, goes into the toilet that has a vent opening on the warehouse.

1922. From that same vent the fourteen-year-old Noodles (SCOTT TILER) is spying on the beautiful Deborah (JENNIFER CONNELY), a girl of his own age and Fat Moe's sister, who is dancing to the tune of "Amapola" played on a gramophone. Even though she knows he is looking, Deborah nonchalantly changes clothes and goes off to her dancing lesson.

Noodles catches up with her in the street, but the haughty girl snubs him. He meets his gang mates, Cockeye, Patsy and Dominic who have been given the job of extorting from a newspaper. The four of them, carrying a pump, spray the newsstand with gasoline and set it on fire.

They are rewarded by Monkey, proprietor of a speakeasy, who lets them chose a customer of his to rip off. The boys eye a valuable watch sticking out of the pocket of a drunk. They follow him into the street but, as they are about to attack him, a wagon loaded with household goods passes and blond Max jumps down, lifts the man onto the wagon and gives him a ride. The neighborhood cop chases the kids away brusquely.

When Noodles gets home he holes up in the toilet to read *Martin Eden*. Peggy (Julie Cohen), a curvaceous and provocative young girl, joins him there. They joke and touch each other, but if he wants her she demands a charlotte russe with whipped cream. Noodles leaves her in the toilet.

In the street he meets Max who is moving with his family. Noodles waits until he is busy unloading a chandelier to steal the drunk's watch from him. The same cop turns up and seizes the stolen watch.

At dawn the four delinquents, joined by Max, attack a black trumpet player and rob him of his trumpet and wallet. Max decides that they are not going to work for others anymore.

Patsy, who has bought a charlotte russe to pay Peggy with, cannot resist his own greediness and devours it in an instant as he is waiting for the girl on the stairs. As a result he has to be satisfied with spying on her when she meets the neighborhood cop on a roof terrace. The friends, who are quickly informed of what is happening, photograph the couple in a compromising position and blackmail the policeman: besides giving them back the watch he must no longer protect Bugsy, the little boss of the neighborhood, and must allow Max and Noodles to enjoy Peggy's charms free of charge. They do so at once.

On one Passover day, when everyone is at the synagogue, Noodles and Deborah kiss in the back room of Fat Moe's place. Then, when Max and Noodles are in the courtyard, Bugsy (James Russo) and his gang arrive. Max and Noodles, guilty of working on their own, are beaten up savagely. When Noodles, bleeding, knocks on her door, Deborah does not open to him.

In the clandestine distillery of the Capuano brothers, Noodles presents a system he has thought up for salvaging the whisky that the bootleggers habitually are forced to dump into the sea when the police boats arrive. It is a question of filling sacks with salt that break after a few hours underwater and let the cargo tied to buoys come to the surface. Noodles tries it out in a barrel.

The invention works even when it is repeated in the bay. The boys are enthusiastic – they will get ten per cent of every salvaged cargo.

At the train station, the five boys, dressed up in new clothes, put the suitcase containing the gang's joint fund in a locker and solemnly swear fidelity. The key to the locker is entrusted to Fat Moe.

Outside the station they run into Bugsy who pursues them in a rage (in a scene that was not shot, Bugsy is arrested while Max and Noodles deride him from a distance) and he shoots little Dominic (Noah Moazezi). In self defence, Noodles plants a knife in his adversary's stomach, then, in a panic, also hits a policeman who comes to break up the brawl. A second policeman stuns him with his truncheon.

The police van, with Noodles inside, enters the prison. From far off his three friends wave goodbye to him.

1968. Noodles enters the chapel of the cemetery where his three friends are buried. Automatically a tape begins playing a march that Cockeye used to play on his flute to accompany the gang's activities. A small key hangs from a tablet.

[The director of the cemetery appears and says that she does not know who had this tomb built. In the street Noodles has the impression that a black limousine is following him and he writes down the license number.]

In the train station Noodles uses the key taken from the tomb to open a locker. There he finds a suitcase full of banknotes and a note: "This is in payment of your next contract." While he is walking cautiously under an elevated road, a frisbee flies over his head.

1932. After having spent nine years in prison, Noodles is released and finds Max waiting for him at the wheel of an undertaker's van. Inside there is the pretend corpse of a gaudy redhead who "comes to life" and pulls Noodles in with an inviting air. In a clandestine tavern in Fat Moe's basement, Patsy, Cockeye and Fat Moe are celebrating the convict's release. Also there are Peggy (AMY RIDER), who has become a high-class prostitute, and Deborah (ELIZABETH McGovern) who has become a successful ballerina. The boys go up to the second floor where, during a lunch, Noodles is presented to the boss Frankie (JOE PESCI) and to Joe (BURT YOUNG) who has asked for some men to pull off a jewelry heist in Detroit.

The hold-up takes place. The terrified owner hands over the diamonds held in the safe while Carol (TUESDAY WELD), the secretary who is an accomplice of the gangsters, becomes hysterical and incites Noodles to beat and rape her.

On the outskirts of Detroit the bandits deliver the diamonds to Joe, get their money, and then kill Joe and his men. A survivor tries to hide in a nearby factory in a washing machine. Noodles finds him and eliminates him. On the way back in the car, Noodles, irritated with Max about the bloody end of the affair, presses the accelerator and plunges the car into the lake.

[Everyone except Noodles emerges immediately...]

1968. [Near Senator Bailey's villa where a mysterious garbage truck is parked, Noodles sees the black limousine again, which blows up with an enormous blast.] A television broadcast shows how the remains of the car are salvaged in the course of an investigation on Senator Bailey who has been accused of corruption. Seated in Fat Moe's bar, Noodles happens to see the program and recognizes Jimmy Conway (TREAT WILLIAMS) among the people interviewed, the old Truckers' Union president.

1932. In a deserted slaughter house, Jimmy, then a young union man has gasoline poured over him by two gangsters who threaten to make him into a human torch if he does not call off a strike. Noodles and his men arrive, having taken Crowning (GERARD MURPHY) hostage, the boss of the truck owners' organization. The two gangs exchange prisoners.

Coming out of a hospital, Vincent Aiello (DANNY AIELLO), the chief of police, talks jokingly with reporters. He is on cloud nine because after four daughters his wife has finally given birth to a boy.

Dressed as doctors, Noodles and his men get into the hospital nursery, where they change identification tags for all the newborn babies, having first made a note of the real identity numbers.

In his wife's room, Aiello discovers that his baby is a girl. At that very moment a phone call arrives from Noodles: if he wants his son back, Aiello must call the police out of the factory where scabs have replaced the striking workers. But Patsy has lost the numbers indicating the identities of the newborn babies, so Aiello is given one at random.

Noodles has telephoned from a cathouse where he recognizes one of the girls as Carol, the secretary-accomplice of the Detroit hold-up. The four friends think up a joking way of getting her to recognize them: they cover their faces with handkerchiefs and unbutton their pants.

[While waiting for Deborah at the stage door of a Broadway theater, Noodles has a bitter exchange with his chauffeur, a Jewish refugee from Germany.]

Noodles has dinner with Deborah in a seaside restaurant. The two dance in a romantic atmosphere. On the beach he tells her that he had constantly thought about her during his long years of prison and asks her to be his woman. But Deborah is consumed by her career and tells him that she is leaving for Hollywood the next day. Later, in the car, Noodles misunderstands her affectionate behavior and gives vent to his disappointment by raping her.

[At Fat Moe's, Noodles tries to drown his guilt feelings in alcohol. He picks up a young hooker, Eve, but in the bedroom he immediately falls asleep.]

[The next day Noodles catches a glimpse of Deborah seated at a table in the station restaurant and he follows her along the track.]

The train leaves and Deborah pulls down the shade of her carriage window, thus excluding him definitively from her life.

At a meeting of the gang in Fat Moe's office, Noodles meets Max, more overbearing and megalomaniac than ever, in the company of Carol, who has become his girl. The phone rings. It is Jimmy calling from a public phone booth and an instant later he is gunned down.

Coming out of the Plaza, Crowning's two bodyguards are killed by Max and Noodles hiding in a wardrobe. Crowning is terrified.

In a hospital room, Jimmy, with a wounded leg, celebrates the union's victory, primarily due to the activities of the gangsters. A politician is present who proposes that the boys enter the business world. Max is agreeable, Noodles not.

Noodles and Max, together with Carol and Eve, are enjoying themselves on the beach in Miami. They read about the imminent end of Prohibition. They are out of work but have a million dollars. To end their career with a bang, Max proposes a hold up of the Federal Reserve Bank of Manhattan. Noodles tells him he is crazy and Max punches him.

[1968. Carol, living in a retirement home, tells Noodles that Max was about to go insane like his father.]

1933. In a car, Carol and Noodles plan to squeal on Max to keep him from the absurd attempt of holding up the Federal Reserve Bank and bringing about a pointless massacre.

While the end of Prohibition is being celebrated at Fat Moe's, Noodles phones the police to inform them that the gangsters are about to escort a last load of bootleg whisky. He is expecting them all to be arrested, himself included, but it is the only way to foil Max's crazy plan. The latter dispenses him from going with the escort, and when Noodles calls him crazy he goes into a rage and stuns him with the butt of his pistol.

1968. At the retirement home Carol tells Noodles that Max did not want to end up in an insane asylum, so he planted the idea in his friends' heads of denouncing him and when the police stopped the truck he was the one who opened fire.

[In a theater, Deborah is playing the death of Cleopatra. Sitting in the audience, Noodles watches her.]

In her dressing room, while she is taking off her make-up, Noodles asks her if he should accept the mysterious invitation to Senator Bailey's party, Deborah's companion of many years.

She tries to discourage him from going so as not to ruin the memories of their youth. As he leaves the dressing room, Noodles runs into Senator Bailey's son who is the spitting image of Max as an adolescent.

On the night of the party the villa is crowded with guests. [In one room, Jimmy is talking to Senator Bailey who is none other than Max resuscitated. He tries to convince him to kill himself to prevent an investigating committee from bringing their past to light.]

Max, now alone, receives Noodles. The old Senator's invitation has a precise purpose: seeing that he must die, he wants it to be by the hand of his old friend. Bailey owes him a big debt: he took his money and his woman and left him to bear the remorse for all those years. Of course, the charred corpse in the truck was not his. The police were in on the game.

Noodles refuses the job. He continues to call Max "Mister Bailey" and pretends not to recognize him, his friend Max died many years ago.

As Noodles goes out into the night, he thinks he sees Max, but a garbage truck passes by and as soon as it is gone the avenue appears deserted. In the park, Noodles sees three antique cars full of Max's guests to the party dressed with typical clothes of the thrities.

1933. Noodles enters the opium den above the Chinese shadow theater, stretches out on a mattress and begins to smoke blissfully.

Materials

CRITICS

Here, we are in the presence of a film-maker of such stature that whoever it was who commissioned him to make such a magnificent piece of entertainment was attempting to sell a dream. An American dream, that great Jungian sort of dream we Europeans have all experienced through cinema. We can understand why Americans do not like the film. It's not their cup of tea, it's ours. If we are looking for realism, for authenticity, for pertinence, the film fails to make the grade: it is not an American film, but rather an Americanist film. The opium that De Niro is smoking in the opening scene (shades of Cocteau, for we are surely looking at a surrealist work) might stand for the cinema-as-a-drug, of Californian origin, which has fed us, amazed us, excited us for almost a century. *Once Upon a Time in America* offers us a veritable overdose, espousing Fellini and Howard Hawkes. It is a film, which, overall, fails to say all the things Leone would like it to say. We cannot see it simply as the story of an impossible romantic relationship marred by rape (a sort of hard-core version of *The Great Gatsby*) or the umpteenth Flaubertian variation of the love-hate, friends-enemies theme (the parallel lives of De Niro and James Woods inexorably bound together, come rain or shine, till they are consumed or destroyed by their own lives), nor is it a neo-realistic apology of the "milieu" from which the characters emerge (Sabbath at Hester Street, the Jews wearing their white scarves, is an unforgettable scene). Rather than describe the story of the film, we feel persuaded to evoke the finer details. Just like in a dream, the main themes are less important and pithy than the more trivial impressions. The legendary teaspoon that stirs and stirs, tinkling, the coffee in the cup. The dawn over the Atlantic when De Niro gets out of the limousine after raping Deborah. The comings and goings with the locker at the railway station and the suitcase full of cash that disappears and reappears like a magic trick.

[Tullio Kezich, "La Repubblica", 29 September 1984]

Leone doesn't bother to develop his characters – to him, they're mythic as soon as he puts them on the screen. And in his movie, though he gives almost an hour to the childhood years of his gang of six Jewish boys (and a couple of girls), the camera solemnizes and celebrates these kids of ten and twelve and fourteen from the start. It's like watching the flamboyant childhood of the gods. In a sense, what Leone gives us is predigested reveries; it's the ultimate escapism–a dream begotten dream, but a feverish one, intensified by sadism, irrational passions, vengeance, and operatic savagery. Leone has found the right metaphor here; the movie begins and ends in an opium den, where Noodles puffs on a pipe while episodes of his life of killings and rapes and massacres drift by and a telephone rings somewhere in the past. In its full length, the movie has a tidal pull back towards the earliest memories, and an elegiac tone. Partly, I think, this the result of De Niro's measured performance. He makes you feel that Noodles never forgets his past, and it's his all-encompassing guilt that holds the film's different sections together. But Leone doesn't provide what seems essential: a collision between Noodles and Max – or, at least, some development of the psychosexual tensions that are hinted at. By not exploring the two mens' competition and love-hate undercurrent, the film chokes off its dramatic core. Noodles often seems to be contemplating his life instead of living it. Leone wants his characters to be as big as the characters he saw on the screen when he was a child, and he tries to produce that effect with looming close-ups and heroic gestures; the key thing for his actors is to have the right look. After you have seen his *Once Upon a Time in the West*, you can't get the iconographic faces (Henry Fonda, Charles Bronson, Jason Robards, Woody Strode, Claudia Cardinale, Jack Elam...) out of your mind. But it's almost impossible to visualize all of the five adult gang members in America, even right after you've seen the movie. Worse, they don't have the basic movie-gangster characteristic: they don't exude danger.

Pauline Kael ("The New Yorker", 27 May 1985)

The second paradox is that Leone's film, despite everything, has turned out to be, in reality, fundamental in the way it designs and anticipates the contours within which post-modern and neo-baroque cinema has subsequently found an identity. The dominant logic of film-making in the nineties has been fragmentation, or perhaps more accurately, the accumulation of fragments in which it would be pointless to seek out an organizing principle. The dominant idea behind post-modernism is that of an infinite number of possible orders and that whatever we chose to communicate is neither reality nor the truth, but merely fragments of the truth that contradict and refute one another reciprocally. The main characteristics of post-modern cinema are precisely self-reference, a taste for quotation, a jumbling of genres, while the "neo-baroque" is characterized by the ambiguity of first-person narrative (resulting in the fallibility of the information offered), the splitting up of a seemingly straightforward narrative and the proliferation of unexpected twists and turns (Bryan Singer's *The Usual Suspects* is the most eloquent example of this trend), the abnormal enlargement of the plot, the tendency to breakdown the story (*Pulp Fiction* in particular), the mixing of genres, the ostentation of "all things wonderful" and/or "poetical" (in other words, an attempt to elicit in the viewer an emotional reaction using "technical" tricks such as slow motion, "shifts" in the sound etc.) During the Nineties, American cinema implemented a decisive Baroque revival: think of such films as Coppola's *Dracula,* Scorsese's *Casino*, Stone's *Natural Born Killers*. This move has had two consequences: on the one hand the transformation of the viewer, no longer merely passive and immature; on the other a "drift in the story" towards more complex, hypertrophic forms, in which no one seems to worry about revealing the artificiality of the cinematographic narrative. This type of cinema first builds up appearances then reveals them. *Once Upon a Time in America* was instrumental in creating this contradiction.

[Marcello Garofalo, *Tutto il cinema di Sergio Leone*, 1999]

Cutting *Once Upon a Time in America* by an hour and 22 minutes, doing it without Leone's approval, and jettisoning the *Kane*-like structure for a movie that proceeds in strict chronological order, at first glance seems like an act of desecration akin to re-editing Joyce's *Ulysses* into a Dublin travelogue. But, surprisingly it isn't. The Ladd Company version makes more sense. It has considerably more emotive force. It is a stronger, more cohesive film. The short version begins with Deborah's dance. A few scenes later, it introduces Max as a voyeur spying on the love scene between Deborah and Noodles. Thus, it establishes the boys' rivalry as a metaphorical battle for the heart of fair Deborah. (It, however, cuts the 1968 scenes in which Deborah appears, so we don't know that she ended up in a liaison with Max and bore his child.) It discards most of the early adventures of the young gang, trims a few of the bloodier scenes and Deborah's rape. And it "solves" the very questionable ending of Leon's film. In the long version, Noodles is called to the home of Christopher Bailey, a rich man recently appointed to be "secretary" of some government department. Bailey – a sort of Great Gatsby who has outlived his romantic past – turns out to be none other than Max, who had faked his death in 1933 with the connivance of the police. Having ruined Noodles' life, Max now wants Noodles to end "Bailey's". Noodles refuses and walks out. On the street, he sees a garbage truck parked in front of the Bailey mansion. The truck starts up and passes Noodles. Its blades are churning some unidentifiable refuse – Max, presumably. In the short version, the scene between Noodles and "Bailey" (here a trucking magnate) is the same but shorter. Noodles walks outside, pauses, and hears a loud shot – from the gun Max had pleaded with Noodles to use on him.

[Mary Corliss, "Film Comment", 1984]

The film-event, the film-life story of Sergio Leone, brings to fulfilment a long and tormented gestation. Born to be remembered, like it or not, as a singular case of vehement passion towards America and cinema. How are we to talk about a film that cost its director more than ten years of his life, endless emotions and never-ending misgivings? How are we to limit our judgement of *Once Upon a Time in America* to something as concise as a road sign? And what else can we add if the director is Sergio Leone, erstwhile inventor of a Western without a past, a stylistic curb on European cinema, and his own, violence? We are, quite understandably, suspended in a state of conflictual solidarity, of negotiated agreement: admiring, troubled, dead beat and provoked. He has chased after a scheme without end, a fable of an imaginary America conceived of through cinema, an immense apologue on the cinema envisaged as an adventurous code, so huge and overflowing that the American distributors asked that it be cut, taxed, punished, in accordance with the contract and the belief that you can say everything you want to say in two and a half hours, instead of the original (almost) four. The funny thing is that the two claims actually seem to concur: Leone's right to have his work accepted in its entirety, the Americans' plan to cut it, to "explain" it according to the very same Hollywood codes that Leone has borrowed and upended, possibly once and for all. Leone's merit as a director, albeit somewhat belatedly and grudgingly acknowledged, is precisely this ability to upset the proverbial apple cart. *Once Upon a Time in America* is stretched out like a gigantic body for three hours and forty minutes, plus an extra hour in the TV version; but even a shred of *Once Upon a Time in America* is the whole film. It is an ambitious and extraordinary adventure that repeats itself over and over again but always with a difference, that envisages the development of the story as a stylistic stratagem rather than a narrative (even though the plot does have a "cops and robbers" structure!). The very idea of dividing the film into three parallel, yet interconnected sections (the main character's childhood, his adult years, his old age) discloses right from the start that the narrator has abandoned time in favour of a sentimental, continuous, all-absorbing, even tiring present. It doesn't matter that we know what happens, but how Leone makes it happen, what his priorities, his skills, his insights, his indulgencies are. This America re-invented from the Twenties to the Seventies is cinema re-invented, but also commemorated. Leone said: "I know as much about gangsters as anyone else." In other words, not much, but implying: I know everything about cinema, my soul is full of it, in fact it's overflowing. So, quite naturally, his long, suspended, Western phase has evolved into a more even rhythm that garners every detail, the ellipses dear to American cinema have become hyperboles, the spaces and the long pauses that in Leone's Westerns were filled with a satirical suspense, are filled here with method and sentiment. The adventurous Leone here becomes the sentimentalist. It's like saying: I'll tell you about the dream of my nostalgia, no I won't, I'll explain what nostalgia is. But can you? *Once Upon a Time in America* in all its majesty bears witness, not to the history of America, not even the history of the cinema, but the story of a relentless passion for pictures that has dragged on for years, like a wounded body, through adversity to the final, incredible salvation of a finished work of art. [...] The cinema and life itself are alike in this: that all the best is soon over and the only gratification is remembrance. Even for two gangsters with no future, for two imaginary criminals. The film is full of twists in the plot like a dramatic mockery of the genre (the sex scene in the back of a hearse, the babies who all get swapped over in their cots in the hospital, the lunch at the empty Grand Hotel): signs of the pacified sadism with which the director views the world, like a carnival of violence, assassins, blood, explosions, in which the women (two prolonged rape scenes) are the victims, but also the accomplices, a celebration of murder that is only slightly alleviated by a feeling of nostalgia, to the extent that it seems like a worn-out, vindictive and naive excuse, like the notes of *Amapola* that accompany De Niro, a pen pusher of crime, never so lonely, never so humiliated.

[Stefano Reggiani, "La Stampa", 21 May 1984]

Sergio Leone manages to transform even the harshest conditions of everyday life into a fairy tale. The film is a successful reinvention of a theme, that is at once clear-cut and nuanced, notwithstanding its many facets; but it is above all an amazing walk down memory lane, a search for one's roots, elicited, and not by chance, by the shadow figures dancing on the little screen in the opium den and from the drug-induced dreams that cloud and seduce our hero's mind until we reach the final frame (the sad face of a disillusioned Noodles, a loser but still with a smile). Not an easy subject to bring to the screen, but accomplished here with lyrical force, underscored by a disconsolate bitterness. It is as if to say that, at the end of this journey, from the vulnerable years of adolescence to an adulthood as rich as it is cynical and cruel, there is only death. Or, for those who have, either through laziness or fear, made a choice, there can be, before death comes, refuge in dreams and the evocation of a bygone era. Apart from these two assumptions (everyday life and memory lane), the other essential theme and strong point of Leone's film is the deep-seated and sincere, albeit competitive, friendship between Noodles and Max; the former more circumspect, the latter a more determined adversary. Noodles, without doubt a violent man where necessary, but ultimately more compromising and romantic, Max, cruel-hearted, avid and self-possessed. Leone does not dwell on fifty years of American life, or on the question of small-time gangsterism, likewise he does not dwell on our two "minor heroes", rather, he celebrates and commemorates them. Though they can hardly be painted as heroes, the walk down memory lane consigns them to a world of adventure, shootouts and blood, the features of which are highlighted but without pretension, leaving us with a transfigured reality. A big risk and an arduous undertaking, but nonetheless, film-making at its best. Despite everything, Deborah gone forever, Max white-haired and running scared, Noodles is not completely defeated and he knows it. True, he is a loser, but the importance he continues to attribute to friendship is absolute and unreserved. Moreover, he is still alive and walking free. Free to dream, to smoke some opium, to fantasize about a time that will never be the same again, about the blossoming of a tender love affair and a friendship which, born in the mean streets of the city, he refuses to destroy with a crime. The last, for which he has already paid the price. For his part, Morricone has composed a beautiful theme, at times reminiscent of Mahler, which symbolizes and recapitulates, suffused as it is with gentle charm and nostalgia, everything in the film that is memory, tenderness and regret. A motif that recurs, alive and poignant, like a warning or a reminder. Or maybe a glimmer of hope. The film is classified as restricted, given one or two licentious or brutal moments, and two episodes of sexual violence.

[Review by Centro Cattolico Cinematografico, 1984]

b) Films Partially Directed by Sergio Leone (Uncredited)

1959
The Last Days of Pompeii

Director: Mario Bonnard, Sergio Leone; *story*: from the novel of the same name by Edward Bulwer-Lytton (1834); *screenplay*: Ennio De Concini, Luigi Emmanuelli, Sergio Corbucci, Sergio Leone, Duccio Tessari; *music*: Angelo Francesco Lavignino; *photography:* Antonio Ballestreros, Enzo Barboni (Totalscope-Eastmancolor*); set decoration*: Aldo Tomassini, Ramiro Gomez; *costumes*: Vittorio Rossi; *editing*: Eraldo Da Roma; *second unit director*: Sergio Corbucci; *first assistant directors*: Duccio Tessari, Sergio Leone.

Cast and Characters: Steve Reeves (Glaucus Leto), Christine Kaufmann (Ione), Fernando Rey (Arbaces, high priest of Isis), Barbara Carroll (Nydia), Anne-Marie Baumann (Julia), Mimmo Palmara (Gallinus), Carlo Tamberlani (Olinto, Christian leader), Mino Doro (Roman consul), Guillermo Marin (Ascanius), Ángel Aranda (Antoninus Marcus).

Origin: Italy/Spain/Germany.
Producer: Giuseppe Maggi.
Associate producers: Lucio Fulci, Paolo Moffa.
Production: Cineproduzione Associate, Domiziana (Rome), Procusa (Madrid), Transocean Film (Munich).
Filming (interiors): Cinecittà (Rome), CEA Studios (Madrid).
Filming (exteriors): Pompeii (Italy).
Running time: 100' (Italy), 103' (USA).
Distribution: Filmar, later Fida Cinematografica.
Release date: 12 November 1959.

1973
My Name is Nobody

Director: Tonino Valerii, Sergio Leone; *story*: Ernesto Gastaldi, Fulvio Morsella, from an idea by Sergio Leone; *screenplay:* Ernesto Gastaldi; *music*: Ennio Morricone; *cinematography:* Giuseppe Ruzzolini in Italy and Spain, Armando Nannuzzi in USA (Technicolor, Panavision); *production design*: Gianni Polidori; *costumes*: Vera Marzot*; editing*: Nino Baragli; *assistant director*: Stefano Rolla.

Cast and Characters: Henry Fonda (Jack Beauregard), Terence Hill [Mario Girotti] (Nobody), Jean Martin (Sullivan), Neil Summers (Squirrel), Leo Gordon (Red), R.G. Armstrong (Honest John), Remus Peets (Big Gun), Piero Lulli (Sheriff), Mario Brega (Pedro), Antoine Saint Jean (Scape), Benito Stefanelli (Porteley), Mark Mazza (Don John), Geoffrey Lewis (leader of the Wild Bunch), Franco Angrisano (railway worker), Alexander Allerson (Rex), Steve Kanaly (false barber), Angelo Novi (bartender), Tommy Polgar (Juan), Antonio Luigi Guerra (official), Carla Mancini (mother).

Origin: Italy/France/Germany.
Producer: Claudio Mancini.
Executive producer: Fulvio Morsella.
Production: Rafran Cinematografica (Rome), Les Films Jacques Leitienne (Paris), Rialto Film

Preben Philipsen (Berlin).
Filming (interiors): De Paolis (Rome).
Filming (exteriors): Almeria (Spain), New Orleans and New Mexico (USA).
Distribution: Titanus.
Distribution USA: Universal.
Release date: 13 December 1973 (Germany).
Release date France: 14 December 1973.
Release date Italy: 21 December 1973.

CRITICS

Nobody is not a person. Nobody is a bizarre creature who lives in the script and is, at the same time, extra-textual. Nobody is a spectator because, clearly, he has seen lots of Westerns (all of them starring Henry Fonda, no doubt) and has a headful of quotes. Nobody is also a script-writer because it is he, basically, who dictates the rules of the script. Nobody even becomes a director when he stages certain scenes (the clash with the Wild Bunch, the bogus final duel) and tells the other actors what to do. Nobody becomes a spectator again when he watches Beauregard's epic battle as he takes on all 150 of the Wild Bunch single-handed. But Nobody is also a creature of the collective psyche that penetrates Beauregard's very essence: according to a classical parable of American cinema (two characters who initially do not like each other but end up by cooperating and developing a friendship), Nobody becomes Beauregard's unconscious memory when the aging gunslinger, Winchester at the ready, sees the saddles of the Wild Bunch shimmering in the distance. [...] Incidentally, no one has told us, or will ever tell us, why the Wild Bunch had packed themselves with dynamite in that way. The bottom line is that Nobody is a sort of perverse polymorph that becomes the true key to the film. Right from the opening credits, it is Hill's character who does the talking and who cheekily introduces himself: my name is Nobody, a contradiction in terms, a playful Homeric parody. Leone often spoke of Homer, sometimes mixed with Goldoni and Trastevere. [...] Italian comedy is in Leone's DNA, as it was in his slow, gentle way of speaking, typical of a Trasteverine, both intellectual and commoner at the same time. This is where Nobody comes from, long before the Trinity films. Nobody is a typical Roman *"rompicojoni"* (ball breaker), a youth who takes the local hoodlum as his role model and attaches himself like a limpet, telling him all the time what a great guy he is. Jack Beauregard, who instead comes from the classical Western, from Ford, where young people know their place, is at first bewildered by this youth, he would really like to make short shift of him, but little by little he begins to understand and finally love him. The affectionate farewell he writes him is really a love letter: "....you can preserve a little of that illusion that made my generation tick. Maybe you'll do it in your own funny way, but you'll be grateful just the same." And if this isn't already a critique of the of the film! There is also the same burning awareness of passing time that was to haunt Noodles at the end of *Once Upon a Time in America* [...] We have no desire to know which scenes were actually shot by Leone personally. We like to think that he shot the more humorous ones: the interminable middle thanks to which Nobody succeeds in highjacking the train carrying the gold, the obsession with the three stupid gunslingers, ridiculed by Nobody. But even the scenes where Hill is clearly playing "Trinity" are perfectly in keeping with the tone of the film. It is no accident that these take place in a sort of macro-sequence, that of a town-amusement park, a sort of run-down proto-Disneyland, where Jack, followed by Nobody, goes looking for Sullivan. Here, it is as though the film comes to a standstill: as regards the narrative tension Valerii and Leone lose the thread a bit, but on a meta-cinema level they pull out all the stops. First the giant on stilts who turns out to be a dwarf, then the cake-in-the-face of the Negroes gag, the scene in the saloon and the whisky glass throwing contest, the Trinity-style punch-up, the house of mirrors reminiscent of Welles, and finally the billiard scene. Here, citations abound: first of all Chaplin (Nobody steals an apple from a child just as Chaplin did in *The Circus*), next DeMille

Once Upon a Time in America.

Once Upon a Time in the West.

Duck! You Sucker.

289

For a Few Dollars More.

Duck! You Sucker.

Duck! You Sucker.

Footware

A Fistful of Dollars.

For a Few Dollars More.

The Good, the Bad and the Ugly.

The Andersonville concentration camp in a photograph taken by A.J.Riddle in 1864 and the camp's reconstruction in Leone's *The Good, the Bad and the Ugly.*

a

Henry Fonda's ice-cold, evil eyes were not invented by Leone in *Once Upon a Time in the West* [b] but hark back to John Ford's *Fort Apache* [a], although the savagery in Ford's film was well hidden, as often happens, behind the mask of heroism.

b

Drawings by Carlo Simi for *The Good, the Bad and the Ugly*.

Drawings by Carlo Simi for *Once Upon a Time in America*.

A Fistful of Dollars.

The Good, the Bad and the Ugly.

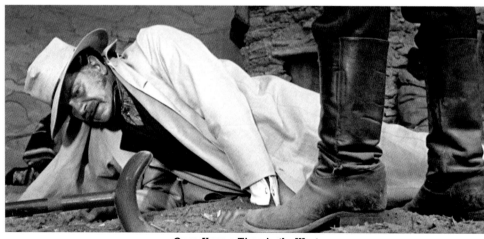

Once Upon a Time in the West.

Once Upon a Time in the West.

Once Upon a Time in America.

Once Upon a Time in America.

Horses' buttocks

"...I told Leone that I really liked the way he filmed horses' buttocks..."
(BERNARDO BERTOLUCCI).

The Good, the Bad and the Ugly.

Duck! You Sucker.

The Good, the Bad and the Ugly.

Duck! You Sucker.

Once Upon a Time in America.

Duck! You Sucker.

*Once Upon a
Time in America.*

*The Colossus of
Rhodes.*

*My Name is
Nobody.*

*The Good, the
Bad and the Ugly.*

Duck! You Sucker.

For a Few Dollars More.

A Fistful of Dollars.

The Colossus of Rhodes.

Gymnastics: rings (*The Colossus of Rhodes*).

Gymnastics: horizontal bar (*For a Fistful of Dollars*).

Gymnastics: parallel bars (*Once Upon a Time in the West*).

You're Darn Tootin' (1928).

Lee and Clint in Oliver and Hardy mode (*For a Few Dollars More*).

The gunslinger without arms (*For a Fistful of Dollars*).

The Blue Angel (1930).

Marlene Dietrich-style gunslinger *(My Name is Nobody)*.

Thumbing one's nose! (*Duck! You Sucker*).

Snaky/Jack Elam listens to the match on the little radio (*Once Upon a Time in the West*).

Juan/Rod Steiger's twist (*Duck! You Sucker*).

Colonel Mortimer/Lee Van Cleef walks off chatting on his cell phone.
(*For a Few Dollars More*).

The Good, the Bad and the Ugly.

For a Few Dollars More.

Duck! You Sucker.

(the mirrors in the saloon, reminiscent of the scene in *Union Pacific*), on to, believe it or not, the Vasilyev brothers. Maybe I'm being a bit imaginative, but the billiard scene ("This ball is good, this is bad, this is me", and all balls together representing the Wild Bunch) reminds me of a fantastic scene in *Ciapaiev*, a classic of social realism, in which the Bolshevik commander explains his tactical ideas using potatoes and tomatoes, laid out on the table to represent the conflicting forces. Anyway, back to Bachtin. For a good half hour Valerii and Leone take us into a carnevalesque world that reproduces the entire film "upside down". Here, it is clear, once and for all, that Beauregard is the King and Nobody his carnevalesque doppleganger, the court jester who aspires for one day to wear the crown. It is precisely the derisive carnevalesque nature of the film that permits the classic relationship between the Old and the Young to be turned upside down. The difference between most Westerns and *My Name Is Nobody* is the same as an equatorial forest, formed naturally over thousands of years, and an example of post-modern architecture in which, in a timeless present, citations from radically different eras happily co-exist. There is at the same time, an "allusion" to the past (the riders of the Bunch who, exploding, turn into yellowed photos) and the negation of the past. The present in *My Name Is Nobody* symbolically embraces the end of a century (it is 1899) and moves in the rarefied and all-encompassing dimension of myths and games. The myths meet up, each has its own crossroads and within these myths time stands still, the names are also myths and our heroes never grow old. It's not worth growing old because, says Jack, "the years don't make wisdom, they just make old age".
[Alberto Crespi, "Segnocinema", July-August 1994]

c) Leone: Producer, Actor, Screenwriter, Assistant Director, Advertiser

La Bocca sulla Strada (1941)
by Roberti Roberti
among the actors: Sergio Leone (a child)

The Mad Marechiaro (1944/1951)[73]
by Roberto Roberti
assistant director: Sergio Leone
among the actors: Sergio Leone (an American lieutenant)

Rigoletto (1946)
by Carmine Gallone
assistant director: Sergio Leone

Bicycle Thieves (1948)
by Vittorio De Sica
assistant director: Sergio Leone
among the actors: Sergio Leone (a young German priest)

Fabiola (1949)
by Alessandro Blasetti
assistant director: Sergio Leone

Il Trovatore (1949)
by Carmine Gallone
assistant director: Sergio Leone

Outlaw Girl (1950)
by Mario Camerini
assistant director: Sergio Leone

The Force of Destiny (1950)
By Carmine Gallone
assistant director: Sergio Leone

The Legend of Faust (1950)
by Carmine Gallone
assistant director: Sergio Leone

Night Taxi (1950)
by Carmine Gallone
assistant director: Sergio Leone

Il Voto (1950)
by Mario Bonnard
assistant director: Sergio Leone

---

[73] See footnote page 131.

Materials

Quo Vadis? (1951)
by Mervyn LeRoy (and Anthony Mann)
assistant director second unit: Sergio Leone[74]

Three Corsairs (1952)
by Mario Soldati
assistant director: Sergio Leone

Girls Marked Danger/White Slave Trade (1952)
by Luigi Comencini
asssistant director: Sergio Leone

Frine, Courtesan of Orient (1953)
by Mario Bonnard
assistant director: Sergio Leone
co-screenplay writer: Sergio Leone

Man, Beast and Virtue (1953)
by Steno
assistant director: Sergio Leone

Marsina Stretta, segment of **Of Life and Love** (1954)
by Aldo Fabrizi
technical direction: Sergio Leone

Betrayed (1954)
by Mario Bonnard
assistant director: Sergio Leone

La Ladra (1955)
by Mario Bonnard
assistant director: Sergio Leone

Helen of Troy (1956)
by Robert Wise
assistant director second unit: Sergio Leone[75]

They Stole a Tram (1956)
by Aldo Fabrizi (and Mario Bonnard)
assistant director (and co-director?): Sergio Leone

Allow Me, Daddy! (1956)
by Mario Bonnard
assistant director: Sergio Leone

Teacher and the Miracle (1957)
by Aldo Fabrizi
assistant director: Sergio Leone

---

[74] He was assistant director to war scenes and to the burning of Rome sequences.

[75] According to Luciano Vincenzoni, Leone directed quite a number of scenes because Bonnard was often ill.

Aphrodite, Goddess of Love (1958)
by Mario Bonnard
co-screenwriter: Sergio Leone
assistant director: Sergio Leone

Nel Segno di Roma (1958)
by Guido Brignone and Michelangelo Antonioni
co-screenwriter: Sergio Leone

Ben Hur (1959)
by William Wyler
assistant director second unit: Sergio Leone [76]

Son of the Red Corsair ((1959)
by Primo Zeglio
assistant director: Sergio Leone

La Legge mi Incolpa / Quai des Illusions (1959)
by Emile Couzinet
consultant for the Italian version: Sergio Leone

The Nun's Story (1959)
by Fred Zinnemann
assistant director and director of a number of sequences: Sergio Leone[77]

The Seven Revenges (1960)
by Primo Zeglio
co-scriptwriter: Sergio Leone

Duel of the Titans (1961)
by Sergio Corbucci
co-scriptwriter: Sergio Leone

Il Cambio della Guardia (1962)
by Giorgio Bianchi
director of certain scenes: Sergio Leone[78]

Sodom and Gomorrah (1962)
by Robert Aldrich
director second unit: Sergio Leone[79]

Slave Girls of Sheba (1962)
by Guido Zurli
co-scriptwriter: Sergio Leone

Cemetery Without Crosses (1968)
by Robert Hossein
among the actors: Sergio Leone (a hotel employee)[80]

---

[76] Leone was assistant director to the charriot race scene, directed by Andrew Marton.

[77] He directed the Congolese scenes.

[78] Leone took Giorgio Bianchi's place for the last week of shooting, but he wasn't accredited.

[79] Leone directed the battle scene near Marrakech with more than a thousand horsemen.

[80] This scene was cut off during the editing.

Materials

12 Dicembre – Documenti di Giuseppe Pinelli (1970)
by Elio Petri, Ugo Pirro and Nelo Risi
co-director (?): Sergio Leone[81]

A Genius, Two Partners and a Dupe (1975)
by Damiano Damiani (and Giuliano Montaldo)
executive producer and director of one sequence: Sergio Leone[82]

Il Gatto (1977)
by Luigi Comencini
producer: Sergio Leone

An Almost Perfect Affair (1979)
by Michael Ritchie
among the actors: Sergio Leone (himself)

A Dangerous Toy (1979)
by Giuliano Montaldo
executive producer: Sergio Leone

Fun is Beautiful (1980)
by Carlo Verdone
co-producer: Sergio Leone

Bianco, Rosso e Verdone (1981)
by Carlo Verdone
executive producer: Sergio Leone

Troppo Forte (1986)
by Carlo Verdone
executive producer, writer, screenwriter and director of one sequence: Sergio Leone[83]

---

[81] The few witnes of this "counter-intelligence dossier on the murder of Piazza Fontana" (and about the unclear death of the anarchist Giuseppe Pinelli misteriously fallen from the window of a police station in Milan) agree, more or less, that Leone signed it just for sympathy (together with Brass, Loy, Monicelli, Visconti) without being involved in the direction of any of the scenes.

[82] In a way, for some elements, the prologue is reminiscent of some initial sequences of *Once Upon a Time in the West*.

[83] Leone directed the first sequence. He gave his contribution to the screenplay, too. That's why he's accredited in the opening titles.

COMMERCIALS (1976-1983):

Gervais Ice creams (Dany Danone)
Renault 18: *Petra*
Renault 18: *Il Diesel si Scatena*
Riz Lustucru
Pain Bonne Fornèe
J&B whisky
Europ Assistance
Palmolive
Talbot Solara
Renault 19

In the first (*Petra*), filmed in Jordan, the birth of the Renault 18 takes place in a temple. The car comes out of the darkness, leaves the temple (with an invisible driver), descends the steps and meanders around Petra. Occasionally a goddess appears to block its path: the car blinks its headlights, a flirtation takes place. Finally the goddess lets it pass and the car drives away onto the superhighway. In the second commercial (*Il Diesel si Scatena*) a car leaps out of control in the middle of an arena. ("They wanted me to shoot it in a marble quarry in Carrara, but I preferred the Roman arena in Tunis. It is much more impressive – it seems like the Coliseum.") The music is Ennio Morricone's. This film won the platinum Minerva, the Oscar of commercials.

Another commercial for Renault was filmed in January 1989 in Zimbabwe. Here, the adventurous car even carries out a rescue operation, holding up a wooden bridge which risks collapse when a herd of elephants crosses it. Leone died while he was editing the commercial together with Nino Baragli (who proposed the music of the three-way duel in *The Good, the Bad and the Ugly*"). This was the last work Leone directed.

3. Filmography of Babel

My Name is Nobody.

Film Projects Never Realized

Grand Slam
Leone was supposed to direct this film in the mid-Sixties. Before he left for Egypt to begin filming, he quarrelled with the producers who had originally proposed the film to him, Giorgio Papi and Arrigo Colombo. The film was offered to Giuliano Montaldo.

Cent'Anni di Solitudine (*One Hundred Years of Solitude*)
A television movie in ten episodes based on Gabriel Garcia Marquez's novel *One Hundred Years of Solitude*. "Television asked me to direct *Garibaldi* and *Marco Polo* (the Chinese wanted either me or Wertmuller), but they constantly rejected Marquez."

Colt. Una Leggenda Americana (*Colt. An American Legend*)
A TV-series in six episodes born from a Sergio Donati's idea and inspired by Anthony Mann's novel *Winchester '73*, in which the legendary gun changes hands many times.

Don Chisciotte (*Don Quixote*)
Sancho Panza and Don Quixote perplexed in modern America.

Leningrad
"The movie is to open with Shostakovitch composing his *Leningrad Symphony*[84] in his room. This music is the background for a long helicopter sequence starting from Shostakovitch's house and following the crowd coming into the street armed with rifles, getting onto trams and reaching the front lines on the outskirts of the city. The camera continues moving until it reaches the line of German panzers ready to launch an attack. The idea came up in the sixties. Speaking with various intellectuals, Italian and French ones included, I became aware that they were confusing the battle of Leningrad with that of Stalingrad. So this made me want to read Harrison Salisbury's book *The Nine Hundred Days*. I was struck by these people's readiness to sacrifice their lives. In three years forty per cent of the population of Leningrad died – 1,300,000 people. In a documentary of the time, one sees the workers when the siege was announced. The camera pans their faces from which one understands that the Germans would never enter. And Hitler was counting on a blitz. He had tickets printed up for a concert of Wagner's music that was to take place at the Leningrad Philharmonic ten days after the start of the siege. There were some cruel facts too, episodes of cannibalism and scenes of women who could not manage to transport the dead because their bodies were frozen. I was moved by that little girl, a kind of Anna Frank, who

---

[84] Namely *Symphony n. 7*, 1941.

made dailyentries in her diary about the deaths of her relatives – her grandmother, her sister '... and today I have been left alone.' Only her diary was found...

"De Niro is the typical American reporter, first cynical and then more willing to become involved, like in *For Whom the Bell Tolls*. He expected to stay there a few months. Instead he stayed there forever. The woman will be a party member. We don't yet know quite what her profession should be. If they found her together with a Westerner it meant twelve years of prison for her. An American and a Russian, the two world powers that today hold the destiny of the world in their hands – and all around the apocalypse. But with many little intertwining stories. It is no *Zhivago*; it is a difficult movie to construct. At the end he dies, a worker's death, but which we will not see directly. In a movie house they show a documentary he shot with a hand camera on the last day of the siege. Germans fleeing, the Russians pursuing, grenades coming from all sides, and then an explosion in front of the camera. The Russian woman is in the theater. She has their little girl in her arms, a few months old.

"... I can't mention Salisbury, for the Russians don't have good memories of him. Instead I have chosen a book recommended by Giulietto Chiesa, the Moscow correspondent of *L'Unita*, a book written by two Russians recounting the siege day by day.

This is Russia seen through the eyes of an American, which are almost my eyes. However I am going to do plenty of research; it will rake a year to write the script, five months of which will be spent in Russia. I will write it with Arnold Yanovich Vittol who wrote a television movie on the siege, with an American – I think it will be Alvin Sargent – and two Italians, Benvenuti and De Bernardi. I hope to leave in a few days. I've been sent an article from the Leningrad *Pravda* announcing the movie."
(From an interview conducted by Oreste De Fornari that appeared in *L'Europeo*, March 25, 1988.)

Un Segreto che solo Mary Conosce (*A Secret Only Mary Knows*)
This is the story of friendship during the American Civil War. The title came from a poem by Edgar Lee Masters. Mickey Rourke and Richard Geer were to star, Enrico Gastaldi was to write the screenplay while Luca Morsella was to direct.

Stalingrad
An Italo-Soviet co-production, the film was to begin with a cannonade and a boy falling out of bed. The whole battle is seen through the eyes of this fourteen-year-old boy.

Vado, l'Ammazzo e Torno
With Marcello Mastroianni. The story of Gaetano Bresci, the anarchist who assassinated King Umberto I in Monza in July 1900.
"He was a half-hearted anarchist who had left America to escape from a difficult family situation and who tried to vent his hatred of the world by participating in the plot against Umberto I. He was a man full of doubts, uncertainties, impulses, losses of will power – a very human personage and thus well-suited to Mastroianni's temperament." (From an interview with Angelo Lucano that appeared in *La Rivista del Cinematografo,* January 1967.)

La Vera Storia della Monaca di Monza (*The True Story of the Nun of Monza*)
From the trial documents that the Church authorities have finally made public.
"It is a great temptation for me to shoot a movie entirely within the walls of a convent. It is far from my usual subject matter, but my way of shooting, which pays attention to psychological states, could be suited to this kind of story."

Gone with the Wind
"It's not a remake of the original. I saw that again recently and I didn't like it this time any more than I did the first time I saw it. I want to write my own screenplay from Mitchell's novel and film everything exactly where the action took place. I would get four unknowns for the lead roles and then I would rehearse with them for at least six months. The only thing from

the original film that cannot be replaced are the main actors, Gable, Leigh, De Havilland, and Howard. There's no point choosing four big stars, much better to have four newcomers. The big names, such as Brando or De Niro, I could use in supporting roles [...]Anyway, the Americans seem interested. I would like to end my career with *Gone with the Wind*, my finale, a definitive challenge to Hollywood." (From an interview by Gianni Rondolino for La Stampa, 28 June 1986).

Viaggio al Termine della Notte
From Celine's novel *Journey to the End of Night.* "It remains the dream of my life. But I ask myself if it weren't better left alone, all the more since I, for better or worse, am a desecrator. It's an enormous risk."

Viale Glorioso
A film of memories that takes its name from the Trasrevere street where Leone spent a good part of his adolescence. Written before Fellini's *I Vitelloni,* it was proposed to producers in vain after the success of *A Fistful of Dollars.*

Other Projects Considered (☺) or Refused (☹)

☺ *Le Aquile di Roma*, a sword-and-sandal film that was planned but never realized due to its high costs (after *The Colossus of Rhodes*)

☺ A realistic Western with Sophia Loren in the role of Calamity Jane and Steve McQueen as Wild Bill Hickock (after *For a Few Dollars More).*

☹ *Caravans*, a high-budget American Western produced by Metro-Goldwyn-Mayer (1967).

☺ *Ricordati di Abilene*, a Western starring Jean-Paul Belmondo and Ursula Andress for United Artists (1967).

☺ A remake of *Viva Villa!* Directed by Jack Conway and Howard Hawkes (1934), with Toshiro Mifune or Burt Lancaster in the role of the Mexican revolutionary.

☹ An American Western, which eventually became the splendid *The Life and Times of Judge Roy Bean*, directed by John Huston in 1972.

☺ *Cocaine,* from a novel written by Pitigrilli in 1921, a story of love and drugs in a bygone era.

☹ *Flash Gordon*, produced by Dino De Laurentiis (made by Mike Hodges in 1980).

☹ An opera-film adapted from Bizet's *Carmen* (probably the project later offered to Francesco Rosi in 1984).

☹ A film adaption of Corto Maltese's comic-book hero Hugo Pratt.

☹ A pirate story proposed to Leone by George Lucas.

☺ An American version of Eduardo De Filippo's *Filumena Marturano*, with Robert De Niro and Barbra Streisand (1985).

☺ A film version of the French graphic novel *The Black Order Brigade* (circa 1985).

☺ A film version of André Malraux's *Man's Fate* (between 1985 and 1989).

☹ A biography of Gioacchino Rossini, later refused by Robert Altman and eventually directed by Mario Monicelli *(Rossini! Rossini!).*

☹ *Vita di Garibaldi* for Italian television, suggested to Leone by the former Prime Minister Bettino Craxi.

For a Few Dollars More.

Once Upon a Time in America.

Duck! You Sucker.

4. BIBLIOGRAPHY

Books on Sergio Leone

Franco Ferrini, *L'Antiwestern e il Caso Leone*, «Bianco e Nero», 1971.

Laurence Staig and Tony Williams, *Italian Western – The Opera of Violence*, Lorrimer, London 1975.

Gilles Lambert, *Les Bons, les Sales, les Méchants et les Propres de Sergio Leone*, Solar, Paris 1976.

Oreste De Fornari, *Sergio Leone*, Moizzi, Milan 1977.

Massimo Moscati, *Western all'Italiana – Guida ai 407 film, ai Registi, agli Attori,* Pan, Milan 1978.

Christopher Frayling, *Spaghetti Westerns – Cowboys and Europeans from Karl May to Sergio Leone*, Routledge & Kegan Paul, London / Boston / Henley 1981.

Alain Petit, *20 Ans du Western Européen*, Les Editions de la Meduse, Paris 1981.

Gian Lhassa, *Seul au Monde dans le Western Italien*, Ed. Grand Angle, Mariembourg 1983 [in 3 volumes].

Lane Roth, *Film Semiotics, Metz and Leone's Trilogy*, Garland, New York 1983.

Gilles Cébe, *Sergio Leone*, Henry Veyrier, Paris 1984.

Oreste De Fornari, *Sergio Leone*. the great Italòian Dream of Legendary America, Gremese, Rome 1997.

Diego Gabutti, *C'era una Volta in America – Un'Avventura al Saloon con Sergio Leone*, Rizzoli, Milan 1984.

Robert C. Cumbow, *Once Upon a Time – The Films of Sergio Leone*, Scarecrow Press Inc., Metuchen (New Jersey) 1987.

Noël Simsolo, *Conversations avec Sergio Leone*, Stock Cinéma, Paris 1987.

Marcello Garofalo, *C'era una Volta in America – Photographic Memories,* Editalia, Rome 1988.

Francesco Mininni, *Sergio Leone*, La Nuova Italia, Florence, 1989.

Gilles Gressard, *Sergio Leone*, J'ai lu, Parigi 1989.

Roberto Pugliese (edited by), *Sergio Leone*, Venezia Circuito Cinema, Venezia 1989.

Carlos Aguilar, *Sergio Leone*, Ediciones Catedra, Madrid 1990.

Gianni Di Claudio, *Directed by Sergio Leone,* Libreria Universitaria Editrice, Chieti 1990.

Philippe Ortoli, *Sergio Leone. Une Amerique de Légendes*, L'Harmattan, Paris 1994.

Claver Salizzato, Carlo Cozzi (edited by), *C'era una Volta*, 38° Spoleto Cinema, 1995.

Roserto Lasagna, *Sergio Leone,* Ripostes, Salerno 1996.

Luca Beatrice, *Al Cuore Ramon, al cuore – La Leggenda del Western all'Italiana*, Tarab, Florence 1996.

Adrian Martin, *Once Upon a Time in America*, B.F.I., London 1998.

Marcello Garofalo, *Tutto il Cinema di Sergio Leone,* Baldini e Castoldi, Milan, 1999.

Gianluca Saccutelli, *C'era una volta Sergio Leone*, Ottava Musa Edizioni, Porto Sant'Elpidio / Ascoli Piceno 1999.

Angela Prudenzi e Sergio Toffetti (edited by), *Il Buono, il Brutto, il Cattivo di Sergio Leone*, «Quaderni della Cineteca», Fondazione Scuola Nazionale di Cinema, Rome 2000.

Michael Carlson, *Sergio Leone*, Pocket Essentials, Harpenden, 2001.

Roberto Granata, *Leone*, Giuseppe Maimone, Catania, 2002.

Christopher Frayling, *Sergio Leone: Something to Do With Death, Faber & Faber, London 2000*

Fabio Zanello*, Sergio Leone. C'era una Volta il West*, Libreria Universitaria Editrice, Chieti 2003.

Roberto Donati, *Sergio Leone. America e Nostalgia*, Falsopiano, Alessandria 2004.

John Fawell, *The Arts of Sergio Leone's Once Upon a Time in the West*: *A Critical Appreciation*, McFarland & Company Inc., Jefferson / London 2005.

Marco Giusti, *Dizionario del Western all'Italiana*, Mondadori, Milan 2007.

Jean-Baptiste Thoret, *Sergio Leone*, Cahiers du Cinéma, Paris 2007.

Alessandro Paronuzzi (edited by), *Vado l'Ammazzo e Rido. Battute dai film di Sergio Leone*, Stampa Alternativa, Viterbo 2007.

Italo Moscati, *Sergio Leone. Quando il Cinema Era Grande*, Lindau, Turin 2007.

Gian Luca Farinelli e Andrea Meneghelli (edited by), *Sergio Leone, uno sguardo inedito*, Edizioni Cineteca di Bologna, Bologna 2009.

Roberto Donati, *Sergio Leone – L'America, la Nostalgia, il Mito*, Falsopiano, Alessandria 2009.

Raffaele De Berti (edited by), *I Film di Sergio Leone e il Genere Western*, CUEM, Milan 2009.

Sergio Donati, *C'era una volta il West (Ma c'ero anch'io)*, Omero, Rome 2009.

Fabio Melelli, *Sergio Leone e il Western all'Italiana, tra Mito e Storia*, Morlacchi, Perugia 2010.

Jean-Marie Samocki, *Il Était une Fois en Amérique de Sergio Leone*, Exhibitions International, Leuven 2010.

Alberto Pezzotta, *Il Western Italiano*, Il Castoro, Milan 2012.

Harald Steinwender, *Sergio Leone: Es War Einmal in Europa*, Bertz + Fischer, Berlin 2012.

Christian Uva, *Sergio Leone. Il Cinema Come Favola Politica*, Edizioni Ente dello Spettacolo, Rome 2013.

Rodrigo Carreiro, *Era una Vez no Spaghetti Western – O Estilo de Sergio Leone*, Estronho, São José dos Pinhais 2014.

Christopher Frayling, *Once Upon a Time in Italy: The Western of Sergio Leone*, Abrams, New York 2005.

Daniel and Dino Jarach, *Sergio Leone, Backstage of a Genius*, Daniel Clemente Jarach Editore, Milan 2018.

Peter J. Hanley, *Behind the Scenes of Sergio Leone's "The Good, the Bad and the Ugly"*, Il Buono Publishing, 2016.

Philippe Chanoinat e Charles Da Costa, *Il Était une Fois Sergio Leone*, Editions Bourguet-Gachon, London 2017.

Roberto Donati, *C'era una Volta il West*, Gremese, Rome 2018.

Ilaria Feole, *C'era una Volta in America*, Gremese, Rome 2018.

Alireza Vahdani, *The Hero and the Grave: the Theme of Death in the Films of John Ford, Akira Kurosawa and Sergio Leone*, McFarland & Company, Jefferson 2018.

Selected essays and articles on Sergio Leone and his films:

Mario Soldati, *Nascita del Western Italiano*, in «L'Europeo», 28 November 1964 (then in *Da spettatore*, Mondadori, Milano 1973).

Domenico Paolella, *La Psicoanalisi dei Poveri*, in «Midi-Minuit Fantastique», n. 12, May 1965.

Ugo Pirro, *Da "Caltiki" a "Un Pugno di Dollari"*, in «Ulisse», n. 56, October 1965.

John Francis Lane, *La Strada per Fort Alamo*, in «Films And Filming», vol. II, n. 6, 1965.

Alberto Abruzzese, *Mito della Violenza e Pistole Scariche*, in «Cinemasessanta», n. 54, 1965.

Goffredo Fofi, *Lettre d'Italie: le Western et le Reste*, in «Positif», n. 76, 1966.

Enzo Natta, *Il Buono, il Brutto, il Cattivo*, in «Cineforum», n. 61, January 1967.

Angelo Lucano, *Intervista a Sergio Leone*, in «La Rivista del Cinematografo», January 1967.

Tino Ranieri, *Il Western Casalingo*, in «Teatro e cinema», n. 1, January-March 1967.

Massimo Negarville, *Il Buono, il Brutto, il Cattivo*, in «Ombre Rosse», n. I, May 1967.

Pio Baldelli, *Western à l'Italienne*, in «Image et Son», n. 206, May 1967.

Nuccio Lodato e Gianni L. Dalla Valle, *Western all'Italiana: Morte Presunta di un Genere*, in «Civiltà dell'Immagine», n. 4, August 1967.

Umberto Rossi, *È Già Iniziata la Resa dei Conti?*, in «Civiltà dell'Immagine», n. 4, August 1967.

Tullio Kezich, *Il Western all'Italiana*, in Catalogo Bolaffi del cinema italiano, Torino 1967.

Materials

Sylvie Pierre, *Le Bon, le Brute et le Truand*, in «Cahiers du Cinéma», n. 200-201, April-May 1968.

Raymond Durgnat, *The Good, the Bad and the Ugly*, in «Films And Filming», November 1968.

Fernaldo Di Giammatteo, *Che Guaio Avere Sognato la Rivoluzione*, in «Bianco e Nero», n. 1-2, January-February 1969.

Michel Mardore, *Il Était une Fois dans l'Ouest*, in «Le Nouvel Observateur», August 1969.

Serge Daney, *Il Était une Fois dans l'Ouest*, in «Cahiers du Cinéma», n. 216, October 1969.

Jean A. Gili, *Un Univers Fabriqué de Toutes Pièces*, in «Cinéma 69», n. 140, November 1969.

Guy Braucourt, *Intervista a Sergio Leone*, in «Cinéma 69», n. 140, November 1969.

Michel Ciment, *Il Était une Fois dans l'Ouest*, in «Positif», n. 110, November 1969.

Sylvie Pierre, *Il Était une Fois dans l'Ouest*, in «Cahiers du Cinéma», n. 218, March 1970.

Andrew Sarris, *Once Upon a Time in the West*, in «The Village Voice», 6 August 1970.

Mike Wallington, *Italian Westerns – A Concordance*, in «Cinema» (Cambridge), n. 6-7, August 1970.

Christopher Frayling, *Sergio Leone*, in «Cinema» (Cambridge), n. 6-7, August 1970.

Sandro Graziani, *Western Italiano – Western Americano*, in «Bianco e Nero», n. 9-10, September-October 1970.

Pierre Lachat, *Der Italo-Western*, in «Cinema» (Adliswil, Svizzera), n. 61, 1970.

Stefan Morawski, *Spaghetti Western Wedtug Leone*, in «Kino», n. 6, 1970.

Gaston Haustrate, *Faut-il Briller les Westerns Italiens?*, in «Cinéma 71», n. 154, March 1971.

Pierre Baudry, *L'Idéologie du Western Italien*, in «Cahiers du Cinéma», n. 233, November 1971.

Guy Braucourt, *Il Etait une Fois la Révolution*, in «Ecran 72», n. 5, May 1972.

Guy Braucourt, *Intervista a Sergio Leone*, in «Ecran 72», n. 5, May 1972.

Manuel Dori, "*Sergio Leone*", in *Il Western*, Feltrinelli, Milano 1973.

Ljubomir Oliva, *Western Krizem Krazem*, in «Film a doba», n. 7, 1973.

Stuart Kaminsky, *The Grotesque West of Sergio Leone*, in «Take One», May 1973.

Noël Simsolo, *Notes sur les Westerns de Sergio Leone*, in «La Revue du Cinéma», n. 275, September 1973.

Richard Jameson, *A Fistful of Sergio Leone*, in «Film Comment», March-April 1973 and March-April 1974.

Stuart Kaminsky, *The Italian Western Beyond Leone*, in «The Velvet Light Trap», n. 12, 1974.

Eduardo Geoda, *Mitologia e Iconografia del Western-Spaghetti*, in «Cinefilo», n. 25, 1974.

Ignacio Ramonet, *Westerns Italiens – Cinéma politique*, in «Le Monde Diplomatique», October 1976.

Roberto Pugliese, *Intervista a Sergio Leone*, in «Segno Cinema», n. 12, March 1984.

Michel Chion, Serge Le Péron e Serge Toubiana, *Intervista a Sergio Leone*, in «Cahiers du Cinéma», n. 359, May 1984.

Giuseppe Rausa, *Interni Rapporti di Complicità tra Western e Melodramma in Sergio Leone*, in «Segno Cinema», n. 13, May-June 1984.

Jean A. Gili, *Intervista a Sergio Leone*, in «Positif», n. 280, June 1984.

Claver Salizzato, *Sweetwater, New York*, in «Cineforum», October 1984.

Mary Corliss, *Once Upon a Time in America*, in «Film Comment», 1984.

Piera Detassis, *C'era una Volta in America*, in «Bianco e Nero», n. 4, 1984.

Paulin Kael, *Once Upon a Time in America*, in «The New Yorker», 27 May 1985.

Reports of the Conference *Il Western all'Italiana. Stage di Analisi e Studio*, Turin, 7/13 July 1985.

Claver Salizzato (edited by), *Il Cinema di Sergio Leone*, in «Cinecritica», n. 11-12, October 1988-March 1989.

Bill Krohn, *La Planète Leone*, in «Cahiers du Cinéma», n. 422, July-August 1989.

José Maria Latorre, *Hasta que Llegó su Hora*, in «Dirigido por...», n. 133, February 1986.

Vincent Ostria, *Il Était une Fois dans l'Ouest*, in «Cahiers du Cinéma», hors-série 1993: 100 films pour une vidéothèque.

Serge Toubiana, *Il Était une Fois en Amerique*, in «Cahiers du Cinéma», hors-série 1993: 100 films pour une vidéothèque.

Marcello Garofalo (edited by), *Il Cinema-Leone* (writings by Garofalo, Silvestri, Pittante, Giusti, Caprara, Avondola, Pugliese, Canova, Crespi, Morandini, Ghezzi), in «Segno Cinema» n. 67, May-June 1994, e n. 68, July-August 1994.

David N. Meyer, *Once Upon a Time, an Epic Was Shorn of Grandeur*, in «New York Times», 14 February 1999.

Antonio José Navarro, *Sergio Leone. Mas alla del Oeste*, in «Dirigido por...», n. 336, July-August 2004.

Paolo Speranza (edited by), *Speciale Sergio Leone*, in «Quaderni di Cinemasud», year 7 n. 1, 2010.

Screenplays

A Fistful of Dollars: complete shooting script after final editing and original dialogues, by Luca Verdone, Cappelli, Bologna, 1979.

Duck! You Sucker: complete shooting script after final editing, and original dialogues, in Franco Ferrini, op. cit.

Once Upon a Time in America: only the complete shooting script of scenes cut in the Italian release version; *Il Cinema di Sergio Leone*, cit., edited by Claver Salizzato.

Writings by Sergio Leone

A John Ford, un suo allievo: dal *West con Amore*, «Corriere della Sera», 20 August 1983.

Preface in Harry Grey, *Mano Armata,* Longanesi, Milano 1983.

Introduction to Joe Hembus, Western Lexicon, Hanser-Verlag, Monaco, 1976.

Preface in Diego Gabutti, *C'era una Volta in America*, cit., 1984.

Per i Novant'Anni del Cinema, «L'Unità», 28 December 1985.

Introduction to Gianni di Claudio, *Il Cinema Western*, Libreria Universitaria Editrice, Chieti, 1986.

Per il Decimo Anniversario della Morte di Chaplin, «L'Unità», 26 December 1987.

Introduction to Marcello Garofalo, *C'era una Volta in America – Photographic Memories,* Editalia, Roma 1988.

Venivamo da Ogni Parte della Terra, «Bianco e Nero», n. 4, October-December 1988.

Films and Videos on Sergio Leone

Tommaso Chiaretti, Mario Morini, W*estern Primo Amore*, presented by Franco Parenti (Sergio Leone comments the mythology of the Western), RAI.

Gianni Minà, *C'era una volta il cinema. Sergio Leone e i Suoi Film*, RAI, 1985.

Luca Verdone, *Sergio Leone*, Presidenza del Consiglio dei Ministri, Dipartimento Editoria, 1996.

Claver Salizzato, *Sentieri Selvaggi. Scene Segrete di Sergio Leone*, Sergio Leone production, 1996.

Howard Hill, *Once Upon a Time: Sergio Leone*, 2001.

Luca Morsella, *I Sogni nel Mirino. Omaggio a Sergio Leone*, Sergio Leone Productions, 2002.

Carles Prats and Manel Mayol, *Sergio Leone – Cinema, Cinema*, 2002 (DVD edited in Italy, 2010).

Giulio Reale, *Sergio Leone – Il Mio Modo di Vedere le Cose*, 2006.

Michael Arick, *Tre Voci: Three Friends Remember Sergio Leone*, 2007.

Mike Siegel, *Marisol: Sergio Leone's Madonna in the West*, 2018.